BONDED LABOR

BONDED LABOR

TACKLING THE SYSTEM OF SLAVERY IN SOUTH ASIA

Siddharth Kara

Columbia University Press
New York

Columbia University Press
Publishers Since 1893
New York   Chichester, West Sussex
cup.columbia.edu
Copyright © 2012 Siddharth Ashok Kara
All rights reserved

COVER IMAGE: Erik Messori / OnAsia.com

Library of Congress Cataloging-in-Publication Data
Kara, Siddharth.
  Bonded labor : tackling the system of slavery in South Asia / Siddharth Kara.
    p.   cm.
  Includes bibliographical references and index.
  ISBN 978-0-231-15848-0 (cloth : alk. paper)—ISBN 978-0-231-52801-6 (e-book)
  1. Peonage—South Asia.   2. Forced labor—South Asia.   3. Slave labor—South
Asia.   I. Title.

  HD48475.S567K37   2012
  331.11'730954—dc23

                                                          2012008188

Columbia University Press books are printed on permanent and durable acid-free paper.
This book is printed on paper with recycled content.
Printed in the United States of America

c 10 9 8 7 6 5 4 3 2 1

References to Internet Web sites (URLs) were accurate at the time of writing. Neither the
author nor Columbia University Press is responsible for URLs that may have expired or
changed since the manuscript was prepared.

For Aditi, my endless all

There—they stand with bowed heads mute
Chronicling centuries of pain-drawn lines
on their haggard faces.
Their shoulders bent forever under weary loads
Slow they move
as long as they have life.
And after—
leave the legacy to their sons—
for generations and generations.

—"EBAR FIRAO MORE," RABINDRANATH TAGORE

Contents

Tables and Figures

Preface

After I finished writing my first book on the subject of contemporary forms of slavery, I was not sure that I would write another. I did have two other books in mind for which I had already conducted numerous research trips, but the process of writing the first book, which was focused on the bleak and disheartening subject of sex trafficking, proved a greater challenge than I anticipated. Reliving painful memories, narrating the immense suffering I had witnessed, and trying to do justice to the courage of the hundreds of slaves who had shared their stories with me took a heavy toll on my heart, mind, and health. However, as the months went by after *Sex Trafficking* was released, I began to feel compelled to write again—to continue documenting the breadth of contemporary slavery I had researched around the world, in the hopes that doing so might result in more effective efforts to combat these unconscionable crimes.

My second book on slavery focuses squarely on the practice of bonded labor[1] in South Asia. The four main countries in which bonded labor in South Asia takes place are India, Pakistan, Bangladesh, and Nepal. There are small amounts of debt bondage in Afghanistan and Sri Lanka, but India, Pakistan, Bangladesh, and Nepal constitute roughly 97 percent of the debt bondage in the region. More narrowly, one could cover the preponderance of the nature and functioning of bonded labor across South Asia within India alone. The giant of the region has been dealing with bonded labor longer than any of its immediate neighbors (who, aside from Nepal, were all part of India up to 1947), and it also has produced by far the most extensive body of research and legal reasoning on the issue. Approximately seven out of ten of the roughly fifteen to eighteen million bonded laborers in South Asia at the end of 2011 toiled in India, and there is almost no single industry of bonded labor exploitation present in any other South Asian nation that is not also present in India. There are, of course, important regional differences in how debt bondage in one industry or another has evolved. There are also very different social responses and legal traditions on the issue in each of the four main countries in which bonded labor takes place. Most important, the faces and narratives from one country to another are distinctive in crucial ways. For these and other reasons, I endeavored to research bonded labor as extensively as possible across the four main countries in South Asia (as well as debt bondage more generally on several continents around the world), in order to provide the most comprehensive overview possible.

The field research for this book dates back to the year 2000 and was completed in 2011. My research was completely self-funded until 2010, when I received the gracious support of the human rights foundation Humanity United. Across eleven years of research, I spent more than ten months in the field throughout India, Nepal, Bangladesh, and eastern portions of Pakistan. I made five trips to India, covering the states of Rajasthan, Punjab, Haryana, Uttar Pradesh, Bihar, West Bengal, Madhya Pradesh, Maharashtra, and Tamil Nadu. In three trips to Nepal I spanned the breadth of the country from Mahendranagar in the west to Biratnagar in the east. In one trip to Bangladesh I covered the southwestern reaches of the Sundarban region all the way to the far northeast near Sylhet, across the border from Assam. With Pakistan, I was limited to the Sindh and Punjab provinces along the border with India. I had planned a more comprehensive trip to Pakistan, one focused on gathering data and narratives deeper in the country, but I was prevented by the government's failure to grant me a visa.

I applied for a visa to Pakistan for my second trip to the country at the embassy in Los Angeles in May 2010. As of January 2012, I have still not received one. I visited the embassy in person nine times and was told repeatedly that the application was under review in Islamabad—unlike most visas, which were approved on site. The office of Senator Dianne Feinstein of California contacted the embassy several times on my behalf, to no avail. Pakistani colleagues at Harvard University contacted diplomatic ties in the Pakistani government, again with no result. Not to be dissuaded, I attempted to secure a visa from a Pakistani embassy in another country in South Asia, but it was immediately clear that the only way it was going to happen was if I offered a substantial bribe, which I was unwilling to do. While it has definitely become more difficult for me to obtain visas after the publication of *Sex Trafficking: Inside the Business of Modern Slavery*, it was also made clear to me by an official at the embassy in Los Angeles that my Indian ethnicity was an impediment. As a result, I have thus far been unable to conduct more comprehensive field research in Pakistan. I did, however, succeed in conducting several direct interviews with nomadic *hari* bonded laborers during a week-long camel trek through the Thar Desert, and I also managed to hold direct interviews with brick-kiln bonded laborers in Punjab province, when I was granted a meager three-day visit back in 2001. Beyond this, more detailed field research in Pakistan was not entirely necessary, as the nature of debt bondage in agriculture, brickmaking, carpet weaving, and other sectors in the country functions similarly to other South Asian nations. Rather, my primary research need was gathering data and narratives. For this, I have relied on the indispensible efforts of trusted colleagues in Pakistan. These colleagues have been working on bonded labor for many years and were able to conduct the random sampling, demographic data gathering, and other research I needed. They also documented numerous narratives from bonded laborers in several sectors on my behalf. I must here note that they undertook this work at considerable personal risk. They and other activists probing bonded labor in Pakistan have been regularly harassed by police and detained without cause. Their phones have been tapped, and their personal safety has been threatened. The sociopolitical interests that maintain the system of bonded labor in rural Pakistan are more impervious to disruption than almost anywhere in South Asia, and I am exceedingly grateful for the risk these colleagues took in assisting me with my research.

When I completed my final research trip for this book, I had simultaneously completed more than eleven years of research into human trafficking and contemporary slavery. During that time, my research spanned six continents and twenty-four countries, most of which I visited more than once. I interviewed and comprehensively documented the cases of more than one thousand current and former slaves of all kinds, more than five hundred of whom were bonded laborers in South Asia. In addition to these cases, I observed and more casually interacted with thousands of former and current slaves. Without question, bonded labor proved to be one of the most complex, intractable, and exploitative modes of human enslavement I encountered. While it is not always as barbaric or nearly as profitable as sex trafficking, bonded labor is a form of slavery that ensnares approximately six out of ten slaves in the world today. Saying this, of course, necessitates answers to several important questions: What is slavery? How many slaves are there, and of what types? And is bonded labor a form of slavery?

My thinking on these questions has evolved considerably since the publication of *Sex Trafficking* in 2009. I take up these questions in detail in chapter 1 and appendix A of this book, and I encourage the reader to spend time on these sections. I believe that efforts to understand and combat contemporary slavery more effectively have been hampered by a lack of careful thinking on these issues. Rather than sensationalize these terms and invoke them carelessly, scholars and activists must take pause to be more precise in their understanding of the nature and extent of contemporary slavery, including the definition and use of the term itself.

As for bonded labor, this revolting mode of servitude is a remnant of Old World barbarism that has persisted into modern times as a result of a cocktail of highly complex sociocultural forces. The system also persists by virtue of its deft adaptation to meet the needs of a global economy that feeds on systems of labor exploitation with remarkable efficiency. Unlike human trafficking, there is a longstanding legal and scholarly tradition with bonded labor, which negates the possibility of facile analysis. Scholars and activists in South Asia have been studying bonded labor for decades, and in the face of their expertise and commitment, I feel uneasy offering any sort of novel insight or approach. With *Sex Trafficking*, I was able to provide some degree of new analysis, given the newness of the field and the relative paucity of truly strategic, economic, or legal analyses of the issue at the time my book was released. With bonded labor, this is not the case. There are giants in this field, and, as I write this book, I feel out of place suggesting that there may be new ways of understanding bonded labor— and of eliminating it.

Nevertheless, I attempt in this book to portray the extent and overall functioning of the system of bonded labor in South Asia. I share the voices of numerous bonded laborers directly with the reader, and I try to provide some degree of analysis and argument on what should be done to tackle this system of servitude more effectively. If nothing else, I hope these efforts may reinvigorate global action to combat bonded labor, commencing with the societies and governments of South Asia themselves. Of course, tackling bonded labor requires an attack on other forms of forced labor and child labor simultaneously, as there is considerable overlap among these various modes of slavelike exploitation. It is often difficult to determine where bonded labor ends and forced labor or child servitude begins. In that way, tackling bonded labor really means tackling slavery and all the systems that promote it. However, there are distinctive elements to the nature and functioning of bonded labor that can and must be targeted in order to respond most effectively to this specific form of human bondage.

There are countless activists in the far reaches of South Asia who fight anonymously and against unimaginable odds to eliminate bonded labor each and every day. I have met many of these individuals, and I have learned a tremendous amount from them. They have inspired the deepest respect and admiration in me. My only hope is that this book may motivate greater efforts to assist these crusaders and, in so doing, help liberate the millions of destitute, exiled, and oppressed citizens of South Asia who are exploited by brutes day after day in relentless slave labor.

Acknowledgments

I am profoundly grateful to each and every woman, child, and man who shared their stories with me. The dignity and courage of the exploited and enslaved individuals I met across the years has both humbled and inspired me. In trying to do justice to the suffering they shared, knowing fully that very little benefit might accrue to them for doing so, I hope I have not let them down.

In addition to several local translators and guides who assisted me across South Asia, numerous people offered invaluable goodwill, knowledge, and assistance throughout my research. I would like to thank each of them: Swami Agnivesh, Nirmal Gorana, S. A. Azad, Shri K. S. Money, Dr. Sanjay Dubey, Rajeev Shukla, P. K. Basu, Krishnendu Ghosh, Debjit Dutta, Anuradha Talwar, Ujjal Biswas, Pabitra Roy, Pratima Sardar, Ruchira Gupta, Sheila Gupta, Aftab, Sheik, Arshad Mahmood, Ali Farooq, Omar, Gul, Zafarullah, Saki Mohammed, Mustafa Bakuluzzaman, Zakir Hussain, Satchidananda Satu, Sumaiya Khair, Ridwanul Hoque, Sharffudin Khan, Sanjoy Majumder, Mostafa Nuruzzaman, Mukhul Datta, Khondoker Aynul Islam, Erica Stone, Bruce Moore, Aruna Uprety, Kamala Adhikari, Kamal Rana, Deepak Bhattarai, Deepak Adhikari, Fakala Tharu, Bijaya Sainju, Elisha Shrestra, Mahadev Besi, Sapana Malla, and Nina Smith.

I am grateful to Humanity United for its generous funding of the longest research trip I took for this book (and two trips for my next book). I am especially thankful to Lori Bishop, for her cherished friendship and faith in me.

Rebecca Merrill provided meticulous and crucial assistance with the legal research required for this book.

My agent and dear friend Susan Cohen continues to work tirelessly to ensure that my books (and their author) have the best support possible.

I remain deeply indebted to my editing mentor Peter Dimock, who helped me find the only voice with which I could relay the immensity and urgency of what I have seen around the world.

Columbia University Press and Anne Routon continue to provide the best home for my books and all the backing and goodwill a writer could desire. I am very grateful for the leap of faith the press took in commencing this journey with me.

My parents, Dinaz, Ashok, Rani, and Vijay, I thank for their unconditional encouragement. I could not have completed this book without everything they did to guide me and facilitate this mission. My mother, in particular, ensured that I embarked on life on the right path and would have the strength to stay on it, no matter what.

More than anyone, and forever, there is my darling wife, Aditi. I cannot express my gratitude for everything you are and everything you do to bring light, love, and meaning into my life. Your love has carried me much farther than I could have ever gone otherwise. Whatever I am, and do, and become—is thanks to you.

BONDED LABOR

{ 1 }

Bonded Labor

AN OVERVIEW

The system of bonded labour has been prevalent in various parts of the country since long prior to the attainment of political freedom and it constitutes an ugly and shameful feature of our national life. This system based on exploitation by a few socially and economically powerful persons trading on the misery and suffering of large numbers of men and holding them in bondage is a relic of a feudal hierarchical society which hypocritically proclaims the divinity of men but treats large masses of people belonging to the lower rungs of the social ladder or economically impoverished segments of society as dirt and chattel. This system . . . is not only an affront to basic human dignity but also constitutes a gross and revolting violation of constitutional values.

—CHIEF JUSTICE P. N. BHAGWATI,
BANDHUA MUKTI MORCHA VS. UNION OF INDIA, 1983

A MAN NAMED AJAY

An elderly man named Ajay led me to his thatched hut to have a cup of tea.[1] We sat on mats in the dirt, amid his meager possessions and a small cot on which he slept. Dust, insects, and lizards abounded. I gave Ajay a bottle of water, which he heated in a dented pot over a small firepit dug into the ground. With shaky hands, he produced two small metal mugs. As we waited for the water to boil, Ajay rubbed his fragile legs. His skin was so brittle, I feared it would crack if he pressed any harder.

Depleted after a long day of research, I turned my gaze outside, toward the setting sun. A bright orange light set the heavens afire, and a resplendent golden hue radiated from the vast mustard fields. Sensing twilight was near, swarming blue jays erupted into song, and intrepid mosquitoes emerged to track down fresh blood.

The water warmed slowly, so Ajay added another piece of wood to the fire. It hissed and cracked as it burned to ash. Though his workday was completed, his two sons and grandchildren were still toiling not far away at brick kilns. His beloved wife, Sarika, was no longer with him. Barely able to make it through each day, Ajay's withering body and weathered face cried countless tales of woe. His frayed skin scarcely covered the crumbling bones beneath, and he labored to draw sufficient air into his lungs. He had no money, no assets, nothing of his own, not even the dilapidated roof over his head. The spark of life had long ago been extinguished from Ajay's body when I met him that day in the rural reaches of Bihar, India, after he had suffered almost five decades of exploitation as a bonded laborer. No one I ever met had been a slave longer than he.

The water did not quite come to a boil, but Ajay asked for the tea. I broke open a few tea bags from my backpack and poured the tea into the water. A few minutes later, Ajay poured two cups for us to drink. Interspersed with long pauses and painful recollections, Ajay shared his story:[2]

I took the loan of Rs. 800 ($18) for my marriage to Sarika. My father and mother died when I was young, so it was up to me to arrange our wedding. I promised Sarika after we finished our *pheras*[3] that I would make her a happy life. I felt so proud. I was only seventeen at that time. What did I know?

Since the time of our wedding, we worked in these fields for the landowner, who loaned me the money. When he died, we worked for his son. From the beginning, we were promised wages each day of a few rupees. I felt my debt would be repaid in two years at most, but the landowner made so many deductions from our wages, and each year we had to take more loans for food or tenancy. Sometimes, the landowner would tell me at the end of the season that I owe him this amount or that amount, but I could never know what the real amount was. He did not allow us to leave this place for other work, even when there was no work here to do. My brothers and I have worked in this area all our lives. My two sons will inherit my debt when I am gone.

When Sarika became very ill three years ago, the landowner refused to give me a loan for medicines. There was no doctor here, and he would not send us to a medical clinic. He said my debts were too high and I was too old to repay this expense. I pleaded with him to save Sarika, but he told me only God can determine her fate. I was desperate, but I did not know what to do. Sarika did not want our sons to take more debts for her medicine, so she forbade me from telling them when she was ill. How could I deny her wish?

Our lives are filled with so much pain. I did not give Sarika a good life. For many years, I wanted to take my life. I told Sarika I had cursed us, but she said that the suffering in our lives was not so great as others. I told her she should have married a rich man and been happy. Maybe then she would still be alive.

I am old now, and I can no longer work. The landowner has little use for me. My life is almost over. I wait only for the end. No one in this country cares about people like us. We live and die, and no one but ourselves knows we have drawn breath.

WHAT IS BONDED LABOR?

Bonded labor is the most extensive form of slavery in the world today. There were approximately eighteen to 20.5 million bonded laborers in the world at the end of 2011, roughly 84 percent to 88 percent of whom were in South Asia. This means that approximately half of the slaves in the world are bonded laborers in South Asia and that approximately 1.1 percent of the total population of South Asia is ensnared in bonded labor.

Bonded labor is at once the most ancient and most contemporary face of human servitude. While it spans the breadth and depth of all manner of servile labor going back millennia, the products of present-day bonded labor touch almost every aspect of the global economy, including frozen shrimp and fish, tea, coffee, rice, wheat, diamonds, gems, cubic zirconia, glassware, brassware, carpets, limestone, marble, slate, salt, matches, cigarettes, bidis (Indian cigarettes), apparel, fireworks, knives, sporting goods, and many other products. Virtually everyone's life, everywhere in the world, is touched by bonded labor in South Asia. For this reason alone, it is incumbent that we understand, confront, and eliminate this evil.

In its most essential form, bonded labor involves the exploitative interlinking of labor and credit agreements between parties. On one side of the agreement, a party possessing an abundance of assets and capital provides credit to the other party, who, because he lacks almost any assets or capital, pledges his labor to work off the loan. Given the severe power imbalances between the parties, the laborer is often severely exploited. Bonded labor occurs when the exploitation ascends to the level of slavelike abuse. In these cases, once the capital is borrowed, numerous tactics are used by the lender to extract the slave labor. The borrower is often coerced to work at paltry wage levels to repay the debt. Exorbitant interest rates are charged (from 10 percent to more than 20 percent per month), and money lent for future medicine, clothes, or basic subsistence is added to the debt. In most cases of bonded labor, up to half or more of the day's wage is deducted for debt repayment, and further deductions are often made as penalties for breaking rules or poor work performance. The laborer uses what paltry income remains to buy food and supplies from the lender, at heavily inflated prices. The bonded laborers rarely have enough money to meet their subsistence needs, so they are forced to borrow more money to survive. Any illness or injury spells disaster. Incremental money must be borrowed not only for medicine but also because the injured individuals cannot work, and thus the family is not earning enough income for daily consumption, requiring more loans and deeper indebtedness. Sometimes the debts last a few years, and sometimes the debts are passed on to future generations if the original borrower perishes without having repaid the debt (according to the lender). In my experience, this generational debt bondage is a waning phenomenon, though it does still occur throughout South Asia. More often, the terms of debt bondage agreements last a few years or even just a season. However, because of a severe lack of any reasonable alternative income or credit source, the laborer must return time and again to the lender, which recommences his exploitation in an ongoing cycle of debt bondage. This vicious cycle of bonded labor is represented in figure 1.1.

The term "bonded labor" is typically used interchangeably with "debt bondage," though the former term has been more often used to describe the distinctive mode of debt bondage that has persisted in South Asia across centuries. Beyond South Asia, there have been numerous variations on tied labor-credit economic arrangements spanning centuries of human history, commencing with the early agricultural economies. Aristotle wrote about bonded labor and other forms of slavery in his *Politics*,[4] and various forms of bonded labor were prevalent in ancient Rome and Egypt. The medieval Western European economy from the ninth to the sixteenth centuries was typified by a manorial arrangement between a landed class of lords that exploited the unpaid agricultural labor of landless serfs. The agricultural system of Mughal India (1526–1707) constitutes an Indian variant of this traditional European feudalism. The economic system of Tokugawa

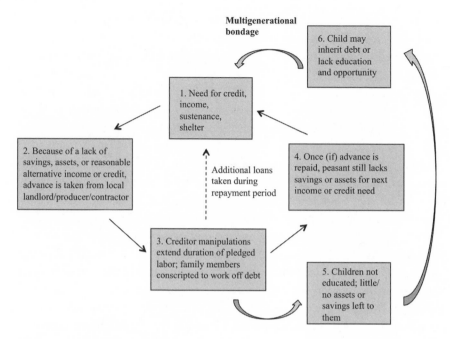

Figure 1.1. Bonded labor vicious cycle.

Japan (1603–1868) provides another example in which a landed class, the shogunate, exploited the bonded labor of landless peasants and untouchables (*burakumin*) within the structure of a highly stratified class society. Finally, the peonage system in the American South after the U.S. Civil War was also typified by exploitative debt bondage arrangements.[5] These and other forms of debt bondage–based economic relations were almost entirely overturned throughout much of the world by a mix of social revolution and transition to industrialized market economies. No such revolution ever took place in South Asia. As a result, more than four out of five debt bondage slaves in the world today reside in the region. There are still informal systems of debt bondage throughout the world—in particular with the widespread practice of recruiting migrant domestic servants into debt bondage[6]—but only in South Asia can one still find a truly systemic, archaic, feudal system of slave-labor exploitation of one class of individuals by another. This system represents a severe and reprehensible violation of basic human rights. It is a form of slavery that is perpetuated by custom, corruption, greed, and social apathy. It is an oppressive arrangement that degrades human dignity through the pitiless exploitation of the vulnerable and desperate. The phenomenon is complex and ever evolving, but there are several salient features that are almost always shared by bonded laborers in South Asia.

KEY FEATURES SHARED BY BONDED LABORERS

Perhaps the most important feature shared by bonded laborers in South Asia is extreme poverty. Each and every bonded laborer I met lived in abject poverty without a reliable means of securing sufficient subsistence income. Almost 1.2 billion people in South Asia live on incomes of less than $2 per day, approximately nine hundred million of whom are in India alone (see appendix F). Adjusting the $2 metric for inflation (especially food inflation) from its inception in 2000 results in a number that exceeds $3 at the end of 2011, which would capture an even greater share of India's population as living in poverty, despite the country's stellar economic growth across the last two decades. Today, there are more billionaires in India than in the United Kingdom, but the number of people living on less than $2 per day in India is more than fifteen times the entire population of the United Kingdom. This staggering chasm in income distribution utterly debases social relationships. This debasement, in turn, allows one set of privileged people to self-justifiably exploit (or ignore the exploitation of) the masses of "inferior" classes. Both sets tend to accept this formula, the rich with entitlement and the poor with fatalism. This self-entitlement may also explain the embarrassing lack of charity among rich and middle-class Indians. Individuals and corporations in India are responsible for only 10 percent of the nation's charitable giving, whereas in the United States the number is 75 percent and in the United Kingdom 34 percent.[7] Unethical and unsustainable income asymmetries and acute and grinding poverty across South Asia are unquestionably among the most powerful forces promoting numerous forms of suffering and exploitation, including bonded labor.

The second feature shared by almost all bonded laborers in South Asia is that they belong to a minority ethnic group or caste. The issue of caste will be discussed in more detail later in this chapter, but, in summary, it is crucial to understand that there remains a stratum of human beings in South Asia who are deemed exploitable and expendable by society at large. Be they *dalits* or *tharu, adivasi* or *janjati*, minority ethnicities and castes in South Asia are the victims of a social system that at best exiles them and at worst disdains them.

Almost all bonded laborers lack access to formal credit markets. This is primarily because, other than their labor, they typically have no collateral to offer against a loan.[8] Coupled with an inability to earn sufficient income to save money, this lack of access drives poor peasants to informal creditors, such as exploitative local moneylenders, landowners, shopkeepers, and work contractors (*jamadars*), who capitalize on their desperation to ensnare them in bonded slavery.

Other common features shared by bonded laborers include a lack of education and literacy, which renders them easier to exploit, especially when it comes to keeping track of their debits and credits. Landlessness is another near-universal feature shared by bonded laborers. Without land, individuals have no security or means to cultivate basic food for consumption. As a result, they often mortgage their labor simply to secure shelter and food, and the threat of eviction is often used to ensnare them in severely exploitative labor conditions. Bonded laborers are almost always socially isolated, and they tend to be located a great distance from markets, which renders them reliant on lender-slaveowners to monetize the output of their labor (agricultural products, bricks, carpets, etc.), and these lenders do so inequitably in order to extend the bondage.

Finally, the most important quality aside from poverty and minority ethnicity shared by each and every bonded laborer I met is a *lack of any reasonable alternative*. The power of this force should not be underestimated, as it is the absence of alternative sources of income, credit, shelter, food, water, and basic security that drives each and every bonded laborer I met to enter into a debt bondage agreement with an exploiter.[9] The lack of reasonable alternative also provides immense bargaining power to the lender; he can all but dictate the terms of credit, wages, and employment and manipulate the contracts at will, because the destitute laborer has no other option that would empower him to bargain for better terms or walk away. I believe this essential duress negates any argument that the bonded laborer is entering into the agreement voluntarily, which some have suggested as a reason that bonded labor is not a form of slavery. On the contrary, it is a well-established tenet of contract law that duress to person (physical threats), duress to goods (the threat to seize or damage the contracting party's property or, in the case of a bonded laborer, to evict him), and economic duress (forces of economic compulsion without a reasonable alternative to the original agreement or renegotiations) render the agreement voidable.[10] Consent is vitiated in the presence of any of these forms of duress, and in almost all cases of bonded labor that I have documented, one if not all of these forms of duress was present at the time of the supposed agreement. Accordingly, few if any of these agreements can be construed as voluntarily entered.

There are other qualities shared by many of the bonded laborers I have documented—such as an inability to diversify household occupations (which would help attenuate the lack of income when one sector is depressed or out of season), a propensity to migrate for income opportunity (migrants are inherently more isolated and vulnerable to exploitation),[11] a sense of fatalism that bondage is the only life available to them, and the tendency of male heads of household to abuse alcohol or abuse their family members.

Tables 1.1 and 1.2 provide a summary of some of the overall statistics from the bonded laborer cases I have documented across South Asia. Average initial debts range from $151 in Pakistan to $169 in Bangladesh, with a regional weighted average of $161. The average debt outstanding for the laborers at the time of my interviews ranged from $254 in Nepal to $282 in India, with a regional weighted average of $276. The initial debts in Bangladesh skewed slightly higher because of the disproportionate level of bonded laborers in aquaculture (shrimp and fish farming), who must take out very high loans to lease land on which they farm. The increase in overall debt outstanding at the time of my interviews versus the size of the original loan taken is caused by additional loans that were taken across time—as well as the accrual of interest expense. Nepal and Bangladesh had slightly lower durations of bondage at 5.5 and 5.7 years, respectively, while India and Pakistan were higher at 6.5 and 6.8 years, respectively. The average annual interest rates on loans were enormous, ranging from 51 percent in Bangladesh to 62 percent in India. Though it was difficult to confirm, my sense was that the lower level of interest in Bangladesh was partially a function of the proportionally higher availability of microcredit, whose interest rates tend to hover around 15 percent to 20 percent per year. In many cases, the annual interest rates on bonded labor loans exceeded 100 percent. By my calculation, the total aggregate debt of all bonded laborers in South Asia at the end of 2011 was $4.5 billion dollars.[12] Of course, the solution to bonded labor is not as simple as coming up with $4.5 billion and freeing every bonded laborer in South Asia. First, it is morally questionable

TABLE 1.1

Bonded Labor Cases Documented by Industry

Bricks	110
Agriculture	94
Construction	67
Carpets	57
Stonebreaking	55
Bidis	32
Shrimp	29
Domestic	18
Tea	18
Other	24
Total	**504**

The number of cases by sector that I have captured is not rigidly proportional to the incidence of bonded labor occurring in those industries in relation to the others, particularly for agriculture. Even though agriculture has by far the highest gross number of bonded laborers of any industry in South Asia, it has a comparatively low incidence of bonded labor, because there are at least 440 million laborers in agriculture in South Asia. There will be some bias in the data by virtue of the industry weightings of the cases I managed to document, but I do not believe that a strictly proportional data set would result in materially different metrics from the data I present in this book.

to respond to slavery of any kind by freeing slaves through the payment of supposed debts. Second, all bonded debts are specifically illegal in India, Pakistan, and Nepal. (Bangladesh, Afghanistan, and Sri Lanka do not have specific laws abolishing bonded labor.) Third, much more than $4.5 billion would be necessary for the long-term training, education, asset acquisition, basic consumption, microcredit expansion, and other assistance (along with a host of systemic and social changes) that would be required to allow individuals to achieve a self-sustaining existence in which they are no longer vulnerable to exploitation. Having said this, the $4.5 billion number provides a general sense of the overall credit needs of South Asia's bonded laborers. A significant multiple of this number would represent the overall credit needs that remain unmet by formal credit markets for the poor across South Asia.

TABLE 1.2

Summary Statistics on Bonded Labor Cases Documented

	No. of Bonded Laborers Documented	Average Initial Debt ($)[1]	Average Debt Outstanding ($)[2]	Average Aggregate Duration of Bondage (yrs.)	Average Duration of Each Loan (yrs.)	Average No. of Loans Taken During Bondage	Average Interest Rate on Loans (%)
India	327	162	282	6.5	2.5	2.6	62
Nepal	76	153	254	5.5	1.4	4.0	56
Bangladesh	71	169	277	5.7	1.6	3.5	51
Pakistan	30	151	266	6.8	2.4	2.8	60
Total/Avg.	**504**	**161**	**276**	**6.3**	**2.2**	**2.9**	**59**

Dollar values in 2011 U.S. dollars.

These data represent averages of all the cases I documented across all industries. Even though there are wide ranges in the sizes of advances and interest rates from one case to another, in general there is remarkable similarity across industries and across countries in terms of the average size of advances, average interest rates, and average aggregate durations of bondage, which indicate at some level that there are efficient market forces at play within the bonded labor industry. Also, the number of cases I documented in each country is not strictly proportional to the overall incidence of bonded labor in each country relative to the others; however, I do not believe that extrapolating for data based on the proportional incidence of bonded labor in each country would yield materially different results.

[1] 2011 U.S. dollar valuation based on country-specific CPI adjustment from the date initial loan was taken.

[2] For those laborers still in bondage, calculated at the time of interview; includes 2011 U.S. dollar valuation on aggregate loans taken as well as aggregate interest accrued based on country-specific CPI adjustment. In many cases, these values had to be calculated based on data gathered from the laborers, as they did not have a sufficiently precise sense of debt outstanding.

KEY FEATURES OF BONDED LABOR AGREEMENTS

The specific mode of entry into bondage and the nature and function of bonded labor agreements vary by industry and region, though there are several common features to most agreements. For example, bonded laborers in construction will typically be recruited by *jamadars* who solicit them with advances in exchange for work at the construction site. Once on the site, the debt bondage begins, typically in the form of subhuman work conditions and severely underpaid wages. In the western Terai of Nepal, *kamaiya* bonded laborers enter into one-year debt bondage contracts each season during Maghi (early January), in which they are offered advances that can include a plot of land, paddy,[13] cash, meals, and clothes, in exchange for one full season of agricultural labor, which may on rare occasions include

TABLE 1.3
Reasons for Taking a Loan

Reason	Percentage
Consumption	24
Income-generating activity	17
Repay previous loan	15
Wedding	12
Medicine or illness	12
Funeral	8
Repairs	6
Home upgrade	4
Other	2
Total	**100**

As with table 1.2, the data in this table represent an aggregate of all cases I documented across all industries and
countries. The proportions of the reasons for taking a loan
will vary from one industry or region to the next, but the
aggregate data give a sense of the overall credit needs of
the bonded laborers I documented across South Asia.

a small share of the output. The *kamaiya* almost always end the season in
debt, which is carried over to the next season when they enter a new contract. In Bangladesh, many shrimp farmers take loans to lease land, but
their yields are almost always below the prevailing lease rate—not to mention that they need additional advances for food or medicine, so they also
enter into perpetual states of indebtedness from one year to the next. Seasonal brick workers in all four major South Asian countries similarly take
advances of various kinds, including cash, food, and shelter, which they
attempt to work off for seven to eight months during the brickmaking season. Manipulation of debts, underpaid wages, and exorbitant interest rates,
among other tactics, exacerbate debt levels for these individuals at the end
of the season, and the debt is carried over, year after year.

Since loans are the fundamental vehicle of entry into the condition of
bonded labor, it is important to understand the spectrum of reasons for
which the loans are taken. Table 1.3 shows the primary reasons that loans
were taken among the bonded labor cases I documented. Once a peasant
takes a loan, he must always pledge to repay the advance with the only asset he has—his labor. Typically, the labor of family members is added to

the bargain (including children), in order to meet exorbitant production requirements by the lender (a certain number of bricks per month, a certain number of kilograms of rice per season, etc.). The agreements are rarely written or put down in print, and when they are, the illiterate bonded laborer signs the agreement with a thumbprint, relying solely on the lender to describe the terms of the agreement. There are always high exit costs to the bonded laborer for breaking the agreement. Landless bonded laborers can be evicted, physically beaten or tortured, or denied future credit, and, in some cases, family members may be forcibly sold to human traffickers to repay the outstanding debts. Fellow bonded laborers may even apply pressure to finish repaying debts as a matter of custom or duty. Exploitative terms are almost always introduced into the agreement after it is formalized. Deductions of wages for debt repayment may exceed what was promised, along with deductions from wages for breaking rules or working poorly (according to the lender). Movement is restricted on threat of punishment, and no other employment or sources of credit are allowed. There is almost always highly asymmetric information between the lender and the laborer. The laborer rarely has access to any sort of balance of accounts or statement of his debits and credits. Even if he does, there is little he can do about any discrepancies. Where a share in the output of the labor (usually agriculture) may be the primary form of compensation, only the lender knows the final prices of the products sold at the market, and what is reported back to the bonded laborer is invariably much lower than reality.

In sum, bonded labor agreements are typified by numerous features that deeply disfavor the laborer and extend the term of his indebtedness and servitude. Ongoing labor pledged toward repayment of a fictitious debt becomes nothing less than slave labor.

THE ECONOMICS OF BONDED LABOR

From an economic standpoint, bonded labor agreements are highly inefficient for all parties involved, including society at large—except the exploiter. Total output in most any industry in which bonded labor takes place is by necessity less than it would be if free and fair market forces were allowed to prevail.[14] This is largely because in a freer market environment, producers must compete for workers through the payment of competitive wages and benefits, and workers are in turn incentivized to perform well (which increases overall productivity) in order to pursue better and more productive opportunities for themselves and society. The only party in the more competitive environment that suffers is the producer-exploiter, who enjoys less profitability, given the increased labor and recruitment costs that result from the absence of a tied and low-wage labor force that is readily available during peak production times. The compensation provided to the worker at the outset must only exceed the laborer's alternative less an insurance premium. The "insurance premium" means having the fixed wage in the form of an upfront loan, as opposed to a day wage for the same job, whose rate on a daily basis is usually higher than the amortized daily value of the loan but is not guaranteed from one day to the next. This is the insurance the bonded laborer receives, and because destitute peasants are highly risk averse and often exist at the brink of starvation, they place a high value on this premium. When the peasant's reasonable alternative is nothing or next to nothing, he values the perceived fixed wage and insurance as even greater, which empowers the producer-exploiter to offer the lowest possible terms, in order to entice the peasant into the bonded agreement. At that point, the insurance often transforms from a fixed wage for a period of time into outright enslavement. The more destitute the peasant, the more severe his absence of any alternative opportunity, and the more he values any level of fixed income in the form of a loan, the lower that loan has to be in order to secure a bonded agreement. In some cases, loans as small as $20 or $30 have resulted in years of bonded labor.

The producer-exploiter can, and almost always does, leverage his position in society to ensure that the peasant's alternatives remain almost nonexistent.[15] With the help of an apathetic society and an ineffective, if not corrupt, system of law enforcement and justice, the landowner easily keeps the peasant's alternatives close to nil. Closing off access to other sources of income, credit, assets, unionization, or opportunities of any kind negates bargaining power for the laborer, which renders him readily available, pliant, and desperate to accept even the most exploitative of agreements. Reinforcing the lack of alternatives with a stratified caste (or gender) system that dictates a pathetic horizon of opportunity for the lowest stratum of society further consigns an entire subclass of individuals to slavelike exploitation. The system clearly benefits those who control land, local government, assets, and means of production in the rural and informal sectors, but the economy at large and each individual laborer suffer considerably. Fair opportunity to access reasonable wages, land, and credit would not only increase overall incomes (because the lender must always exceed the laborer's alternate income, less the insurance premium, or credit, less the interest rate), but it also would incentivize production by providing the laborer with a stake in the output. In other words, if the laborer is working for himself rather than for the exploitative producer-lender, he will typically be motivated to work harder. Multiplied across millions of bonded laborers in numerous industries, overall output (and perhaps quality) would be significantly increased, boosting both the economy at large and the human-development potential of each and every laborer in the system. Only the producer-exploiter suffers in a scenario of fair and competitive labor agreements that are reinforced by the rule of law and more equitable bargaining power. It is an unfathomable mystery of modern times that South Asia's bonded labor exploiters have managed to repress the lives of millions of peasants across the region, as well as their overall economies at large, for so many decades, solely for the sake of maintaining their interests in maximizing profits through this ignoble and unlawful practice. Furthermore, when one sector of society is allowed to flaunt justice and basic human rights, the entire society suffers from a general disregard for the rule of law. This human debasement seeps into and permeates the consciousness and conscience of a society, rendering it more difficult to overcome the degrading systems that promote bondage and slavery. The Supreme Court of Pakistan put it best in the Court's first bonded labor case, *Darshan Mashih vs. State*: "This total degradation of this section of society is bound to affect the entire social fabric of our society if allowed to continue. The open violation of the Fundamental Rights of the supreme law of the land will give way to a 'non-respect' to laws of the country."[16]

THE BUSINESS OF BONDED LABOR

From its ancient beginnings in feudal agricultural economies, bonded labor has expanded to dozens of industries in the era of the global economy.[17] Transnational competition to provide the lowest-cost production environments to both domestic and international businesses has resulted in the growth of informal, underregulated labor markets in developing nations—be it sweatshops or outright slavery. For almost any legitimate business in the world, labor is typically the largest component of that business' operating expenses. Thus throughout history, producers have tried to find ways to minimize labor costs. Slavery is the extreme outcome of this impetus. Slaves afford a virtually nil cost of labor, which in turn reduces total operating costs substantially, allowing the slaveowner to maximize profit. Drastically reduced labor costs also allow producers to become more competitive, by lowering retail prices. The retail price of any product or service is largely based on the costs of producing, distributing, and marketing that product or service, along with the available supply of the product or alternatives and whatever brand premium the market will bear. If a major component of cost is stripped out of the production model, then producers can finely balance their desire to maximize profit and lower retail price. Because consumers in general almost always prefer the lower-priced version of the same product or service (if all other variables, such as quality, are the same), producers often compete with one another by minimizing price, and one of the most effective ways to do so while retaining profitability is to exploit labor. Bonded, forced, and child labor are three of the many faces of this phenomenon.

While agriculture, brickmaking, and construction are the industries that tend to exploit the highest number of bonded laborers across South Asia, I have also documented bonded labor exploitation in numerous other sectors, including carpet weaving, domestic work, stonebreaking, fish and shrimp farming/catching/processing, tea harvesting/processing, bidi rolling, leather processing, silk production, sari embroidery, glass bangle making, mineral mining, precious stone and gem cutting, and commercial sex. Other industries that often exploit bonded laborers that I did not personally document include pottery, coffee harvesting/processing, rubber production, rice mills, match manufacture, and fireworks production.

In appendix B, I provide sample profit-and-loss tables for some of the key bonded labor industries in South Asia. In appendix C, I provide supply chain charts for select industries, in which I have reliably traced goods tainted by bonded, forced, or child labor in South Asia to consumers in the United States and European Union. This profit and supply chain data is vital for identifying the most strategic points of intervention in the highly variegated sectors in which bonded laborers are exploited (discussed in more detail in chapter 8). The brickmaking sector is easily the most cash-profitable bonded labor industry in South Asia, with average annual net profits per bonded laborer of approximately $1,990 U.S. dollars (see table B.3 in appendix B). At the other end of the spectrum, agricultural bondage such as the *kamaiya* and *hari* (tables B.1 and B.2) generate average annual cash profits per bonded laborer closer to $300 and $380 respectively. Construction and glass bangle production are closer to the middle range of all bonded labor sectors, at approximately $1,000 and $900 in average annual net profits per bonded laborer, respectively (tables B.6 and B.10). The net profit margins for most bonded labor industries hover between 45 and 55 percent, with shrimp farming in Bangladesh being by far the most profitable, at almost 68 percent. Overall, I calculate that approximately $15.0 billion in net profits was generated in South Asia during 2011 through the exploitation of bonded laborers ($17.6 billion worldwide). On the one hand, this is a comparatively small sum that represents less than 1 percent of the combined GDP of South Asia in 2011. On the other hand, it is a considerable number for the producer-exploiters, a number that clearly motivates their ongoing demand to maintain this ancient system for their economic benefit.

A HISTORY OF SLAVERY AND BONDAGE IN SOUTH ASIA

Though bonded labor continues to evolve into the modern era, the contemporary manifestation of the phenomenon in South Asia is shaped by an ancient history of slavery dating back to Vedic times, up to and including the British colonial period. When discussing "ancient India," this includes the territories that would become present-day Pakistan and Bangladesh after 1947 and 1971, respectively. Until that time, "India" refers to all three countries. Understanding the history of slavery in ancient India is vital for formulating more effective efforts in tackling all forms of bondage and servitude in the region.

Slavery in Ancient India

The concept of slavery in ancient India begins with the word *dasa*. This word appears often in Sanskrit, Prakrit, and Pali texts and is generally translated as meaning "slave." However, it is a complex term that covers a range of subservient conditions, classes of individuals, and even certain tribes in ancient India. Aryan invaders identified the people they conquered and forced into servile labor in the Indian subcontinent as *dasas*.[18] Throughout ancient texts, different categories of *dasas* are described as being held in complete servitude or other forms of limited or conditional bondage. Certain categories of *dasas* could own property; others were listed as a master's assets alongside animals.[19] Unlike the ancient Western civilizations of Greece and Rome, there were no stark opposites of free and enslaved peoples in ancient India but rather a continuum of various degrees of subservience based on numerous qualities, including class, gender, tribe, economic condition, and caste. From these complex beginnings, a spectrum of servitude continues to the present day and evades more simplistic Western concepts or legal definitions of slavery and forced labor. This complexity necessitates a deeper understanding of the evolution of servile labor in South Asia and its treatment in the modern context.

While signs of slavery have been documented in South Asia as far back as the Harappan period (2600–1900 B.C.E.) at Mohenjo-Daro in present-day Pakistan,[20] it was not until the significant expansion of the agricultural economy in South Asia during post-Vedic times (after 500 B.C.E.) that a wide-scale class of servile laborers developed across the region. As agriculture expanded, land became an increasingly valuable asset whose ownership was concentrated in the hands of the upper-class *gahapati* ("householder") stratum of society. This wealthy landowning class utilized the labor of landless *dasas* and *karmakaras* (laborers) to work their land. The *gahapati* had complete control over the *dasas* and *karmakaras* and could treat them however they pleased. Pali texts from the fourth and fifth centuries B.C.E. describe the extreme poverty and destitution of the *dasas* and *karmakaras*, who lacked assets, land, and capital and were forced to sell their freedom (*dasas*) or low-wage labor (*karmakaras*) in order to survive.[21]

During the Mauryan period of the second and third centuries B.C.E., the *Arthashastra* ("The Science of Material Gain" or "The Science of Political Economy") as set down by the Hindu scholar Kautilya codified comprehensive regulations on labor and slavery for the first time. Kautilya defined nine categories of *dasas*, including the first definition of the concept of debt bondage (*ahitaka*) as an individual who becomes a slave upon acceptance of money from a master. The *Arthashastra* also refers to the *dasa-karmakaras* as *visti*, or "those who provide free labor."[22]

The next and perhaps most important development in the evolution of slavery and bondage in ancient India occurred during the post-Mauryan

period, with the Brahmanical scholars Yajnavalkya, Narada, and Katayayana. These scholars established caste as an increasingly forceful determinant
of destiny among ancient Indian people, a force that continues today to
shape the fates of tens of millions of low-caste South Asians. As part of
their efforts, these scholars also expanded the number of *dasa* categories.
Narada provides the most comprehensive classification, one involving fifteen different categories of slavery:

1. *grihajata*: One born at his master's house of a female slave
2. *kreeta*: One purchased by the payment of a price
3. *lubdha*: One received as a gift
4. *dayadopaguta*: One obtained by inheritance
5. *ankulabritta*: One whose life was saved during famine in exchange
   for enslavement
6. *ahita*: One pledged to be a slave upon acceptance of money by a
   master
7. *rinadasa*: One who becomes a slave upon release from a heavy debt
8. *joodhprapta*: One acquired as a slave during war
9. *punajita*: One won during a wager (i.e., "If I lose this bet, I will be
   your slave")
10. *oopagata*: One who voluntarily offers himself as a slave
11. *prubrujeabusita*: One who has faltered from the vow of asceticism
12. *kritakala*: One enslaved for a stipulated period of time
13. *bhuktadasa*: One who becomes a slave in order to receive basic
    maintenance
14. *burrubabhritta*: One who marries a female who is a slave
15. *atmavikrayee*: One who sells himself as a slave.[23]

Categories 5, 6, 7, and 13 contain those that would later be called bonded
laborers.

The Role of Caste in Ancient India

One of India's most revered crusaders against bonded labor, Swami Agnivesh, told me in the New Delhi headquarters of his organization Bandhua
Mukti Morcha (Bonded Labour Liberation Front) that "India's abominable

caste system" was the distinctive force that promoted the "parallel social and economic exploitation" of tens of millions of people in the country. The former lawyer and government minister who founded BMM more than thirty-five years ago explained that India's caste system was "abominable" because it consigned individuals to an inescapable fate, which may be fine if you happened to be born at the top of the hierarchy, but it proved a bleak sentence if you happened to be born at the bottom. Estimates vary, but most studies calculate that 95 to 98 percent of all bonded laborers across South Asia belong to subordinated castes and ethnic groups. My own data indicates the number is 97 percent. Along with poverty, caste is the single most powerful force that continues to promote the exploitation of bonded laborers in South Asia.[24]

Each South Asian country has its own distinctive system of caste and social stratification, but these systems are largely based on the caste system that evolved in ancient India during the post-Mauryan period. Set down at some point between 200 B.C.E. and 200 C.E., the *Manusmrti*, or *Laws of Manu*, represent the laws of all social classes as ostensibly established by the Hindu god, Brahma, which he taught to his son, Manu, the father of mankind. Consisting of 2,694 verses, the text outlines legal rules to govern society. These rules include strict social stratifications based on four Varnas, or "types," which are said to be created from different parts of Brahma's body.[25] In descending order of prominence, the Varnas were: Brahmin (teacher, scholar, priest), created from Brahma's mouth; Kshatriya (royalty, warrior), created from Brahma's arms; Vaishya (trader, landowner), created from Brahma's stomach; and Shudra (craftsman, agriculture, service provider), created from Brahma's thighs. Shudras were created to serve the other three groups, and slavery was deemed innate to them.[26] Even if freed by their masters, they were still slaves, because this was their nature.[27] There was absolutely no mobility between castes, so if an individual was born to the servile caste, this was his destiny, and he should perform it dutifully in the hopes of being reborn to a higher caste in his next life.

Within this basic four-part system there are literally thousands of subdivisions, known as *jati*, or subcastes. These subdivisions are based on professional specializations, geography, and other factors. Beneath all castes and subcastes, subsisting even beneath the Shudras at the lowest level of all, are the "untouchables," deemed so because they were relegated to tasks considered impure, such as clearing sewage, leather processing, and handling carcasses. Later called *dalits* and then Scheduled Castes,[28] there are at least three hundred million such individuals across South Asia. Along with the indigenous tribal people referred to as Scheduled Tribes,[29] these are by far the most severely impoverished, disenfranchised, and frequently exploited individuals in the region.

While the strict caste system that solidified in the post-Mauryan period may no longer be quite as forceful to day-to-day South Asian social life as it once was, legacies persist, particularly in rural areas. These legacies promote the exploitation of lower castes and *dalits* by upper castes, and they continue to limit access to reasonable income, opportunity, security, health, and justice for lower-caste groups. Across the centuries, the caste system has been increasingly internalized by South Asian society, resulting in its self-perpetuation, even among those who are most exploited. In speaking with numerous *dalit* bonded laborers, many told me that bondage and servility were their divinely ordained fates, which they must perform dutifully if they hoped to accrue a positive karmic balance that may elevate them upward in the next life. The sedimented and centuries-old fatalism inherent to the caste system of ancient India is a deplorable anachronism in modern times. In discussing India's caste system, the great anthropologist Claude Lévi-Strauss once wrote:

> It is tragic for mankind that this great experiment failed; I mean that, in the course of history, the various castes did not succeed in reaching a state in which they could remain equal because they were different. Men can coexist on condition that they recognize each other as being all equally, though differently, human, but they can also coexist by denying each other a comparable degree of humanity, and thus establishing a system of subordination. India's great failure can teach us a lesson.[30]

The inability to achieve comparable humanity for all people in South Asia is perhaps the region's greatest failure. In a time of rationality and the pursuit of basic human rights for all, the persistence of severe caste-based (and gender-based) asymmetries can only be construed as indicating that the preponderance of those in power in South Asia—if not the preponderance of South Asian society at large—deem these people to be less than human. So long as this is the case, the disgraceful exploitation of subcastes by upper castes will continue.

Bondage and Slavery in Medieval India

Across the next several centuries spanning ancient to medieval India, the Brahmanical tradition that took hold during the post-Mauryan period continued to evolve in ways that promoted caste-based slavery and bondage. In the tenth century, a new form of interest, called *kayika*, was levied against bonded laborers. This interest was paid by manual labor, and the labor could not be applied toward the principal. If the labor was insufficient to repay the accrued interest, another form of interest, *chakravriddhi*, or compound interest, was applied.[31] The specific interest rate to be applied to a loan was determined by Brahmanical scholars based on the caste of the borrower. The lower the caste, the higher the interest rate. These and other tools helped create an expanding and permanent class of lower-caste, bonded laborers across India.

Beginning with the Turkish conquest of northern India in 1206, Islam was introduced to the region, but its comparatively egalitarian ideals (toward fellow Muslims) and more humanitarian approach to slavery did little to stem the ongoing expansion of slavery and bondage in India. On the contrary, domestic slavery, debt bondage, slave trading, and urban slave markets all expanded during this time. Turkish and later Mughal rulers centralized power in urban centers, developed efficient tax-collecting mechanisms, and increased the use of money in the economy. These and other developments promoted new urban slave markets, which were populated by trafficked, low-caste Indians as well as by Africans and other conquered peoples. New revenue policies under Mughal rulers specifically promoted the enslavement of peasants, whereby the inability to pay taxes could be punished by enslavement to the state. Entire peasant families were transported to urban slave markets and sold to secure the desired tax revenues. Droughts and famines throughout the sixteenth and seventeenth centuries were followed by massive increases in rural peasants being sold in urban slave markets. Slave labor was also used to construct Muslim monuments during this period, such as the Qutb Minar in New Delhi and the Taj Mahal in Agra.[32]

Even though Muslim laws on slavery tended to be more liberal than the Hindu laws set down by the Brahmanical scholars (these differences are detailed in chapter 7), domestic slavery, slave markets, and the large-scale bondage of low-caste rural peasants expanded significantly during medieval India, right up to the arrival of European colonizers.

The Role of Colonialism in Expanding Debt Bondage in India

The Portuguese established the first European settlement in India at Calicut (southwestern India) in 1498. Numerous French, Dutch, and British settlements followed across the next century. The British East India Company (EIC) first took hold in India at Surat in 1612 and operated a trading monopoly for the British Empire until 1813 from the port cities of Bombay, Madras, and Calcutta, focused on exports of textiles, raw silk, and spices. The EIC had early aspirations of controlling the subcontinent, but Mughal rulers were too powerful for it to challenge until after the death of Aurangzeb in 1707. A series of internal wars and a major Persian invasion in 1739 weakened the Mughals to the point that the EIC was able to consolidate power across India. After its military victory in 1757 at the Battle of Plassey, the EIC controlled Bengal. It took control of Madras and Bombay provinces in 1803, and by that time it had also driven French and Dutch interests from India. The EIC controlled the subcontinent until the British government dissolved it in 1857, in favor of direct rule—the British Raj—which lasted until India gained its independence in 1947.

Despite Britain's global abolitionist leadership during the eighteenth and nineteenth centuries, the economic and legal policies of the British Raj very directly expanded slavery throughout India, in particular bonded labor. Bonded labor was utilized as a mode of slave labor exploitation deemed—thanks to contracts and advances of credit—to be something different from the chattel slavery that was abolished throughout much of the British Empire by the Slavery Abolition Act, 1833, and, similarly, the trading in such slaves that was abolished by the Slave Trade Abolition Act, 1807. One vital aspect of the 1833 act that is often overlooked is that the territories of the EIC were specifically excluded, which allowed slavery to persist legally in India for many years after 1833. When pressures finally arose to abolish slavery in India as well, bonded labor soon became a means of achieving the continuation of slavelike exploitation.[33]

One must be clear, however, that the European colonizers did not introduce slavery to India. On the contrary, traditional caste-based slavery was firmly entrenched by the time the Europeans arrived, which by then mostly consisted of untouchables who provided a large and systemically perpetuated slave labor force. Even some Shudras owned untouchable slaves. These slaves were sold and bartered like livestock, and there was virtually no avenue for freedom or any alternative once an untouchable became a slave.

However, two specific expansions in slave levels in India can be directly attributed to British colonial rule: the expansion in urban slave markets and slave trading of Indians throughout the British Empire and the expansion and solidification of debt bondage as the primary means of securing slave labor across India and the British Empire.

The Expansion of Urban Slave Markets

The expansion of urban slave markets in India dates back as early as the 1600s straight through to the nineteenth century. During this time, British as well as Portuguese and Dutch colonizers vastly expanded existing slave-trading markets in port cities including Bombay, Calcutta, Goa, and Madras. For the British after the 1833 act, Indians became a primary replacement for lost African slaves. From the 1830s straight until the 1920s, much of the British Empire filled with millions of trafficked and indentured Indian slaves, including its colonies in Mauritius, Burma, Malaysia, Fiji, the Caribbean, British Guiana, East Africa, South Africa (after the Boer War), and of course throughout the Indian subcontinent. A vast human-trafficking network was established by the British from Indian port cities, a network more complex than the North Atlantic slave trade. To meet the needs of this network, Indian slave markets were expanded, and a multilevel system of licensed recruiting agents was formed, which reported to the British commercial entities that operated the slave markets to fill orders for specific types of Indian slaves required by specific colonies. For example, tens of thousands of Indian females were trafficked across five decades to Surinam beginning in the 1870s, specifically for domestic servitude.[34] At the bottom of the recruitment ladder was an unlicensed agent, called the *arkatia* (precursor to the modern-day *jamadar*), who used his knowledge of local villages, shantytowns, temples, bazaars, and railway stations to recruit the most vulnerable and desperate individuals. Recruitment in general was a sham, relying on outright deception and bait-and-switch tactics, with promises of shorter terms of work, comfortable living conditions, and higher wages than were provided. Deeply indebted individuals were specifically provided offers to purchase their freedom in exchange for favorable work conditions in a British colony. Transportation by ship was as deadly as the slave trade journey across the Atlantic, and exploitation in the destination colonies was brutish, violent, and designed to extend the servitude of the bonded laborer through spotty wage payments, arbitrary wage cuts, and severe penalties for breaking rules (for example, £10 or one month's imprisonment in British Guiana for one day's absence from work). These and other tactics conspired to ensnare the trafficked slave in debt bondage for years, often until the slave perished.[35]

Simultaneously and continuing well after the 1807 act outlawing the slave trade from Africa, Africans (called *coffrees* in India) were traded by the British into India from Africa and Arabia, where they were auctioned at the burgeoning Indian slave markets, usually for agricultural labor or domestic servitude. One article in the *Calcutta Journal* in 1823 noted the two-way slave trading of Africans to Calcutta and Indians back to the other way:

> This great capital is in short at once the depot of the commerce and riches of the East and the mart in which the manacled African is sold like the beast of field to the highest bidder. . . . It is known too that these ships are in the habit of carrying away the natives of the country, principally females, and disposing of them in Arabia in barter for African slaves for the Calcutta market.[36]

Economic and Legal Policies That Expanded Debt Bondage

The second expansion in slavery that can be attributed to British colonial rule relates to specific economic and legal policies that broadened caste-based debt bondage as a means of securing slave labor. First, the general commercialization and expansion of agriculture and textiles by the British strongly reinforced debt bondage in India. These expanding industries required a large and captive labor force, and this was increasingly secured through debt bondage of various forms. In Orissa, untouchable castes such as *mehtars*, *doms*, and *dhobis* were routinely ensnared in agricultural debt bondage, bartered, mortgaged, and rented out by their owners. In Bihar, untouchables such as *ghatwards* and *santals* were caught in debt bondage through loans for subsistence or life ceremonies. In Gujarat, *halis* were conscripted into generations of agricultural debt bondage in order to meet basic consumption needs. Across India, impure and untouchable castes that lived on the brink of starvation were provided the most meager of advances in exchange for contractual agreements to pledge their labor and the labor of succeeding generations until the debts were repaid.[37] In that way, two forces combined to expand bonded labor under the British: the need for a large, captive labor force to support expanding British industrialization and the entrenched cultural subordination of untouchables. In essence, while the British accelerated industrial production throughout India, they did not alter the mode of debt bondage–based labor, which resulted in a massive increase in the levels of bonded labor. Further, as pressures from abolitionists back in England increased during the mid- and late 1800s to abolish slavery in India, slaveowners responded by substituting deeds for sales of human beings with contracts of pledged labor to repay debts. Legislation passed by the British reinforced this process, in particular the Workman's Breach of Contract Act, 1859, which made any breach-of-contract terms a legally punishable offence. Bonded laborers who had contractually agreed to pledge their labor until their debts were repaid could not escape servitude without harsh punishment (see chapter 7 for further details). The 1859 act gave British slave masters the legal ability to enforce bonded labor, which most masters viewed as being the same as chattel slavery anyway, simply under a different name.[38]

The next force that expanded slavery and bondage in India under British rule has to do with British land-revenue policy during the 1700s and 1800s. These policies directly led to the mass dispossession of the peasantry of India (especially in the north), who were in turn forced to take loans for subsistence or to migrate for low-wage, debt bondage, or forced labor conditions in factories, mines, agricultural fields, and the rapidly expanding tea plantations in Assam and present-day Bangladesh. Surveying land plots and assessing taxes was a major revenue-generating activity of the EIC, resulting in a 10 percent increase in revenues generated from village units as compared to the land-tax policies under the Mughals.[39] This activity accelerated after the Permanent Settlement of 1793 under Governor General Lord Cornwallis. The Permanent Settlement was an effort to impose Western concepts of private property and land taxes in Bengal, northern India, and later Sindh and Punjab provinces in present-day Pakistan. Previously, *zamindars* were the wealthy landowners who owned the land and all the peasants who lived on it. Under the *zamindari* system, taxes were collected by the *zamindars* from the peasants on behalf of the Mughals, and the *zamindars* eventually assumed the same role for the British. It should be noted that the *zamindars* did not need any assistance in being ruthless toward the peasants living on their land, often exploiting them in debt bondage and forced labor. However, inconsistent and inefficient collections (as perceived by the British) led to a new system of formalized assessment of land titles, valuations, and fixed taxes under the Permanent Settlement. The capitalist logic of the British was that once landowners felt secure in their ownership of private land and knew that taxes would be fixed, they would maximize the economic value of their land by investing in infrastructure and production. Unfortunately, the tax rates assessed were even higher than those back in England, and no concessions were made for times of famine or drought, which led to countless *zamindars* going into default, who were then forced to sell the land to officials within the EIC or to wealthy bankers and aristocrats back in England. *Zamindars* were subsequently reduced to revenue-collecting intermediaries between these new British landowners and the peasants still living on the land. Most peasants could not afford the tax rates (due in cash only) and were forced either into debt bondage in order to pay their debts or to migrate for work across the subcontinent, where they typically found equally, if not more, exploitative working conditions.[40] One of the worst examples of this phenomenon was the mass trafficking of destitute and landless peasants from Orissa and Bihar into the tea plantations of Assam and Bengal during the early and mid-1800s. On arrival, these individuals were met with outright slavery that eventually became legally enforceable under the 1859 act, including coercion to sign five-year contracts (in which the work conditions were invariably misrepresented), steep taxes and fines, beatings, torture, and a minimal compensation of five rupees per month (four for women, three for children), which was one-third the wages being paid to labor migrants in other British colonies.[41] I witnessed the devastating outcome of this trafficking and exploitation more than 150 years later when I visited the tea plantations in Bangladesh near Sylhet and Srimangal (see chapter 4), all of which were populated by the exploited, isolated, and destitute descendants of these trafficked migrants from Bihar and Orissa a century and a half earlier.

Finally, one cannot complete a survey of the effects of the British colonial period on slavery and bondage levels in India without commenting on the massive extraction of wealth from India by the British and the concurrent increase in poverty levels across India, which naturally promoted bondage and slavery. From 1600 to 1947, India had an almost stagnant per capita GDP, whereas per capita GDP in Britain during the same period increased nine-fold. An amount of wealth equivalent to roughly one-fifth the entire net savings of India was extracted by the British Raj, contributing mightily to the economic disparity between the nations. In 1600, India's economy was twelve times the size of the United Kingdom's, but by 1947 the UK economy was approximately 25 percent larger than India's.[42] Of course, not all of this disparity was a result of the extraction of wealth from India by the United Kingdom, but the net flow of resources and income from India to the United Kingdom was a primary contributor to the United Kingdom's considerable economic growth from the 1600s to 1947, at the severe expense and impoverishment of India.

These increased poverty levels, combined with the economic and legal policies of the British colonial rulers, led to the wholesale ruination of India's peasantry, which caused the mass trafficking for extreme labor exploitation and debt bondage throughout India and the broader colonial empire. Dispossession of land, harsh revenue policies, and the acceleration of industrialization all catalyzed the expansion of debt bondage among low-caste groups, especially during the period after the 1833 act, when India became a primary replacement source of trafficked slave labor for the British colonies. Debt bondage became a technically acceptable way of securing slave labor, by virtue of the artifice of contracts and advances of credits. By the latter half of the 1800s, debt bondage had ascended as the primary mode of securing slave-labor exploitation across the Indian subcontinent. Devastating famines in 1876–1878 and 1899–1900 resulted in millions of new debt bondage slaves who traded survival for servitude. From that time, the system of bonded labor has ruthlessly perpetuated itself well into the twenty-first century, culminating in centuries of exploitation of an entire subclass of disenfranchised, low-caste, and utterly deprived South Asians.

IS BONDED LABOR SLAVERY?

Earlier in this chapter, I stated that bonded labor is the most extensive form of slavery in the world today. However, this begs the question of whether bonded labor is indeed slavery. Indeed, in the previous section we noted that the British utilized debt bondage as a supposed substitute for slavery after the latter had been abolished by the 1833 Slavery Abolition Act. The question of whether some or all forms of bonded labor are also slavery centers on whether debt bondage agreements are voluntary choices or not. No one is arguing that a child who inherits a debt from an antecedent and is coerced to continue the debt bondage relationship is not a slave. However, some economists have argued that certain forms of bonded labor are in fact voluntary choices that are "welfare enhancing" to the laborer and that, in these cases, bonded labor is not a form of slavery but rather a reasonable agreement entered into by two rational economic agents: the landlord and the peasant. In the contemporary context, the majority of bonded labor in South Asia is no longer generational, caste-based debt bondage but rather takes the form of these potentially voluntary agreements between destitute laborers and wealthy principals who offer credit in exchange for labor. These agreements may last a few years or just a season, and the laborers may enter into many of them during their lifetimes. Are these people slaves? That is, are they entering into and out of slavelike conditions with each agreement? Or are they rational peasants who are making voluntary decisions not too dissimilar to agreements we may make in developed economies, when we take loans that we work off with income from our labor? The answer to these questions will substantially affect our overall assessment of the scale and nature of contemporary slavery, and it will also determine very significantly the kinds of tactics to be deployed in the fight against bonded labor.

WHAT IS SLAVERY?

To establish whether or not some or all forms of bonded labor constitute slavery, we must first define slavery. Article 1 of the League of Nations Slavery Convention of 1926 defines slavery as the "status or condition of a person over whom any or all of the powers attaching to the right of ownership are exercised." This definition was followed a few years later by the International Labour Organization Forced Labour Convention no. 29 of 1930, which in Article 2(1) defined forced labor as "all work or service which is exacted from any person under the menace of any penalty and for which the said person has not offered himself voluntarily." From this early stage, a dichotomy between the term "slavery" and "forced labor" commenced, whereby the former was regarded as relating more to Old World chattel slavery and actual legal rights of ownership over another human being (which no longer exist in any jurisdiction), and the term "forced labor," which focuses more on coercive and threatening conditions used to extract involuntary labor. The United Nations expanded its 1926 definition in 1956 with the Supplementary Convention on the Abolition of Slavery, the Slave Trade, and Institutions and Practices Similar to Slavery, which included various other forms of slavelike exploitation, such as serfdom and debt bondage. Article 1(a) of the convention defined debt bondage as

> The status or condition arising from a pledge by a debtor of his personal services or those of a person under his control as security for a debt, if the value of those services as reasonably assessed is not applied towards the liquidation of the debt or the length and nature of those services are not respectively limited or defined.

Beginning in 1972 in India and following in other South Asian nations after that, bonded debts of all kinds were deemed illegal. Hence this 1956 UN definition is not as helpful in the contemporary South Asian context, as it is now largely irrelevant whether the services provided toward the liquidation of the debt are reasonably assessed or not. The mere existence of a debt securitized by pledged labor constitutes bonded labor and is illegal.

Following the United Nations' expansion of its definition of the term "slavery," the ILO's Committee of Experts on the Application of Conventions and Recommendations also expanded its definition of the term "forced labor" to include the following eight categories:

1. Slavery and abduction for forced labor
2. Compulsory participation in public works
3. Coercive recruitment practices
4. Domestic workers in forced labor situations
5. Forced labor exacted by the military
6. Bonded labor or debt bondage
7. Trafficking in persons
8. Prison labor

These and other definitions have been internationally reinforced numerous times, including in the 1948 UN Universal Declaration on Human Rights, which held that "no one shall be held in slavery or servitude" (Article 4), and the 1950 European Convention for the Protection of Human Rights and Fundamental Freedoms (the "European Convention on Human

Rights"), which in Article 4 affirmed that "No one shall be held in slavery or servitude" and "No one shall be required to perform forced or compulsory labour." Nevertheless, the early dichotomy of the terms "slavery" and "forced labor" has led to confusion as to what these phenomena truly constitute. Is (chattel) slavery a form of forced labor separate from other forms such as bonded or prison labor? Is forced labor a form of slavery that encapsulates other similar practices, such as bonded labor and forced marriage? Or are all of these abuses different categories of servile labor exploitation that are generally agreed to be a violation of essential human rights? Without question, the absence of choice is critical to any definition of slavery or forced labor, and if certain categories of bonded labor are predicated on a voluntary choice, then those categories would be excluded from either slavery or forced labor.

Recognizing the long history of scholarship on slavery and forced labor, I would like to offer my thoughts as to what constitutes slavery in the modern context. My own thinking has evolved during my last several years of research, since I wrote my first book, *Sex Trafficking*, in which I also offered definitions of "slavery" and "slave trading" (the latter to replace the term "human trafficking").[43] In this book, I use the term "slavery" as a unifying term that captures three primary categories of contemporary servitude: forced labor, bonded labor, and human trafficking.[44] This usage is distinct from the original usage of the term, which focused more narrowly on legal rights of ownership over another human being associated with chattel slavery. I understand and to some extent agree with the reluctance in some circles to use the historically and emotionally charged term "slave." This emotionalism has often been sensationalized for personal or organizational gain by would-be activists focused more on fundraising or selling stories. We can either allow these individuals to take control over this important word and corrupt its usage for their own gain, or more genuine scholars and activists can reclaim this term and adapt it responsibly to the modern context. One could also select a different unifying term—such as unfree labor or human servitude—but I believe "slavery" may be the best choice for now. I do, however, remain circumspect about using the word, and I do so only as a synonym for these other unifying terms. I hope that additional scholarly efforts will be undertaken to clarify the term further and set the conditions of its responsible usage. In that spirit, the following is my current definition of slavery as applied to the modern context:

Slavery is the condition of any person whose liberty is unlawfully restricted while the person is coerced through any means to render labor or services, regardless of compensation, including those who enter the condition because of the absence of a reasonable alternative.

Bonded labor is the condition of any person whose liberty is unlawfully
restricted while the person is coerced through any means to render
labor or services, regardless of compensation, including those who
enter the condition because of the absence of a reasonable alternative,
where that person or a relation initially agreed to pledge his labor or
service as repayment for an advance of any kind.

Per these definitions, bonded labor is a type of slavery in which the servitude commences with an agreement whereby credit is provided in exchange for pledged labor. While labor is the dominant mode of credit repayment, repayment may also occur through the sale of the bonded laborer
to another creditor or the sale of family members to other exploiters such
as human traffickers.[45] The nature of the credit is irrelevant, be it cash,
payment in kind, tenancy, or other consideration. Unlawful restrictions to
liberty primarily indicate restrictions to a person's lawful freedoms of
movement and employment, as well as loss of sovereignty over self and
family. Where any such restriction to liberty is linked to the coercion of
labor or services, then the extent and duration of the restriction should be
irrelevant—be it partially or fully restricted (extent), or be it restricted only
a few weeks or for a lifetime (duration). Similarly, once coercion is linked
to restriction of liberty, then the manner in which the labor or services are
coerced should be irrelevant, be it coercion through physical or psychological violence or threats, conscripting additional family members or de-
pendents to render labor, or coercion through means that extend the duration of pledged labor, such as wage deductions, manipulated debts or interest
on debts, less-than-market prices for goods and services used to repay
debts, or similar tactics. Where any exchange of credit for pledged labor is
said to exist by an individual claiming to be a bonded laborer, it should
be presumed that there was an agreement to do so, regardless of written
evidence.

Depending on how one interprets and qualifies the key phrases "restriction of liberty," "coerced," and "reasonable alternative," the total number of
slaves in the world can vary considerably. The most restrictive interpretation and narrow qualification of these terms would result in *22.4 million*

slaves in the world at the end of 2011. A more reasonable interpretation and qualification of these terms, which I believe is reflective of the broader nature of contemporary servitude, results in a tally of *30.5 million slaves* in the world at the end of 2011. In this case, "restriction of liberty" includes the qualification "unlawful" and can be partial or for various periods of time, so long as some degree of freedom of movement or employment is limited and some degree of sovereignty over self and family is limited; "coercion" includes the qualification "through any means" and can include forms of physical, psychological, economic, social, or cultural duress as well as manipulations to extend or increase bonded debts; and a "reasonable alternative" means, at a minimum, sustained subsistence-level income and security. The linked conditions of coercion of labor or services without the lawful ability to move freely or pursue alternate employment should always be sufficient to establish some form of slavery in the modern context, but the narrowness or breadth with which we construe these terms will alter our quantum of slavery significantly. Though I typically err on the side of conservatism in my estimates and definitions, I believe these terms should be construed as widely as reasonably possible, particularly given that every category of restriction tied to coercion that is excluded provides a loophole that shrewd criminals can use to exploit slaves to the fullest, while using their power and influence to make it appear that they are meeting the conditions of the loophole they have been granted. Defining slavery in the contemporary context is more than just an academic exercise. Real people are suffering real servitude every day, and our ability to identify, liberate, and protect such individuals can only be as effective (and broad) as is our definition.

Whether the number of slaves in the world at the end of 2011 was 22.4 million or 30.5 million, neither sum is large enough to justify the oft-repeated statement in sensationalistic antislavery circles that there are more slaves today than at any point in human history. This is a *false* assertion unsupported by historical fact. There are *considerably fewer* slaves today than at many points in human history (particularly when the same definition is applied to past and present), but there are certainly far too many slaves today *given that slavery is illegal everywhere in the world*, a fact that has not been the case for the majority of human history. The numbers I have provided above represent midpoints of 95 percent confidence intervals that I have calculated based on several years of data gathering around the world, and I urge the reader to review appendix A in detail, where the logic of these calculations and further details on the definitions used are discussed.

A few words on "compensation" and "lack of alternative" are in order before proceeding to the discussion of whether bonded labor can be considered slavery. Most NGOs and activists working in the field of modern slavery use a definition of "slave" as a person held captive and coerced against their will to perform labor or services, where compensation does not exceed basic subsistence. I believe the inclusion of compensation as a consideration in whether a person is being exploited as a slave or not is largely irrelevant given the realities of modern forms of slavery. Where a person is held captive and coerced to perform labor or services, it is almost always the case that compensation is unreasonable, but it may often times exceed subsistence. Advances to bonded laborers can certainly exceed subsistence, and bribes or other payments provided to slaves or families of individuals caught in slave labor also often exceed nominal amounts. Where lawful freedoms of movement, employment, and sovereignty of self and family are restricted in conjunction with coerced labor, and where no reasonable alternative is available, then my experience tells me that this person is probably a slave, regardless of the level of their compensation in cash or in kind.

With regard to the lack of a reasonable alternative, I have previously discussed my reasoning for including this qualifier as crucial to the definition of bonded labor, and I believe it equally applies to all forms of slavery, especially for human trafficking, where victims often enter into agreements with traffickers knowing the risks but do so regardless, because of the lack of a reasonable alternative. Duress to person or goods and economic duress following from a lack of sustained alternative sources of subsistence income and security negate any potential for the voluntary entry into deeply exploitative or slave-labor conditions. Conversely, the presence of a reasonable alternative does not negate the possibility of a tied credit-labor agreement being construed as bonded labor, when liberty is still restricted and labor is still coerced through any means, including manipulation of debts. However, if a reasonable alternative is present, and if liberty is not restricted and coercion not used to extract or extend labor or services, then the individual would not be considered a slave of any kind. There are easily tens of millions of people in South Asia and around the world who would fall into this category.

My arguments on reasonable alternatives are perhaps the most aggressive in relation to what I consider to constitute and not constitute bonded labor, so additional discussion is in order.

BONDED LABOR AND SLAVERY: THE QUESTION OF VOLUNTARY AGREEMENTS

Some economists have posited that some or all forms of bonded labor are not forms of forced labor or slavery because they constitute agreements freely entered into by rational parties.[46] The economist Garance Genicot summarized the typical argument well:

> Interestingly, bonded labour is ex-ante voluntary. In the case of debt-bondage, a tenant or debtor voluntarily places himself in a servile position, even though he may have little or no choice in the matter. Just as a serf is tied to his master by apparently voluntary acts of fealty, the bonded labourer is a technically free wage labourer whose state of servitude may be terminated on payment of the debt. So, although once bonded, a worker is unfree, the act of choosing to be bonded is usually one freely made to avert acute poverty or starvation.[47]

By this logic, even if after a debt bondage agreement is entered by a laborer with little or no choice, and if the laborer is subsequently exploited in slavelike conditions, if he chose to enter into the contract from the outset, it is a free and rational choice that must not be considered involuntary, and, by extension, it cannot be considered slavery or bondage. The laborer's choice of debt bondage is deemed to be welfare enhancing, even if it is only the best choice in a spectrum of bad to worse options. This logic suggests that banning debt bondage agreements would cause harm to the peasant, as he would then have to select from a worse set of options. Thus, if an individual chooses the debt bondage agreement, it is because it is his best option, and this freely made and rational choice negates the element of coercion required to establish slavery or forced labor.

Certain categories of bonded labor would nevertheless remain outside the scope of this argument: bonded laborers who inherit debts and are forced to continue working to repay them, bonded laborers who would rather seek alternative employment but are prevented by the creditor-exploiter from doing so, family members of the contracting party who are forced to contribute their labor to work off the debt, and any other category whereby at the outset or before entering an agreement the choice is not strictly voluntary and no provision to escape the agreement is allowed.

Still, this "voluntary debt bondage" argument proposed by some economists would exclude millions of the bonded laborers in South Asia and around the world today, where season after season, or every few years, individuals appear to enter voluntarily into agreements in which credit is exchanged for labor for some period of time, because this is their best option. As previously discussed, the key error in this line of reasoning is the assumption that the peasant has made a fully voluntary and rational choice to enter an agreement—which he often knows will result in some sort of manipulation or exploitation by the lender—and that his entry regardless of this knowledge indicates that he has made a voluntary choice to enhance his welfare because the alternative will be worse. "Better" and "worse" are typically understood by economists to relate to levels of income, food, shelter, security, and other primary goods. While it may be true that the bonded labor agreement will provide enhanced income, security, and shelter for a period of time, this does not necessarily mean the individual is "better off." Were these economists to speak to current or former bonded laborers, they would hear a near-unanimous chorus of voices declaring that freedom is always preferable to coercion and abuse. The inherent value to these individuals of freedom, self-respect, and self-sovereignty— even if coupled with destitution, starvation, and abject poverty—far outweighs security of food and shelter in exchange for servitude and exploitation. Far from being evidence of a voluntary choice, the fact that the peasant selects the exploitation over freedom does not mean he rationally values food and security more than freedom; it simply demonstrates that he understands he must remain alive long enough to preserve the opportunity to attain what he values most: freedom. *The choice to enter bondage is a choice to preserve the opportunity to achieve freedom one day; it is not a choice to value food and shelter over freedom.* Time and again bonded laborers told me that, one day, they hoped to have freedom as well as survival. In the absence of this combination being possible, there is no truly voluntary "choice" of bondage, if that bondage is the best of a spectrum of miserable alternatives, most of which involve an inability to survive. Further, the assumption that the peasant is making his choice rationally is also misplaced. In addition to cogent arguments made by behavioral economists[48] that there are any number of irrational impulses that influence decision making for even the most free and empowered of us, a deeply destitute and desperate peasant faces numerous forces that can affect his ability to make rational choices, not the least of which is the highly prevalent sense of caste-based fatalism across South Asia, in which certain subordinated groups have been made to feel for centuries that bondage and servility are the best and only options available to them—and that they should be grateful to have them.

Perhaps the most important argument in this book is that the lack of a reasonable alternative to the exploitative debt bondage agreement directly negates the voluntary nature of the decision to make it. The decision may still be construed as voluntary from a classical economics standpoint, but I would argue that when an individual is faced with starvation, destitution, an oppressive social system, and no other opportunity for any mode of reasonable subsistence, that individual is hardly making a choice to enter servitude rationally and freely. Surely, any decent parent would "voluntarily" enter into abject slavery if they had no other means to ensure that their children could survive. Have they entered by choice simply because there was no alternative? Are they not still a slave? A former chief justice of India, P. N. Bhagwati, summarized this line of reasoning best in the Indian Supreme Court's first case on bonded labor, *People's Union for Democratic Rights vs. Union of India and Others*, 1982:

> Moreover, in a country like India where there is so much poverty and unemployment and there is no equality of bargaining power, a contract of service may appear on its face voluntary but it may, in reality, be involuntary, because while entering into the contract, the employee, by reason of his economically helpless condition, may have been faced with Hobson's choice, either to starve or to submit to the exploitative terms dictated by the powerful employer.[49]

We must never forget that landowners and other producer-creditors possess near-complete control over all local resources, land, access to markets, and oftentimes the law itself. They work assiduously to ensure that the peasant has absolutely no reasonable alternative. Is this to be held against the peasant as reason to declare his agreement as being voluntary? Further, the fact that society at large has failed to provide any reasonable alternative opportunity for subsistence and decent existence to the poor of South Asia should not be held against the poor as an argument that they are choosing bondage freely! On the contrary, society's failure to provide adequate provision of resources and opportunities so that survival does not have to be traded for freedom is hardly an acceptable reason to argue that destitution-motivated debt bondage is not slavery. To do so provides a gaping loophole for ruthless exploiters to manipulate conditions so that the destitute always seem to choose debt bondage freely (or any other form of labor exploitation), which renders debt bondage and many other forms of servitude outside the scope of international and domestic laws against slavery, human trafficking, and forced labor and significantly diminishes those categories of agreements that would be captured by laws against bonded labor in South Asia. Where the parties to a debt bondage agreement are severely asymmetric in power and resources, the presumption must be that the peasant has not entered the agreement by choice, unless this presumption can be incontrovertibly overturned. Economists must appreciate the immense forces of poverty, deprivation, and fatalism that conspire to negate choice and rationality among the poorest and most needy of the world, as well as the immense power asymmetries that keep them enslaved once they enter bonded labor agreements. They should also consider expanding the scope of what is deemed to enhance welfare and utility to include considerations for fairness, freedom, and human dignity. Above all, the absence of any reasonable alternative must be construed as an element of coercion or duress that negates voluntary choice in any debt bondage agreement, rendering it, without question, a form of contemporary slavery.

TWENTY FORCES PROMOTING BONDED LABOR TODAY

Having traced the history of bonded labor in South Asia and explored the contemporary nature of debt bondage agreements, we must now identify those forces that promote the persistence of bonded labor in South Asia today. Most of these forces are common across the four countries covered in this book. These forces are centered on an essential thesis that is vital to understand if we are ever to eradicate bonded labor: *The persistence of bonded labor in South Asia is driven by the ability to generate substantial profits at almost no real risk, through the exploitation of an immense un-derclass of systemically impoverished and vulnerable people.* The first half of this equation is promoted by *demand-side forces* of substantial profit at no real risk; the second half of this equation is driven by *supply-side forces* that promote the systemic availability of a vast pool of potential bonded laborers.

Both supply and demand forces combine to form an enormous system of human exploitation. The twenty specific forces that promote bonded labor can be sorted into these two categories. I have enumerated the forces within the categories by the order in which they should be tackled. The nature and effects of each of these forces will become evident in the chapters that follow. The forces that promote bonded labor are:

I. Demand-Side Forces (Substantial Profit at No Real Risk)

Demand-side forces are divided into legal deficiencies and systemic barriers.

A. Legal Deficiencies

1. INSUFFICIENT MINIMUM WAGES

Government-stipulated minimum wages for low-skilled and semiskilled labor in the sectors prone to bonded labor range from $1.10 to $2.60 per day. Even if these wages were actually paid, they are insufficient to meet basic subsistence needs, let alone allow for savings. The profit margins of the businesses that exploit bonded laborers can easily support substantially higher minimum wages. This may reduce profitability or slightly increase the prices of the products produced, but elevated minimum wages are compulsory.

2. INSUFFICIENT SCOPE OF VICARIOUS LIABILITY LAWS

The absence of a legal standard of strict vicarious liability[50] that in-cludes the relationship between employers and labor subcontractors (*ja-madars*) is a fundamental gap in the legal regimes of South Asia, one that directly promotes risk-free labor exploitation. This absence allows producers in numerous sectors who hire *jamadars* to staff projects, manage labor, and disburse wages to remain almost entirely immune to culpability for the *jamadar*'s exploitation, which is often sanctioned by the employer as a way to minimize labor costs.

3. LAND LAWS THAT PROMOTE THE ONGOING LANDLESSNESS OF PEASANTS AND AGRICULTURAL LABORERS

Because the poor, especially low-caste, tribal, and untouchable groups, lack rights of ownership to land, they are beholden to landowners for a place to live. The threat of eviction renders them easier to exploit, and the lack of land ownership means they have nothing to cultivate for their own subsistence or income.

4. DEEPLY INSUFFICIENT PENALTIES IN THE LAW FOR THE CRIME OF BONDED LABOR

The laws against bonded labor in all four South Asian countries covered in this book (Bangladesh does not actually have a specific law against bonded labor) prescribe penalties that are grossly insufficient as compared to the economic benefits of the crime.

B. Systemic Barriers

5. SEVERELY LACKING ENFORCEMENT OF LABOR LAWS, SUCH AS THEY EXIST, INCLUDING FLAUNTING OF MINIMUM-WAGE LAWS AND VIRTUALLY NO PROSECUTIONS FOR OFFENCES AGAINST BONDED LABOR

Labor laws across South Asia are largely unenforced. Minimum-wage laws in particular are flaunted with impunity. In addition to boosting profits, underpaid minimum wages also ensure that laborers are unable to accrue savings to use in times of economic need. Most important, there are almost no prosecutions anywhere in South Asia for the crime of bonded labor. The absence of prosecution helps create a high-profit, low-risk environment in which to exploit bonded laborers.

6. CORRUPTION IN GOVERNMENT, LAW ENFORCEMENT, AND THE JUDICIARY

Corruption at all levels of society allows bonded labor to persist virtually risk free, whether it is the local law enforcement official or revenue collector who turns the other eye in exchange for a bribe or district magistrates and judges who regularly side with landowners, contractors, and producers when it comes to any issue relating to bonded labor.

7. DIFFICULTIES WITH IDENTIFICATION AND FREEING OF BONDED LABORERS

Many bonded laborers do not want to be identified as such (for fear of eviction, beatings, or other reprisals), and numerous bonded labor situations are cloaked by the veil of "voluntary" agreements, which can render it more challenging to establish the existence of bonded labor.

8. REPORTING MECHANISMS THAT MAKE IT IMPOSSIBLE FOR BONDED LABORERS TO IDENTIFY THEMSELVES SAFELY

The poorly conceived complaint structure for self-identification of bonded labor is highly problematic. Any bonded laborer who wants to identify himself must typically do so in front of both the very individual exploiting him and a revenue collector or other bureaucrat who is usually well known to be the ally of the producer-exploiter.

9. THE *JAMADAR* SYSTEM OF LABOR SUBCONTRACTING

Labor subcontractors (*jamadars*) who recruit laborers with advances and then ruthlessly exploit them through bonded and forced labor are at the root of slave-labor conditions in numerous sectors in South Asia. The insufficiency of vicarious liability laws that capture the employer-*jamadar* relationship further promotes this wanton exploitation.

II. Supply-Side Forces (Promote Vulnerability to Debt Bondage)

Supply-side forces include:

10. POVERTY

With 1.2 billion people in South Asia living on incomes of less than two dollars per day, the pool of available individuals to exploit is virtually limitless. Until poverty is systemically and comprehensively tackled, there will always be individuals vulnerable to debt bondage and other forms of servitude in South Asia.

11. A LACK OF SUFFICIENT CREDIT RESOURCES FOR THE POOR, ESPECIALLY FOR NON-INCOME-GENERATING PURPOSES

Because the poorest of the poor are unable to access sufficient credit at reasonable terms,[51] and because they are unable to access capital for non-income-generating activities (like food, medicine, or home repairs), they are forced into informal credit markets where landowners or *jamadars* are eager to lend them money in exchange for debt bondage.

12. A LACK OF REASONABLE AND SUSTAINED INCOME OPPORTUNITIES FOR THE POOR, ESPECIALLY FORMER BONDED LABORERS

Because the poor do not have alternative opportunities for reasonable and sustained income and security, they must return time and again to those who lend them capital in exchange for labor. Even those who return on a seasonal basis must accept deeply exploitative agreements because they have no alternative other than starvation.

13. INADEQUATE INFRASTRUCTURE OR MEANS OF TRANSPORTATION FOR RURAL LABORERS TO ACCESS MARKETS

Because laborers, peasants, and other rural workers typically lack access to markets, they are unable to generate their own income, even if they do possess their own land or have the means to produce some goods or products for sale.

14. A LACK OF COMPREHENSIVE LITERACY AND BASIC EDUCATION FOR THE POOR

A lack of education means that peasants cannot understand or even read the agreements they sign in exchange for credit and that they are not able to keep track of the debits or credits of their accounts with the lender, which renders them easier to exploit. Lack of education also limits the alternative wage opportunities available to the peasant.

15. VIRTUALLY NONEXISTENT REHABILITATION OF IDENTIFIED AND FREED BONDED LABORERS, OR UNREASONABLE LAG TIME BETWEEN IDENTIFICATION AND REHABILITATION

Even when identified and freed, bonded laborers rarely receive the benefits of government-mandated rehabilitation packages, because of corruption and a painfully slow bureaucracy. Sometimes three or more years can pass before the first trickles of assistance come through, and by then the individual has migrated elsewhere or has been reenslaved into a new debt bondage situation.

16. POORLY DESIGNED REHABILITATION PACKAGES THAT DO NOT PROVIDE SUFFICIENT CASH INCOME AND RELEVANT VOCATIONAL TRAINING TO FORMER BONDED LABORERS

Many rehabilitation packages do not provide sufficient cash income to the bonded laborer in order to meet basic consumption needs for at least two years while training and other support is provided. As a result, former bonded laborers often go back into debt. The training itself may also be irrelevant to the laborer's skills and opportunities or may be incomplete and inadequate.

17. ISOLATION AND PAUCITY OF UNIONIZATION OF RURAL LABORERS

Isolation keeps peasants vulnerable and easy to exploit. Fewer ties to society limits opportunities, and an inability to unionize (often because of powers exerted by local landowners and producers) deeply diminishes the bargaining power of laborers, which often means they must accept heavily exploitative employment conditions.

18. ENVIRONMENTAL DISASTER OR TRANSFORMATION

Environmental disaster and massive environmental transformation attributable to climate change or other forces almost always expand levels of destitution, human trafficking, and debt bondage. In the midst of these calamities, *jamadars*, traffickers, and other exploiters are often the first on the scene, with promises of work opportunities or monetary advances, and these quickly transform into bondage and slavery.

19. INSUFFICIENT ACCESS TO HEALTH CARE AND BASIC MEDICINES

Many bonded laborers enter into debt or exacerbate debt levels after an illness or injury. As a result of isolation, restrictions on movement, and insufficient savings, the only medicines available to most bonded laborers are through their exploiters, and these are provided at high costs through loans.

20. SOCIAL AND SYSTEMIC BIASES AGAINST SUBORDINATED CASTES AND ETHNIC GROUPS

Longstanding biases against minority castes and "untouchable" groups in South Asia are among the most powerful forces that promote the persistent exploitation of these people. As long as these severe asymmetries of rights and opportunities are tolerated in South Asia, there will be no end to the crime of bonded labor and numerous other forms of exploitation.

There are other forces that promote bonded labor in South Asia, including some that may be more country specific. However, these twenty forces are by far the most powerful and pervasive, and they allow the system to persist today. If these twenty forces were swiftly and comprehensively addressed by a fully resourced and sustained campaign across all levels of government, civil society, and citizenry, I am confident that bonded labor would become an offense consigned to history. To the extent that the commitment and resources are more limited, then, at a minimum, tackling the demand-side forces will provide a significant dent in overall levels of debt bondage, without having to alleviate in the near term the vast forces that promote the supply of potential bonded laborers.

In the hopes that there will be sufficient commitment and resources to tackle all of these forces, here are the ten initiatives I suggest that will help eliminate bonded labor.

TEN INITIATIVES TO ELIMINATE BONDED LABOR

The following ten initiatives, summarized in table 1.4, are intended to address the primary forces that continue to promote the system of bonded labor in South Asia. Tackling these forces will simultaneously address other forms of servitude, such as forced and child labor, as well as labor exploitation more generally. The logic and details of these initiatives will be discussed fully in chapter 8, after we have traveled across South Asia to bear witness to the extent and complexity of contemporary bonded labor. I believe each of these ten initiatives, deployed for at least ten years, will provide an optimal chance at eliminating bonded labor and other forms of slave-labor exploitation across South Asia. Initiatives 2 and 5 are clearly the most ambitious. India must be the nation that takes the leadership role in advancing initiatives such as these, given its overall resources and clear intentions of becoming a world economic superpower. While India's bourgeoning economic might cannot be disregarded, the country can never become a legitimate global leader so long as more than 75 percent of its citizens live on poverty-level incomes of less than two dollars per day and as countless millions are exploited as exiles of humanity.

India has done more than any other country in South Asia to tackle bonded labor, but, by my account, it still has much to do. So long as bonded labor exists in South Asia, the current governments of the region are not very different from the European colonists who exploited the peasant labor of millions of Indians to boost their wealth and power. In fact, I consider today's governments in South Asia even worse, for they exploit not distant people in a time when human rights are less evolved but their fellow man in a time when slavery is rejected by all of humanity and basic human rights are supposed fundamental guarantees of every man, woman, and child on the planet. Bonded labor is a rejection of the most essential human rights to freedom and dignity, and its persistence is a rejection of any semblance of decent society. That lack of decency is not sustainable and will come at a great cost. Bonded laborers are growing angry, and extremists have begun to recruit among their ranks with some success. If nothing else, the risks to security inherent in mass poverty, injustice, exploitation, and suffering should move the powers of South Asia to tackle these issues with alacrity.

TABLE 1.4
Ten Initiatives Intended to Address the Primary Forces That Continue to Promote
the System of Bonded Labor in South Asia

Initiative	Forces Addressed
1. Legal reform, including increase in minimum wages, expansion and enforcement of the legal principle of vicarious liability, redesign of land rights to achieve reasonable land ownership for the poor, and massive increase in economic penalties for bonded labor violations.	1, 2, 3, 4
2. Transnational slavery intervention force that frees bonded laborers, detains offenders, receives bonded labor complaints, enforces minimum wage and other key labor-law provisions, and monitors supply chains for tainted products.	5, 6, 7, 8
3. Fast-track courts for any bonded, forced, or child labor case, with independent observers and judicial review.	5, 6
4. Redesign of the *jamadar* system so that it can be fully and independently regulated or abolition of the system all together, to be replaced by labor recruitment solely by producers in charge of the commercial project.	9
5. Elevated scaling and effectiveness of select government antipoverty programs, focused on (1) massive expansion of microcredit, especially for non—income generating activities; (2) a global economy integration initiative for the poor in rural areas; (3) major expansion of rural infrastructure and manufacturing projects—all focused on achieving effective execution and delivery.	10, 11, 12, 13
6. Expanded and free rural education for all ages, with a particular focus on literacy and small business skills.	14
7. Rapid-response registration and rehabilitation teams for identified bonded laborers.	15, 16
8. Rural integration and information dissemination efforts, including distribution of mobile devices to promote information sharing.	17
9. Rapid-response environmental disaster teams focused on alleviating immediate economic and healthcare needs in disaster areas; also, the expansion of access to healthcare and basic medicines in rural areas in general.	18, 19
10. National awareness and educational campaigns focused on alleviating social and systemic biases against subordinated castes and ethnic groups.	20

WHAT CAN ONE PERSON DO?

In the face of the immense forces that promote the persistence of bonded labor in South Asia, it may seem daunting to contemplate what one person can do to combat these crimes. There are at least seven steps you can undertake today to join the fight against bonded labor:

1. Learn about the issue: Read this book and share it with others who are interested in learning more about bonded labor or child labor in South Asia.

2. Financial support: Each of the NGOs discussed in this book is working mightily to tackle various aspects of bonded labor in South Asia. More important, they are reputable and responsible. Any financial or volunteer support you can offer is of tremendous benefit to their efforts.

3. Contact lawmakers: For those of you not living in South Asia, do not forget that you purchase products every day that are potentially touched by bonded and child labor in South Asia. Demand that your lawmakers do more to ensure that corporations do their part to certify that their supply chains are not tainted by these exploitations. For those of you living in South Asia, do all of this and add to it direct campaigns to your lawmakers to ensure that they combat bonded labor more effectively, employing the kind of initiatives described in this book.

4. Contact corporations: any company that sources raw materials or low-end labor in South Asia must be pressured to investigate and certify that their supply chains are free of slave labor of any kind; consumers must also demand that companies whose products they purchase ensure that this kind of investigation and certification becomes a regular aspect of their operating model.

5. Community vigilance: for those in South Asia, organize yourselves into bonded labor community vigilance committees, identify a nearby geographic area where the kinds of industries described in this book are based, and work with NGOs to help identify bonded or child labor and promote the just and full reempowerment of these individuals. Push relentlessly for the effective prosecution of exploiters. Follow the guidance of NGOs on how you can be most helpful, as they have great experience in this area.

6. Tackle supply-side forces: while most demand-side forces are difficult for individuals to address, anyone in the world can form an organization

that directly combats one or more of the supply-side forces that promote bonded labor. In aggregate, such efforts can make a tremendous difference and will pressure governments to do their part.

7. Social media: use the power of social media to contribute to the fight against bonded labor. You can use these tools to spread awareness, organize community efforts and protest campaigns, or pressure lawmakers and law enforcement to do more. Make videos or documentaries that educate others on the issue; use GPS tagging on your mobile devices to record areas in which you feel bonded or child laborers might be working, then report back to NGOs or reliable law enforcement. Find other creative ways to fight back against slavery by using all forms of social media and technology tools.

If you take some or all of these steps, we will be much farther along toward creating an environment in which bonded labor can no longer exist.

For my part, it is and will remain my lifelong mission to see the end of these crimes. I will continue to research bonded labor, advocate against it, and do everything in my power to promote its elimination. Toward the end of my longest research trip for this book, back in September 2010, I wrote a letter to the chief justice of the Supreme Court of India, outlining some of the bonded labor violations I had documented and offering to share more information from my years of research. My hope was that the letter would be treated as a writ petition under Article 32 of the Constitution of India and would move the court to order an investigation and potentially take action against the exploiters. To date, I have not received a reply. Similarly, my attempts to contact the head of the Ministry of Labour in India to share my research findings have not received a response. For what it is worth, I will continue to combat bonded labor through any and all means available to me. To eliminate bonded labor is to eliminate the most extensive form of slavery in the world today, and though I did not foresee this as my life's calling when I took my first research trip in the summer of 2000, understanding slavery and promoting more effective efforts to combat it have become the fundamental occupations of my life. Despite considerable obstacles, I derive motivation from the thousands of slaves I have met—humbled by their fortitude, inspired by their dignity, and stirred to do justice to their courage. No matter how many times they are broken, no matter how much is taken from them, and no matter how forsaken they feel, they display a strength of spirit that is more transcendent than any force I have witnessed. It is more powerful than the greed, the violence, and the barbaric qualities that are responsible for their enslavement. Their will to be free can only prevail, no matter how long the dark days of human indecency may last.

{ 2 }

Agriculture

KAMAIYA AND *HARI*

Bowed by the weight of centuries he leans
Upon his hoe and gazes on the ground,
The emptiness of ages on his face,
And on his back the burden of the world.

—"MAN WITH THE HOE," EDWIN MARKHAM

THE *KAMAIYA* OF THE WESTERN TERAI

Few people travel to the remote western Terai region of Nepal, home to the majority of the caste-based debt bondage in the nation. I only managed to venture there on my third visit to Nepal, having spent the previous two trips in the central and eastern portions of the country. Nepal is a strikingly beautiful land. Try to imagine two continents colliding into each other in a sixty-million-year-old shoving match. The result is Nepal, and the Terai is the narrow strip of gently sloping flat land that borders the Indian state of Uttar Pradesh to the south. Above the Terai, the full drama of the shoving match is revealed, first with the steep folds of the Mahabarat Range, which rise up to nine thousand feet, followed by the wide valley called the Pahar, or Hill Region, in which half the population of Nepal lives. Finally, beyond the Pahar the landscape launches into the sky with the magnificent Himalayas. While the Himalayas rightfully capture the attention of most visitors to Nepal, the Terai possesses a serene beauty all its own. Verdant rice fields span the horizon, swaying gently beneath the mist-capped Mahabharat peaks. Historically, the Terai is the birthplace of the Buddha, at Lumbini, and Sita (the wife of Rama in the epic *Ramayana*), at Janakpur. For all the Terai's physical beauty and historic legacy, it is also home to a level of human isolation, poverty, and exploitation that is, at times, as severe as anything I have seen in South Asia.

Researching the western Terai commences with a plane ride from Kathmandu as far west as possible, to the town of Dhangadhi. From there, a four-wheel-drive jeep is the only way to penetrate the deeper reaches of the region, where one finds former and current *kamaiya* bonded laborers, child slaves, and other forms of slave labor distinctive from anything else in Nepal. There was no way to avoid taking my third trip to Nepal during the monsoon season of 2010, which was particularly devastating throughout South Asia. The morning of my flight to Dhangadhi, I met my intrepid guide, Bruce Moore, of the remarkable American Himalayan Foundation, at the tiny domestic terminal in Kathmandu. Torrential rains battered the valley outside. Bruce promptly informed me that not one hour earlier, an Agni Air flight from Pokhara to Kathmandu had to circle the airport because of the heavy rains, and it eventually crashed into a mountain, killing all fourteen passengers on board.

"Don't worry," Bruce said, "We're on Buddha Air, and they're pretty safe. Anyway, now that one plane has crashed, we should be okay." Though I knew that the unfortunate crash of one plane that morning had little statistical relevance as to whether another plane might crash the same day, I accepted Bruce's reassurance—but kept my fingers crossed. We boarded our twin-propeller plane about two hours late, climbed out of the turbulent storms inundating the Kathmandu Valley, and an hour later landed in the tiny town of Dhangadhi, the gateway to the western Terai.

The first thing one notices about the western Terai is that it is much hotter than the elevated Kathmandu Valley. The second thing one notices is that it is very sparsely populated. On the other side of the border, in Uttar Pradesh, with roughly the same climate and potential for agriculture, the countryside teems with people and vehicles. In the Terai, one can drive along the well-paved Mahendra Highway for ten minutes without seeing another vehicle. About the only obstruction to travel are the numerous police checkpoints along the highway, intended to prevent the smuggling of drugs, elephant tusks, and people. There are also a few cantonment camps of former Maoist soldiers in the area, all of whom have been waiting since the ceasefire of 2006 for their promised integration into the Nepali army.

For our foray into the western Terai, Bruce and I were joined by Kamala Adhikari, the executive director of the Rural Health Education Services Trust (RHEST) in Nepal, which focuses on the education of minority girls

Photo 2.1. Former *kamaiya* children in school in the western Terai, thanks to the RHEST program.

to help protect them from trafficking and exploitation. We ventured deep into the region, down muddy roads, to reach several settlements of former *kamaiya* bonded laborers. In Himatpur, one such settlement, 405 households of former *kamaiya* eked out a dreary existence that left them vulnerable to various forms of labor exploitation. Some even returned to *kamaiya* debt bondage in order to survive. Every one of them was a member of the darker-skinned, low-caste *tharu* ethnic group. The *kamaiya* system of bonded labor was officially abolished by government decree in 2000, followed by the enactment of the Kamaiya Labour Prohibition Act, 2002,[1] but the suffering of these people before the ban remains fresh in their minds. This is how one former *kamaiya*, a seventy-year-old man named Janatlal, described his life:

In those days, we woke at four each morning to start work. Each family cultivated two or three bigha of land for the *jamindar* (landowner).[2] For this, he gave us one *bukura* (thatched hut) and 650 kg of paddy. We did not receive any money. Some of us might receive one or two *kattha* of land for ourselves, but if the *jamindar* wants he can take our harvest from this land as well. Our first meal was usually at 10 A.M. or 11 A.M. We ate rice and water. We try to have a second meal at 5 P.M. or 6 P.M., but sometimes this was not possible. The *jamindar* made us finish a certain amount of work each season, so sometimes we must stay up all night to finish. Mostly the men did the fieldwork; the women and children would feed the animals or go to the *jamindar*'s home for cooking and cleaning. We were never given holiday. We were forced to work even if we were sick. The *jamindar* would beat us whenever he wanted. If we need to borrow money, a good *jamindar* may give us a loan without interest, but mostly they took interest. If we try to go to a different *jamindar*, he must first pay our current *jamindar* the amount of our debt, and then we must work for the new *jamindar* to pay the debt. We did not know any alternatives. Each year in Maghi we did this contract; otherwise we had no place to live and no food to eat.

Former *kamaiya* such as Janatlal spend most of their lives harvesting rice and wheat under deeply oppressive conditions. Agricultural labor in South Asia is difficult enough without the added elements of coercion, violence, and exploitation. I once spent just half a day harvesting rice in a paddy field in India to experience what it was like. After a few hours spent ankle deep in water, perpetually bent over picking the rice paddies by hand, one by one, under the baking sun, I was dripping with sweat, and my lower back was in agony. This is the life for tens of millions of agricultural workers in South Asia, and it is an even bleaker means of existence for those who do so under servitude and bondage.

As difficult as life was before the 2000 ban for the *kamaiya* of the western Terai, life after the ban has in some ways been more challenging. From the southwestern border town of Mehandranagar to the rural areas near Nepalganj, I met scores of former *kamaiya*, and a man named Saniram living in the hills beyond Mahendranagar typified their plight:

The NGOs informed us about our freedom in 2000. In the beginning, it was difficult. We were scared, and the NGOs had to fight with our masters. Many masters kept us captive after the ban. Many people with larger debts ran away; many others stayed. I took my family to the gov-

Photo 2.2 Bonded laborer planting rice.

ernment resettlement camp, but I could not write, so I could not complete the form they gave me. As a result, we did not receive any land or a home. We came back to our old master and worked for him again. We worked in the *zirayat*[3] system for a time, but I had to borrow money to pay the expenses, so now I am in debt again, more than before 2000. The government has not kept its promise, so many *kamaiya* are much worse than before.

In addition to slipping back into debt bondage because they are unable to pay the upfront expenses for seed and fertilizer involved in the *zirayat* system of sharecropping, many former *kamaiya* have fallen back into debt bondage because of an inability to secure sufficient income for survival. As one former *kamaiya* named Jitendra explained:

The only work for us is agriculture or construction. We can get 100 to 150 rupees ($1.38 to $2.05)[4] each day for agriculture and 150 to 200 rupees

($2.05 to $2.75) each day for construction. But we can only find ten or fifteen days of work each month. This is not enough, so we must take loans. Sometimes we take advances from the shopkeepers, and we must pay off this advance with work. Sometimes we must go back to our masters for a loan, and then we work for months to pay back this debt. If it is a big expense, we do not eat. Many men have also gone with agents to India for work, but they come back, and they are not paid the wages. Every day the agents come to us and make offers to go to India. They promise to make passports and get us good wages. Even though we are not paid, the men keep going with them. The children also go. The agents come for the women, but we know they will send them for sex, so we do not send the women.

Each former *kamaiya* bonded laborer I met was crippled by an intensity of poverty and destitution that was difficult to behold. Many were ill with infections, and their meager frames and gaunt faces betrayed malnutrition and a highly deficient level of food consumption. Most survived on two small meals a day of rice, which they augmented by adding extra water. They felt trapped by poverty and betrayed by a government that promised them true freedom but failed to deliver anything close. Above all, they were desperate for a stable and sufficient source of income. This desperation was worst in the hills around Mahendranagar, where I found the highest levels of former *kamaiya* who had returned to the system. Despite the intense suffering that resulted from their newfound "freedom," almost every former *kamaiya* I met (even those who were forced back into debt bondage) expressed an incontrovertible preference for freedom over bondage.

"Definitely, this is a better life now," Laxmi told me in a government resettlement area for former *kamaiya* called Sri Lanka, so named because the undesirable land was completely surrounded by water and highly prone to flooding. "Now we are free," another member of the Sri Lanka resettlement camp told me. "Before we had to ask the landowner to do anything, even to go outside. Now we are free to do anything." Chaitram, from a village near Dhangadhi, said, "Now we can choose when to wake up and when to work. We can sleep in until eight in the morning if we want. We used to do everything for the landowners; now we do everything for us."

For each and every one of the former and current bonded laborers I met in the western Terai, the power of living in freedom was greater than any force of income or security that was tied to servitude. Every one of them wanted freedom, and the choice of bondage, then and now, was a choice made out of the most powerful duress. The only time I saw a smile on the agonized faces of the *kamaiya* was when they spoke about their freedom. It was, without question, their most cherished possession, and they yearned for a society that would help them retain it.

Unfortunately, 97 percent of the former *kamaiya* I documented belonged to the *tharu*, a marginalized ethnic group that has traditionally been outcast and exploited in Nepal. Mainstream society and the government have demonstrated little genuine interest in transitioning these people to sustained freedom and providing them equal rights and opportunities. The *tharu* I met were not at all the hapless and ignorant class of individuals that the upper-class landowners in Nepal would have me believe they are. On the contrary, I found my conversations with them to be stimulating and intellectually challenging. Many of the *tharu* had a keen sense of the world around them as well as a basic sense of fairness and human rights. Throughout my research, I have always made a point of ending interviews by asking if the interviewee had any questions for me. With uncanny regularity, the former *kamaiya* in several different villages throughout the western Terai would ask me the following three questions: "Do men and women get the same wage in America?" "Do you have a caste system in America like we have here?" and "How does the government give jobs to people in America?"

Gender equality, ethnic equality, and income opportunity are the primary concerns of the former *kamaiya* of the western Terai. In that way, they are hardly any different from the average reader of this book, other than that they are caught in an abyss of inequality and lack of opportunity that scars their lives with perpetual suffering.

THE *KAMAIYA* SYSTEM OF BONDED LABOR

As the narratives from the previous section reveal, the *kamaiya* system of bonded labor takes many forms throughout the western Terai. There are also other forms of agricultural debt bondage in Nepal, such as the *haliya* system (literally, "one who plows"), but these systems are largely similar in modality to the *kamaiya* system.[5] Indeed, the *kamaiya* system—along with the *hari* system of Pakistan discussed later in this chapter—are representative of the general structure of numerous forms of agricultural debt bondage that I documented throughout South Asia.[6] Though several industries such as brickmaking, bidi rolling, and carpet weaving have much higher proportions of laborers caught in slavelike labor exploitation than agriculture, agriculture has the highest gross number of bonded, forced, and child laborers of any industry in South Asia, at approximately eleven to fourteen million,[7] out of a total agricultural labor force in the region that exceeds 440 million.

The exact origins of the *kamaiya* system in Nepal are unclear. In the Indian state of Bihar, the *kamiya* system, which functions similarly to the *kamaiya* system of Nepal, was practiced from antiquity straight up until the 1930s. A similar system of agricultural debt bondage in the Indian state of Tamil Nadu, in which laborers enter into annual contracts with the landlord each year on Ugadi (the first day of the Telegu new year), is still practiced today. Finally, the *kamia-malik* system in the Indian state of Chhattisgarh is also analogous to the *kamaiya* system in Nepal. Scholars typically date the origins of the *kamaiya* system in Nepal as far back as 200 C.E. in the hills of central and western Nepal, though it took a more formalized shape during the thirteenth and fourteenth centuries, when the caste system was solidified under the Malla dynasty.[8] After the Malla dynasty, various forms of forced and bonded labor evolved throughout Nepal, and agricultural bonded laborers in particular became legally tied to landowners, who bought and sold them like chattel. Under the Rana dynasty, the relationship between caste and bondage in Nepal was further solidified. The first Rana ruler, Jang Bahadur Rana, established a legal code known as the Muluki Ain of 1854. This legal code ossified upper- and lower-caste roles in Nepal, including the first definition of the *tharu* caste as enslaveable (though not untouchable). The Muluki Ain of 1854 was eventually abolished by the 1963 Constitution of Nepal, and all discrimination based on caste was officially outlawed; however, more than a century of state-sanctioned, caste-based discrimination had solidified across Nepal, and it remains largely in practice today, especially in rural areas.

The term *kamaiya* was first used to describe the form of agricultural debt bondage among the low-caste *tharu* ethnic group prevalent in the western Nepal districts of Banke, Bardiya, Kailali, Kanchanpur, and Dang during the 1950s. Anecdotally, some *kamaiya* elders describe the period before the eradication of malaria with DDT in the Terai (pre-1951) as characterized by plentiful land with a sparse population, primarily because the *tharu* are said to have a natural immunity to malaria; hence they were the only people able to live in the area. However, following the eradication of malaria in the Terai, upper-caste Nepalis took legal title of the land that the *tharu* had been subsisting on for generations and then conscripted them into debt bondage.

The root of the term *kamaiya* consists of the word *kam*, which means "to work." A *kamaiya* is typically defined as "a tiller of the land" or an "obedient person." In fact, the word primarily refers to a particular type of labor relationship, one in which a peasant works on a farm for a master in order to repay a loan taken by himself or his antecedents. The wife of the lessee (the lessee is always male) is known as a *bukrahi*, and in the traditional system she is responsible for domestic servitude in the home of the master, though she may also work in the fields. The wife's workload varies from full time to part time, and in some cases she may undertake separate labor outside of the *kamaiya* contract. The male children of the *kamaiya* are known as *gaiwar*, and they traditionally tend to animals. The eldest son over the age of sixteen is known as *ghardhuriya*, and he will inherit the debt of his father when he passes. The female children are known as *kamaliri*, and they work as domestic servants in the home of the master. From this origin, a more extensive *kamaliri* system of domestic servitude across Nepal has developed, which I will discuss later in the chapter.

THE *KAMAIYA* CONTRACT

On the surface, the *kamaiya* system is a contractual agreement for one year initiated during the festival of Maghesakranti, or Maghi, (the first day of the Magha month of the Nepali calendar, usually around the middle of January). During Maghi, an agreement is made between an upper-caste landowner and a male *tharu* peasant, where the labor of the peasant's family is exchanged for loans (*saukni*) of various kinds. In the cases I documented, these loans typically fall into one of four categories, as shown in table 2.1.

Each of the contracts also includes allowances for clothes, medicine, and access to future credit. The contracts also include provisions for two meals per day (usually rice), except where land is provided for private cultivation, in which case the *kamaiya* can then cultivate their own food from the paddy provided to them. The valuation of the contracts varies. In the full paddy contract (where the paddy is typically monetized by selling to other *kamaiya* who have their own land or, sometimes, on the market), the

TABLE 2.1
Types of Loans Under the *Kamaiya* Contract

Type of Loan	Percentage of Total
Paddy	8
Paddy and *bukura*	69
Paddy, *bukura*, one to five *kattha* of land for private cultivation	18
One of above plus cash, or all cash	5

amount ranges from 450 to 750 kilograms of paddy per year, depending on the district, with an average of approximately 650 kilograms per year. Small amounts of the paddy may be substituted for maize or wheat. Where *bukura*, cash, or land is included, the amount of paddy is reduced by the estimated value of these assets. Including meals, medicines, and clothes, the total value of the typical *kamaiya* contract ranges from $160 to $180 per person per year. By and large, the meals are the most valuable component of the agreement, constituting roughly $90 to $100 in value per *kamaiya* per year. In exchange for the advance, almost every family member works to varying degrees without additional compensation for one year, generating an average annual net profit of almost $300 per laborer (see table B.1 in appendix B for details) for the agricultural labor alone. The domestic work performed by the wife and children of the contracted male *kamaiya* benefits the landowner through the avoidance of expense as opposed to the direct generation of cash income. This agricultural cash net profit represents a 75 percent return on investment (ROI) per *kamaiya* loan each season. During the season, the *kamaiya* are not allowed to take other work, and they are not allowed to leave the landowner's territory without permission. They report working an average of seventeen hours per day, six to seven days a week, and they can be rented out from one landowner to another to meet additional labor needs. The meager amount of per capita income ($0.45 to $0.50 per day) provided to the *kamaiya* as an in-kind advance is far from sufficient to meet basic subsistence needs, let alone emergencies or family rituals such as a wedding or funeral, so the *kamaiya* invariably borrow more money during the season, which is added to their overall debt. This debt is carried over to the next season, when the *kamaiya* theoretically enter into a new agreement with the landowner. They can only change landowners if the new landowner purchases the outstand-

Photo 2.3. Kamaiya huts in the western Terai.

ing debt from the old landowner and subsequently enters into his own agreement with the *kamaiya*. *Kamaiya* with larger debts are typically unable to secure new agreements with new landowners, but those with smaller debts may be able to change landowners more often.

The argument that the *kamaiya* enter into voluntary agreements as rational actors each Maghi, that they are making choices that optimize their welfare and, accordingly, that the agreements should not be construed as bondage or servitude, is highly misplaced. Numerous forces of duress and coercion negate what appears to be an ex-ante voluntary choice. Poverty, landlessness, social pressure, lack of rights, isolation, seasonal carryover of debt, inheritance of debt, sudden economic crises, and a nearly complete absence of any reasonable alternative mean that the *kamaiya* are pursuing the only option for survival that they have. This holds true of the traditional *kamaiya* system before it was banned in 2000, and it also holds true for those who have returned to various forms of *kamaiya*-like debt bondage after 2000.

THE BAN ON THE *KAMAIYA* SYSTEM

In addition to being exemplary of numerous systems of agricultural debt bondage found across South Asia, the *kamaiya* system of Nepal is of particular interest because it is also the most recent example of a government-level attempt to abolish bonded labor and institute a rehabilitation program for former bonded laborers. These efforts by the government of Nepal are highly representative of how *not* to go about attempting to eliminate bonded labor; hence it is worthwhile taking a closer look.

Throughout the 1960s to the 1990s, there were sporadic protests by *kamaiya* and NGOs seeking to abolish the *kamaiya* system. After the introduction of constitutional democracy in Nepal in 1990, NGOs and international organizations such as the ILO and UNICEF worked more systematically to combat *kamaiya* exploitation. In 1998, the government allocated approximately $700,000 to a "Bonded Labour Debt Relief and Upliftment Program," which was intended to pay off the debts of identified *kamaiya* bonded laborers. The program had little effect, and the morally dubious nature of attempting to repay fictitious debts to landowners was criticized domestically and abroad. In May 2000, a lawsuit brought by nineteen *kamaiya* families who worked for a former minister in the Nepali Congress government, Shiva Raj Patna, provided the tipping point. The families demanded that their debts be canceled, that they be paid minimum wages, that they be provided housing, and that the *kamaiya* system itself be abolished. Mass protests and rallies spread across western Nepal. Roughly two months after the original suit was filed, on July 17, 2000, the government of Nepal issued a decree outlawing the *kamaiya* system of bonded labor and extinguishing all *saukni* pursuant to the system. Minister for Land Reforms and Management Siddha Raj Ojha declared, "From this day, these bonded labourers will not only be free of any obligations but they won't have to pay any money they owe to the landlords and are free from any bonds that are either written or verbal."[9] Victory rallies followed, but the landowners did not comply so easily. The Kishan Hak Hita Manch (Landowners' Rights Protection Forum) was formed within weeks. The forum quickly grew to over eight thousand members, and it formally criticized the government for abolishing the *kamaiya* system and canceling all *sauknis*. Many landowners forcibly imprisoned their laborers and coerced them to continue working; other laborers fled their captors primarily with the help of NGOs. Most important, the government promises for credit, land, clothing, housing, food and water, and vocational training to assist the *kamaiya* in transitioning to freedom remain largely unfulfilled. More than/a decade after the ban, this chaotic and unsupported attempt at emancipation has left many former *kamaiya* materially worse off than before, providing a stark example of the fates that have befallen millions of bonded laborers across South Asia for whom liberation is promised but is not accompanied by adequate and sustained support.

AFTER THE *KAMAIYA* BAN

While it was an important advance for human rights in Nepal, the government's 2000 ban on the *kamaiya* system was made without sufficient programs and resources for the transition of former *kamaiya* to lasting freedom, which has had devastating consequences. Shortly after the ban, the government formed a Coordination and Monitoring Committee to identify and rehabilitate freed *kamaiyas*. The government also promised to construct settlement camps—including brick homes and a half *kattha* of land per family—for liberated *kamaiyas* and to supply them immediately with basic necessities such as food, blankets, and medicine. In August 2000, the government identified 18,400 *kamaiya* households (approximately one hundred thousand total *kamaiya*), grouped into four categories determined by possession of huts and land.[10] This number was widely regarded as exceedingly low. First, many *kamaiya* were not able to register, as they were held captive by their masters. Second, many other *kamaiya*, such as Saniram, were illiterate and unable to complete the registration forms. Finally, the registration process itself required that the landowners sign a form stipulating that the *kamaiya* had actually served as a *kamaiya*, which most were unwilling to do. The bottom two categories of those *kamaiya* who were registered were supposed to receive assistance from the government immediately. However, no assistance was provided to any former *kamaiya* for more than six months after the ban, and only in 2002 did the bottom two categories begin to receive land.[11] The land that was distributed was largely undesirable and isolated. Rather than receive solid brick homes, most of the homes that were provided were mud huts prone to destruction each monsoon season. Very little if any of the promised financial assistance was ever provided to the *kamaiya*, and the vocational training (sewing, bicycle repair, hair cutting, carpentry, masonry, leaf-plate stitching, and pottery) has been sporadic, unsustained, and less available to women than to men.

As a result of these and other deficiencies in postliberation support, the lives of former *kamaiya* in west Nepal remain shackled by poverty, a lack of income, and more modes of exploitation than before, including forced labor, child labor, labor trafficking, sex trafficking, and debt bondage, even now, more than a decade after the *kamaiya* ban. The primary sources of income are sharecropping and casual labor. To earn the same $160 to $180 in value per person from casual labor as the former *kamaiya* contract provided, the average laborer must secure approximately 130 to 150 days of (fully paid) casual labor per year. While some *kamaiya* manage to do this, most secure fewer days than that, and approximately 72 percent reported to me that they were chronically underpaid, which means they must take loans from landowners or are vulnerable to being trafficked or otherwise exploited. While *zirayat* sharecropping has ascended as the dominant mode of agricultural subsistence for the former *kamaiya* of the western Terai, the system is untenable for most *tharu* peasants, who are unable to afford their share of the costs of inputs. They are also not provided an equal share in the output, since the landowners prevent access to markets where the produce is sold. As a result, loans must be taken, and debt bondage ensues. In aggregate, I calculate that approximately 42 percent of former *kamaiya* have fallen back into chronic debt bondage. The majority of the others struggle to survive and are prone to numerous other forms of labor exploitation. This failure of the government of Nepal to emancipate the *kamaiya* effectively is nothing short of a human rights catastrophe. Member of Parliament Sapana Malla explained to me during a meeting in Kathmandu that in addition to corruption and poverty, a general disregard for certain classes of people in Nepal is responsible for the lack of adequate efforts to protect or assist them. "Laws and policies are not enough," Ms. Malla explained. "We also need a change in the mindset and values of people that consider women and certain castes to be second-class citizens. Unless and until that mindset changes, these people will continue to suffer."

The social mindset of disregard toward certain castes in Nepal is symptomatic of broader antipathy toward lower-caste groups across South Asia. This antipathy leads to chronic failures to assist these people when they are emerging from exploitation, which has resulted in countless millions of momentarily freed bonded laborers or other types of slaves falling back into servitude just to survive. The isolated and destitute *kamaiya* of the western

Terai are in particular need of support, lest they continue to fall deeper into an inescapable abyss of the worst kinds of bondage and exploitation.

A WORD ON THE *KAMALIRI* SYSTEM

Before turning to the *hari* of Pakistan, I want to make special note of the *kamaliri* system of Nepal. This system involves extensive internal trafficking of *tharu* female children strictly for the purpose of chattel-like domestic servitude in upper-caste homes in major cities such as Kathmandu, Pokhara, and Nepalganj. With the help of the American Himalayan Foundation and their local partner, Friends of Needy Children, I interviewed fourteen former and current *kamaliri* slaves. Here is how one exceedingly downcast *tharu* girl, Nirmala, described her servitude at a shelter near Nepalganj:

> I am from a village in Banke District. I was ten years old when I first went for work as *kamaliri*. It was a Chhetri home in Kathmandu. There were five people in the home, and I did all the work—cooking, cleaning, washing clothes, washing dishes. I woke each morning at 5 A.M. and went to sleep at 10 P.M. I slept on the floor in the drawing room. I did this work seven days a week. Sometimes the wife would beat me. The husband in the home would rape me. I did not want to be in that home. I was so tired. I was supposed to go home during Maghi, but they did not let me go. After two years, they sent me to another home in Kathmandu. I was in this home for two years. They did not beat me, but I was working all the time. Finally, I was in a third home for three years. I had to do everything. They had two daughters, and I had to take them to school each morning. I wished I could go to school like them. In this home they would beat me very badly. Sometimes they would not let me eat. Eventually, Friends of Needy Children rescued me.

While almost every *kamaliri* slave I interviewed toiled in domestic servitude in upper-caste family homes, some were also sent to businesses and hotels. A soft-spoken, frail young girl named Meena was one of them:

> I am from Kailali district. I started *kamaliri* at age nine. I worked five years in a hotel. I would wake at 2 A.M. each day and do all the cooking and cleaning. I had to prepare the breakfast for the guests. At 10 A.M., if

there was leftover food, they would let me eat breakfast. Many times there was no food, and I did not eat. I had to clean all the rooms and prepare the lunch by 1 P.M. I did all the cooking and cleaning for all the guests in twenty rooms. I did this work seven days a week. They never gave me any days for rest, even if I was sick. I would sleep whenever the work was done. This was usually around 10 P.M. I was so tired doing this work. I wanted to go home, but they did not let me leave the hotel in five years. Eventually, one of the guests helped me escape.

As I dug deeper into the *kamaliri* system, I uncovered a national network of child slavery focused on the *tharu* children. Agents contracting with upper-caste families or businesses in major cities traveled to the western Terai to recruit girls as young as eight. Typically, a payment of around $12 to $14 was provided to the parents. The child was then transported to the contracting family or business, which in turn paid the agent around $40 to $50 for the child. At that point, the child was put into domestic servitude in exchange for room and board. For the most part, wages were not paid, though in some cases, small payments of a few dollars per month were sent to the parents of the *kamaliri* worker. Children were sent from one home to the next until they reached the age of seventeen or eighteen, after which point they were sent home to be married. Not all cases I documented were as exploitative as Nirmala and Meena. In fact, I met four *kamaliri* girls in the homes of their masters who were more than happy to discuss the system.

At an upper-caste Brahmin home in Nepalganj, I met Kavita, a *kamaliri* servant to the family for six years, since the age of eleven. Kavita described her daily routine and relatively decent living conditions. Her father visited every two months, at which time the family paid him approximately $4 for Kavita's work. As the madam of the house explained:

> We give Kavita new clothes, and we send her to school two days a week. We also send her for beautician training, so that she can have a vocation after she leaves. She has her own room, and she eats the same food as we do. She returns home for one week each year at Maghi. She is a well-behaved and sincere girl.

The madam of the home further explained that the *kamaliri* system is a benefit to *tharu* girls: "They would otherwise be starving in their village, or they would be sent to India for sex. At least with us she can get an education. We will make sure she has a job once she leaves. This is much better for her."

A similar rationale was provided by each *kamaliri* owner with whom I spoke, and almost all of them specifically mentioned the threat of sex trafficking to India as something they helped the girls avoid. In their eyes, the *tharu* girls were exchanging starvation and exploitation for security and opportunity, and all they had to provide in exchange was a few years of severely underpaid (or unpaid) domestic labor. In that way, it was a typical debt bondage agreement: security and survival in exchange for labor. On the face of it, the owner was correct—this was a superior outcome for most *tharu* girls. However, as with any debt bondage scenario, it is unacceptable that security and survival must be exchanged for freedom. All societies must provide for the reasonable subsistence, education, health, and human development of all their citizens—regardless of ethnicity or gender—without requiring them to forfeit a period of their lives to slavery. This is particularly true for children, who should never be asked to surrender any span of their lives to domestic servitude—six years and counting for Kavita—simply to survive.

Even though the *kamaliri* system was officially banned by the government of Nepal in 2007, the system is thriving as a result of poverty, ethnic bias, and an absence of rule of law. While Kavita's owner was beneficent, many are not. Several of the homes I tried to visit did not allow me inside, including one, just a stone's throw from the UNHCR office in Nepalganj, in which an eight-year-old *kamaliri* was rumored to be working. I went straight to the UNHCR office to apprise them of the situation, and a concerned officer named Ram Gautam told me that the UNHCR was well aware of the *kamaliri* issue and estimated that at least five thousand children were currently exploited in the system throughout Nepal. The UNHCR had actually convened a Rescue Committee to tackle the issue, but the government had recently ordered all field offices of the United Nations in Nepal to close within a few months, so Ram held little optimism that the situation of the *kamaliri* slaves would improve anytime soon.

THE *HARI:* NOMADS IN THE THAR DESERT

One of my most unique journeys to explore contemporary forms of slavery took place during the earlier days of my research. This trip was focused on meeting nomadic *hari* in the Thar Desert, which crosses Rajasthan in India and Sindh in Pakistan. Though I did not realize it at the time, this trip would comprise all of my direct contact with agricultural bonded laborers in Pakistan. Along with the *kamaiya* system, the *hari* system is exemplary of two of the primary models of agricultural bondage in South Asia: one is predicated on seasonal bondage at the outset (*kamaiya*); the other is predicated on sharecropping that devolves into chronic debt bondage because of, *inter alia*, asymmetric power and access to resources between landowner and sharecropper.

To reach the Thar Desert, I first traveled by train to the magical city of Jaisalmer, at the far western corner of Rajasthan. The 850-year-old fort at Jaisalmer rises out of the desert like a sand castle. It is a captivating outpost lost in time. When the setting sun ignites the golden fort just before twilight, it is among the most enchanting visions one can behold. The Rajput rulers of Jaisalmer accrued their wealth by virtue of the town's strategic position along the camel routes for traders between India and Central Asia. Many nomads still travel these routes today, despite the sporadic military presence along the India-Pakistan border in the heart of the desert. If I was going to meet former or current *hari* bonded laborers directly, traveling these same camel routes was going to be the only way.

From Jaisalmer, I took a jeep roughly fifty kilometers southwest, past the Sam dunes, along a narrow road that was all but swallowed by the desert. We stopped near the Dhanana village, which consisted of little more than a few dozen huts and numerous camels. From there, rolling tides of sand spanned the horizon. My guide, Kisan, hired camels in the village, and together we traveled deeper into the desert for a seven-day trek that would include two meetings with *hari* nomads. Riding camelback along the ancient trade routes of the Thar Desert is one of the most hypnotic experiences a traveler can have. The barren surroundings empty the mind, and the camel's undulating gait lulls one into a meditative trance. Solitude takes over, and hours pass without a conscious thought. Aside from dung beetles and the occasional military jet roaring overhead, Kisan and I were completely alone for hours on end. We stopped only to eat or to explore an ancient ruin. We took shade under khejri trees and sipped delightful morning tea by fireside. Each evening, we rode our camels into the setting sun. Each night, we slept under a star-speckled sky. It was one of the most serene experiences of my life.

Photo 2.4. On our camel trek in the Thar Desert.

The Thar Desert is not completely inhospitable to human life; there are several oases throughout the desert and around five hundred thousand nomads who make a life roaming from one oasis to the next. Portions of the desert are populated by numerous species of trees, shrubs, and animals. Most of the nomads in the desert are Hindu; some are Muslim. Some enter in and out of agricultural debt bondage in the Sindh province of Pakistan; others never leave the desert at all. On the third day of our camel riding, Kisan informed me that we were close to the border with Pakistan, near the Sanghar district of Sindh province, and that we were likely to cross it. I had full faith that Kisan would keep us out of harm's way. He knew the desert down to the dune, and he knew exactly how to avoid unwanted contact. He also knew how to arrange a meeting at what appeared to be a completely random patch of sand in the middle of the desert. Not long into our fourth day, near a gathering of desiccated shrubs, we were met by a caravan of five nomadic *hari* men accompanied by a dozen white goats with black heads. These were the men Kisan had arranged for me to meet, and this was the exact place where he had arranged for us to meet them.

I spent a little less than twenty-four hours with that first group of *hari* nomads. They were all from Sanghar district, which, along with the Umerkot and Tharparkar districts to the south, contains the majority of nomadic *hari* bonded laborers in Sindh province. By firelight, they spoke about their struggles to survive as agricultural workers in Pakistan. They and their families had been *hari* bonded laborers for a few different *zamindars* across several years, but they were severely persecuted, and their debts became insurmountable.

"The *zamindars* treated us like slaves," a nomad named Jawahar told me, "If we did not please them, they beat us." "We could not afford the prices of the seed and fertilizer," another nomad named Hassam told me, "So each year our debts grew more. When the *zamindar* said he would sell our children to repay our debts, we became frightened. He had done this to others. We did not want this to happen to us."

Not soon after this threat, Jawahar and several other *hari* families fled from their exploiters into the Thar Desert to eke out an existence as nomads. This was almost six years before I met them. Many *hari* families from across Sindh had fled into the desert before Jawahar, and many others had fled after him. Survival in the desert was difficult. For some, the struggle was too great, and they returned to their former landlords and reentered agricultural debt bondage. Others sent one or two male family members back to seek out agricultural labor during times of drought or emergency. "This happens especially in Tharparkar district," Kisan told me. "Many *hari* end up in bondage this way. Many others are also trapped by the *zamindars* when they agree to tend the *zamindar*'s animals in the desert, but if one animal falls ill or goes missing, the family must enter bondage to repay this loss."

Finally, there are those former *hari* such as Jawahar who refuse to go back no matter how challenging nomadic life becomes. I spoke casually with Jawahar and the other nomads that night, as they were not terribly keen to relive the details of their former lives. They smoked bhang, ate wet khichdi,[12] and sang a few songs. It was not the most productive session of documenting narratives and gathering data, but it was one of the most memorable nights of my life. There was a serenity in the desert that made all the pains and hardships of the world seem like a dream. The nomads I met the following night shared similar struggles and a similar acceptance of desert life as far preferable to servitude in Pakistan. Despite their desert-worn faces and destitute existences, these nomads were at peace in a way that I could scarcely understand.

The night I met Jawahar, I asked him and the other nomads why they stayed in the desert rather than try to find work in a city in Rajasthan or elsewhere in India, if returning to Pakistan was not an option. "This is our home," Jawahar told me. "In the desert we are safe. In the desert we are free."

THE *HARI* SYSTEM OF BONDED LABOR

Like the *kamaiya*, the *hari* of Pakistan are a highly representative model of agricultural debt bondage in South Asia. *Hari* literally means "wielder of the plow," and the system is based on sharecropping between lower-caste, mostly landless *hari* peasants and landholding, upper-caste *zamindars*. The *hari* system is generally regarded as one of the oldest and most exploitative systems of bonded labor in Pakistan. In fact, the system can be seen as a mode of debt bondage that has existed for centuries in much the same way that the former *kamaiya* system in Nepal has more recently transformed into a sharecropping arrangement that often devolves into debt bondage. The *hari* system is primarily present in the Sindh province of Pakistan, but there are several other modes of sharecropping-based systems of bonded labor throughout Pakistan, in the Punjab, Balochistan, and Khyber Pakhtunkhwa[13] provinces.[14]

There are myriad ways in which the *hari* system manifests itself throughout Sindh province. Some *hari* own small plots of land; others own none. Some are nomadic; others have lived on the same land for years. Some take advances each season—called *peshgi*—while others work off debts that grow year after year, sometimes across generations. Some are recruited by *jamadars*; others seek out a loan themselves. Almost all agreements are verbal, with virtually no written records, contracts, or accounting books. In all cases, the *hari* are lower-caste individuals deeply disenfranchised from mainstream society and with a severe lack of education, opportunities, and rights. Most *hari* are Hindu. They live in extreme poverty, with barely 18 percent of the huts in Sindh province having electricity or toilets. Most *hari* are illiterate, and at least 80 percent of them live on incomes of less than one dollar per day.[15] A third-generation *hari* bonded laborer named Zarafullah, living not far from the city of Hyderabad in the Mirpur

Khas district of Sindh, shared the following narrative with my colleagues in Pakistan:

> My grandfather took the *peshgi* from the *zamindar*. Since that time, my family has been in this area. We harvest wheat and cotton. My father inherited the debt from his father, and I inherited the debt from my father. I do not know how much is the debt at this time. Each season we borrow from the *zamindar* for seed and supplies. He charges very high prices. He is supposed to share these costs with us and also the irrigation, but he does not do this. We must also borrow for food and medicine. The debt grows in that way. At the harvest time, the *kamdar* (overseer) arranges the harvest to go to market. We are supposed to share equally in this income, but we are not given an equal share. We never see any accounts. This is how it has always been for us.

Zarafullah also described other facets of the *hari* system that sounded remarkably similar to the *kamaiya* system in Nepal. The primary similarity was the ability of the *hari* to change landowners, so long as the new landowner purchased their outstanding debt from the old one. Zarafullah said he had done this twice during his lifetime, and it was only at the time of those two transactions that he had any sense of what his outstanding debt was—or at least what the landowner felt it was. In the first case, his family's debt was purchased for roughly $280 in 1986, and twelve years later it was purchased again for $330.

The influence of environmental disaster (and transformation attributable to climate change) on debt bondage, human trafficking, and other forms of slavery is a subject of particular interest to me, so I was curious to investigate the effects of the disastrous monsoon floods of 2010 on the levels of agricultural debt bondage in Pakistan. The results were not surprising. More than eight hundred thousand square kilometers—one-fifth of Pakistan—was underwater during the peak of the floods. More than twenty million people across all four provinces were displaced, primarily rural peasants. Close to seventy thousand square kilometers of agricultural land was flooded, with a nearly complete loss in crop production for 2010 and 2011. Food prices skyrocketed beyond the means of millions of poor Pakistanis, and millions more were left homeless and destitute. One-fourth of the country was already living in poverty before the floods in 2009,[16] and there are no reliable estimates as to how many millions more fell into poverty after the floods. Because of the loss of almost two full seasons of crops, agricultural bonded laborers plunged deeper into debt. One bonded laborer named Ali, from Badin district in Sindh, explained, "After the floods, we lost hope. Everyone was ruined. We have no income at all. We only have debt." Many *hari* in particular who had actually managed to exit debt bondage stated that after the floods, they feared they would be in debt for the rest of their lives. "The government did nothing to help people like us," a *hari* named Iqbal explained. "They left us to die. We had to take very large *peshgi*. There was no work for months. We can never pay back this amount."

The population displacement caused by the floods also caused a massive increase in migration-based bonded labor in numerous sectors, from construction to brickmaking. There is no clear data on just how many of the millions of displaced peasants have been exploited in some form of forced, bonded, or child labor resulting from the utter lack of any means of survival after the floods, but it is clear that the environmental disaster had a devastating effect on the poorest citizens of Pakistan. To this day, very little has been done to assist them, and general estimates are that far more than the traditional 60 to 80 percent of rural Pakistanis have become landless.[17] At the same time, opportunistic traffickers, *jamadars*, *zamindars*, and other slave exploiters have capitalized on the suffering of their most vulnerable countrymen to ensnare them in a tidal wave of increasingly severe exploitation and enslavement.

Another point of interest with regard to the *hari* bonded laborers of Pakistan is the acute level of physical abuse they suffer. Agricultural bonded laborers across South Asia suffer varying degrees of physical violence as part of their coerced labor, but the *hari* in Pakistan have historically suffered some of the most barbaric forms of abuse I have heard of or documented. One elderly *hari* named Arshad described the following incidents, which sounded no better than the treatment of chattel slaves in the Americas during the height of the North Atlantic slave trade:

When I was younger, the *zamindars* would beat us without mercy. They would chain us while we worked. You can see the marks on my ankles here! If we displeased them, they would lock us in prisons without food and water. They would rape our wives in front of us so we suffer shame and indignity. Now there is more attention in this area, but these things still happen today.

Arshad was one of the few *hari* who was willing to talk about the kind of brutish treatment he had suffered in the past and may still be suffering today. Anecdotes about private jails, beatings and torture, and the sexual exploitation of women and children abound in rural Sindh, but virtually no one is willing to speak about it for fear of reprisal. The only other place I encountered similarly brutish conditions in the agricultural sector was with bonded laborers in the state of Madhya Pradesh in India. Here, bonded laborers described outright torture and abuse. They were forced to work and sleep in the fields for weeks on end and were prevented from gathering or talking in groups. Punishments included beatings, needles inserted under their fingernails, and electrocution. A bonded laborer named Bhishma told me that he regularly slept in supply sheds or with animals and that he had not seen his wife in months. "The landowner keeps my wife and two children locked inside his mansion," Bhishma told me. "Sometimes I hear my child is sick or my wife has been beaten, but there is nothing I can do but worry day and night."

As with the *hari*, the sexual exploitation of women and children by the landowners and their men was common with the bonded laborers I met in Madhya Pradesh and throughout the agricultural sector in South Asia. The stigma in Pakistan associated with this abuse is particularly great, so much so that not one single female *hari* was willing to speak to any of my colleagues (nor was I able to meet with any female *hari* nomads during my trek in the Thar Desert). Beyond the *hari*, the wanton exploitation of women in the rural sectors of Pakistan is of particular concern. In its 2009 annual report, the Human Rights Commission of Pakistan summed up the plight of women in the country as follows:

> In 2009 women in the country continued to face multiple challenges resulting from tyrannical social norms, anachronistic traditions and failure of the government to introduce basic institutional reforms . . . the number of honour killings, rape, domestic torture and acid attacks shot up in 2009 as compared to the previous year.[18]

Women represent only 20 percent of the formal labor force in Pakistan,[19] and the rights of women took several steps backward when efforts to quell tribal violence in the Swat Valley in 2009 were achieved by government concessions that women in the region could be governed by Sharia law[20] as opposed to the laws of the government and the Constitution of Pakistan. The level of public floggings, honor killings, and acid attacks in the region escalated soon thereafter.[21] Setting aside Sharia law, there is shockingly still no state law in Pakistan that specifically punishes the crime of an acid attack, which occurs when a male throws sulfuric acid on the face of a female as punishment, often for spurning romantic advances. The skin on the female's face melts, and most suffer blindness. Despite the barbaric cruelty of this offence, attempts to pass a law that punishes this practice in Pakistan remain unsuccessful.

It is difficult to confirm the extent of the suffering occurring throughout the agricultural sector in Pakistan, primarily because of the power of *zamindars* to ensure that their system of exploitation remains intact. Many *zamindars* are in control of law enforcement and the judiciary in their areas, and they use their influence to ensure that their feudal exploitation of *haris* continues. Activists who try to fight back are often harassed, arrested, or otherwise intimidated. The persistence of the system, the abuse and humiliation suffered by bonded laborers—especially women and children—and the endless accumulation of debts lead many *hari* to feel completely helpless. Some find a way to flee, but for most, fatalism sets in. Countless agricultural bonded laborers throughout Pakistan ultimately accept their destinies as unchangeable. For others, the despondency takes a darker turn, and the anxiety to repay debts and be liberated from their suffering leads to desperate decisions. Some bonded laborers sell children to traffickers to repay debts, others sell kidneys, and worse still, some commit suicide. Speaking with colleagues about the state of debt bondage throughout Sindh, Punjab, and other provinces in Pakistan gave me the sense that large pockets of the agricultural sector were little more than forced-labor prisons for millions of peasants. There was very little opportunity for escape, very little chance to become and remain free, and few if any avenues to secure any semblance of justice, rights, and fair treatment. Though the government has passed laws, created a fund to assist liberated bonded laborers, and has in general seemed sympathetic to accounts of bonded labor in Pakistan since the 1990s (see appendix E for details), government officials also turn a blind eye to credible accounts of torture, imprisonment, rape, and even the outright killing of lower-caste peasants caught in agricultural bondage. The prospects for the *hari* and other agricultural bonded laborers in Pakistan remain among the bleakest of any segment of debt bondage that I have researched. One can but pray that a stable, human-rights focused government will take hold in Pakistan soon and will more aggressively address this unfathomable suffering.

THE *PESHGI* SYSTEM

The *peshgi* system of Pakistan functions in an economically similar way to monetary advances provided to peasants throughout South Asia; that is, it is primarily a way of ensnaring individuals in bonded labor. However, there appears to be a larger voice in Pakistan than in other South Asian nations that this system of advances is benign and even beneficial to the debtor. A few specific words on the *peshgi* system are thus in order.

Peshgi is common in numerous sectors throughout Pakistan, from agriculture to bricks to construction to mining. In certain cases, the *peshgi* amounts are fairly low, perhaps $20 or less, and are intended to meet a short-term credit need. These low amounts are rarely in agriculture, construction, or brickmaking but usually in carpet weaving, glassblowing, and economically similar sectors. Workers must typically accept restrictions on movement and alternate employment until the debts are repaid, which usually occurs in a matter of weeks or months, through a 50 percent wage-deduction system. Some economists and government officials in Pakistan argue that this type of *peshgi* is relatively innocuous and provides short-term credit for workers in need. They suggest that the *peshgi* also assures the debtor of income during the time they are working off the debts. Nevertheless, there are countless cases where modest *peshgis* such as these have resulted in the long-term bondage of poor workers who lack any sort of alternative. It is a steep and slippery slope from small loans repaid through wage deductions for a few weeks to long-term, if not endless, debt bondage. In the first Supreme Court case on bonded labor in Pakistan (*Darshan Mashih vs. State*, 1990), which involved the brickmaking sector, the court declared any *peshgi* greater than the equivalent of one week's wages to be illegal and that any restriction on movement or employment can amount to forced labor. In discussing its reasoning, the court stated:

> Prima facie nothing seems to be wrong with the practice of "Peshgi" and in fact on a cursory look it appears to be beneficial to the workers but in practice on lifting the veil, this is the practice which appears to be the

root of almost all the evils in this industry. . . . The next menace emanating from this "Peshgi" system is that this "Peshgi" is advanced to the worker not for his benefit but in fact to enslave him for the rest of his life. . . . It is an "ever-increasing" and "never-diminishing" amount which goes on multiplying on one pretext or another.

In other sectors where the *peshgis* are larger to begin with—such as agriculture, construction, and bricks—the bondage can last years or more. *Peshgis* exceeding $100 to $500 per family are common in these sectors. The level of power exerted by the creditor to extract bonded labor and increase debt levels across years is virtually impossible for the bonded laborers to overcome. The workers are kept in a state of severe deprivation, with just enough food and income to survive and continue working to repay their debts. These levels of *peshgi* are also common during times of strife such as tribal warfare or environmental disaster. Apologists for the *peshgi* system should take a closer look at how even small loans can often lead to extended bondage, and they should also listen to the words of the bonded laborers themselves, who unanimously prefer almost any other source of credit than the local *zamindar* or *jamadar*.

THE BUSINESS OF THE *HARI* SYSTEM

Like much of agricultural debt bondage in South Asia, the roots of the *hari* system in Pakistan can be traced to the land-revenue policies of British colonists during the eighteenth and nineteenth centuries. Cultivating peasants were downgraded to landless tenants as a result of the Permanent Settlement of 1793 under Governor General Lord Cornwallis. These tenants required loans for agricultural inputs, tenancy, and basic consumption. From these roots, centuries of agricultural debt bondage have expanded and remained relatively intact into the modern era.

It is worth noting that shortly after independence, the government of Pakistan did attempt to remedy the rights of landless sharecroppers like the *hari*, first the with Sindh Tenancy Act, 1950; followed by the Land Reforms Regulation, 1972. These laws attempted to protect landless tenants against arbitrary eviction, mandate the equal share in costs and revenues, prohibit the extraction of unpaid labor from *hari* family members (especially women and children), limit the size of landowner landholdings in an effort to redistribute land ownership, and outline other basic duties and obligations between landowner and tenant. However, much of this legislation remains on paper, as the powerful *zamindars* use their political connections to keep the system as exploitative as possible. As recently as February 15, 2009, hundreds of peasants and activists conducted an eleven-day march from the mausoleum of Haider Bux Jatoi[22] in rural Sindh all the way to Karachi to protest the plight of bonded laborers and the lack of enforcement of the regulations under the 1950 and 1972 legislation. However, in the midst of Pakistan's numerous internal issues relating to extremism, poverty, and civil strife, there is little time, few resources, and scant government interest in maintaining the rule of law and fair dealings for low-caste agricultural bonded laborers in Sindh province or elsewhere.

There are four primary types of sharecropping within the *hari* and similar agricultural labor systems in Pakistan. The most favorable and least common system is a 75/25 share in revenues in favor of the sharecropper (type 1). By far the most common is a 50/50 share in costs and revenues (type 2). Approximately seven out of ten *hari* agreements fall into this category. The remaining two systems are 25/75 (the *chauthra* system, or "one-fourth"), and a one-eighth share in income. These latter two types both disfavor the sharecropper. In the 50/50 system, the sharecropper is typically responsible for the upfront costs of tilling and preparing the land for planting, followed by a 50 percent share in the costs of seed, pesticides, and fertilizer. One of the most interesting aspects of the business of the *hari* system, one that has led to increased levels of debt bondage, has to do with increased mechanization and technological development. Unlike the *kamaiya*, many of Pakistan's agricultural laborers make use of tractors, mechanical irrigation systems, advanced pesticides and fertilizer, and other means to increase overall yield. Unfortunately, the sharecropper in Pakistan must avail of these resources from the landowner at inflated prices, which he can almost never afford. Hence, *peshgis* are used to cover these upfront costs. Since the sharecropper almost never receives a fair share of the harvest income, he remains in debt when the accounts are settled at the end of the season, and the debt bondage carries over from one season to the next. It is worth noting that the undervaluation of revenues and overvaluation of costs for the sharecropper that results in extended bondage functions as an indirect way of charging interest on the original *peshgi*, which is convenient for the *zamindar*, since under Islamic tradition charging interest on loans is forbidden.

Table B.2 in the appendix shows the typical economics of a 50/50 *hari* system of bonded labor. *Peshgis* work out to an average of $60 to $65 per acre, with the average family of five working members harvesting around five acres, for an aggregate seasonal advance of $300 to $325 per family. The average *hari* family can harvest one full acre more than the average *kamaiya* family because of increased mechanization. Yields per acre are also higher. The system generates just over $380 in net profit per bonded laborer at an overall net profit margin approximately 10 percent greater than the *kamaiya* system. The increased net profit margin is primarily a result of the asymmetric share in costs and revenues for the bonded laborer (more than 50 percent on the cost side and less than 50 percent on the revenue side). The aggregate dollar values of net profit are relatively low compared to other bonded labor industries, but when one considers that a single *zamindar* can control twenty or more *hari* bonded laborers, the economic value of the aggregate exploitation can be considerable. Similar agricultural bondage systems in other parts of South Asia (especially India) will also tend to generate more net cash profit than the *hari* system of Sindh province or the *kamaiya* system in the western Terai.

Estimates vary on exactly how many agricultural bonded laborers there are in Pakistan. In 2009, the Human Rights Commission of Pakistan estimated that the total number of agricultural bonded laborers in the country was 1.7 million,[23] the highest concentration of which were in Sindh. As a result, the HRCP established camps in Sindh with concrete homes in the outskirts of the city of Hyderabad for families attempting to escape bonded labor. The HRCP says that it assists upward of two thousand bonded labor families each year in these camps.[24] Assuming the assistance is 100 percent successful in keeping families out of bonded labor for the rest of their lives, and assuming five members per family, it would take 170 years to transition all the agricultural bonded laborers in Pakistan to freedom, never mind the bonded laborers in other sectors. Of course, the transition is very rarely successful, and true freedom remains little more than a myth to most bonded laborers in Pakistan, especially for those like Zarafullah, who remain forsaken by a society that allowed generations to be enslaved before him and will most likely allow generations more to come. It is not difficult to see why Jawahar and his companions felt that wandering the Thar Desert as nomads of civilization was far preferable to any sort of life available to them in Pakistan.

{ 3 }

Bricks and Bidis

I have no more to give, all that was mine
Is laid, a wrested tribute, at thy shrine;
Let me depart, for my whole soul is wrung,
And all my cheerless orisons are sung;
Let me depart, with faint limbs let me creep
To some dim shade and sink me down to sleep.

—"TO THE GOD OF PAIN," SAROJINI NAIDU

BRICK BY BRICK BY MISERABLE BRICK

Fifty kilometers southwest of the holy city of Varanasi, India, I hiked through the searing summer heat deep into a remote area of numerous brick kilns. Standing up to two hundred feet high, the distinctive chimneys of the kilns lined the horizon in all directions. Sweat and dust combined to form a sticky paste over every inch of my skin. It was beyond reckoning how the brick kiln laborers could toil underneath the relentless summer sun for fourteen or more hours per day—and more unimaginable still how they could do so next to a kiln that was blazing with heat surpassing one thousand degrees centigrade. Bodies were bent and burnt. Faces were anguished. Children were broken. Though my mortal eyes could not see them, I was convinced there were devils hovering above, exacting this torture on man. The entire scene was a hell on earth.

Upon entering the first kiln area with my local guide, Sanjay, women covered their faces, men eyed us cautiously, and shy children hid behind their mother's legs. Once the workers saw that I was with Sanjay—someone they knew and trusted—they invited us to sit next to their brick huts to talk. One by one, the children came to touch my feet in a gesture of respect. I felt deeply embarrassed and asked Sanjay to convey that I was not someone of such importance. "You are here," Sanjay said. "That makes you important."

The workers at this kiln, like most of the others I visited throughout the state of Uttar Pradesh, were all *dalits*, who have historically subsisted beneath India's traditional four-caste system as outcasts or "untouchables." The very term *dalit* is rooted in the Sanskrit word *dal*, which means "suppressed," "crushed," or "oppressed." No words could better describe the living conditions of these brick kiln laborers. A skeletal man named Gaurav shared their story:

> I was eight years old when my father took an advance for the wedding of my older sister. From that time, I have worked in this brick kiln with my family. In one day, I can make seven hundred bricks. To make a brick, we dig the clay from the earth, then we mix it with water. After that, we put it in the mold and remove it. This wet brick must dry for three days; then the bricks must bake in the kiln for fifteen days. The kiln is kept hot twenty-four hours a day. The firemen wake in the night to add coal to keep it hot. When the bricks are baked, other workers stack them in the field. More laborers come to transport the bricks once they are sold. My part is molding. I can do this work eight months of the year. In the rainy season, I try to find agriculture work near my home in Bihar, but it is very difficult.

After our initial conversation, Gaurav had to return to work in order to meet his minimum quota for the day. Later that evening after the work was completed, I spoke with him again. I asked him more about his story, and with a taut expression, he recounted a life of woe that left me speechless.

> When I was eighteen, my father died and his debt was passed to me. No matter how hard I work, I am always in debt. I have taken so many loans through the years. Each season, I must take an advance to travel here from Bihar and live in this area with my family. I took a loan for my father's funeral. I take loans for food and water and cooking oil. When I was younger, there was a time when I was so desperate to be free from these debts. I took my family from here and went back to my home, but the landowner's men came to my village and forced us to return. They tied me to that tree there and beat me. They electrocuted me and did not let me eat. I was still tied to that tree when they sold one of my daughters

to a *dalal* (trafficker). They said, "This is payment for the work you have not done since the day you tried to cheat us." I could not believe God had done this. I wanted to take my life. You cannot imagine how much pain I felt. I never saw my daughter again.

In seven different states in India, across the Kathmandu Valley in Nepal, throughout central Bangladesh, and briefly in the Punjab province of Pakistan, I comprehensively documented the conditions at forty different brick kilns of varying sizes and conditions, out of a total seventy-two kilns I visited. The smallest kiln I documented was in Bangladesh, which had only twenty-eight workers from nearby rural areas. The largest I documented was in the Kathmandu Valley, with more than one thousand workers who were all from either the western Terai, rural districts to the east and west of Kathmandu, or Bihar in India. Aside from wage deductions that were up to 70 percent, this kiln is remarkable in that it used "Swiss technology" (as the workers described it) to stay open all year, even during the monsoon season. As near as I could ascertain, the "technology" involved a large building with an internal chamber for the drying of molded bricks even during the rainy season, which were then elevated to a second level into a series of four ovens where the bricks were fired, then lowered again. Among all the kilns I visited across South Asia and all the tales of exploitation I documented, Gaurav's story was without question one of the most heartbreaking I heard, but it was far from the only story of pain and torment I recorded. The conditions at South Asia's brick kilns are among the most corrosive and violent of any sector I have researched, and the corresponding mix of resignation in some laborers and simmering anger in others was also the most extreme.

A man named Durga from rural West Bengal sat with me at a brick kiln near a village not far from the Ichhamati River, which borders Bangladesh. Two years earlier, he lost everything in Hurricane Aila. Shortly after the disaster, *jamadars* descended on the area offering advances for work in agriculture, construction, and brickmaking. In a few of the destroyed villages, the landowners offered to rebuild the huts and allow the villagers to stay in them in exchange for a commitment to work in bidi rolling.[1] Homeless and starving, Durga accepted an offer from a *jamadar* for an advance of $44 in exchange for work at a brick kiln at the promised government minimum wage of $1.10 per thousand bricks molded.[2] Durga and his family traveled to the brick kiln and were given a thirty-square-foot brick hut (roughly five feet by six feet) in which to live near the kiln. Here is what his life has been like since:

> We wake at four in the morning to begin work. With my wife and two children, we can mold one thousand bricks each day. Usually we finish work at six or seven at night. At the end of each week, the *jamadar* takes count of our bricks. He gives us a ticket for each sixty bricks. Many bricks that we make are not counted because the *jamadar* says they are damaged. We give the tickets to the accountant, and he pays us on this basis each month. I keep count of my tickets, but the accountant always pays less than the promised wage. He takes half the tickets for repayment of my advance. With the remaining wages, we buy food and water from the landowner, but the prices are very high. The landowner does not let us leave this area, so we cannot buy our food any other place. We must also pay rent of Rs. 400 ($8.90) per month for the hut, and we must also pay for electricity. I have taken more loans during the season just so we can pay these fees.

Durga was illiterate and had no accurate sense of his wages and debt repayment. When we walked through the math together, he began to realize in more detail what he had already known in his heart—he was being severely exploited. With roughly $0.55 per day being deducted for debt repayment, in less than three months Durga should have repaid his debt. However, not only had he worked two full eight-month seasons when I met him, but as near as we could tell his overall debts were now more than twice the original $44 he had borrowed. "What else can I do?" Durga explained, "There is no other work for me. I would like to do better work so I do not have to borrow money and I can send my children to school, but there is no opportunity for people like us."

From the far east of India in West Bengal to the far west in Rajasthan, not far from the town of Alwar, I interviewed several more bonded laborers, some of whom had been tied to brickmaking debt bondage for more than thirty years. Like Durga, they had little sense of their overall debits and credits, other than a vague notion that they were being underpaid. They worked from 4 A.M. to 6 P.M. in the winter. In the summer, they worked from 2 A.M. to 10 A.M., followed by an afternoon shift of 3 P.M. to 9 P.M. I sat down with the laborers and walked them through the arithmetic of their promised wages. Unlike most brick-kiln bonded laborers I met

Photo 3.1. Brick kilns in central Bangladesh.

who were paid every two weeks or on a monthly basis, these workers were only paid in one lump sum at the end of the eight-month season. This major delay in payment tied the workers to the kiln for the full season. We compared the sum that the laborers were told they would be paid each year to what they reported actually being paid the previous year, after the 40 to 50 percent debt repayment deductions. Their actual payment was far below the promised sum less the wage deductions for debt repayment. I asked if they were told that their loans came with any interest rates, in order to explain the variance, but they said the landowner promised he was not charging interest. I asked if he made other deductions for breakage or for not meeting production amounts, and they said that he never talked about these types of deductions and that they always made as many bricks as required. After I worked through the numbers with the laborers, it was clear that they were either working for free almost half of each season, that they were being charged inordinate interest rates, or that there were myriad other deductions from their wages that the landowner had not discussed with them. One of the young men in the village, Sahadev, became particularly irate once the exact magnitude of the exploitation sank in. "You must help us get our wages!" he exclaimed. "The owner of the brick kiln never lets us see the accounts. We have no way to know what our wage should be. Every year we are more in debt. Please help us."

As much as I wanted to help the brick workers, I knew that one visit to the brick kiln's owner would hardly make a difference. More important, even if I took up the laborers' cause, the moment I left, they would be probably punished and evicted from their huts for stirring up trouble and thereby left homeless and without any means of subsistence.

The weathered elder of the group, Ranaji, knew this to be true: "If this man goes to the owner on our behalf, the owner will replace us with other villagers." The threat of eviction was a powerful force that prevented many bonded laborers from fighting for their rights. Still, once these workers had a more detailed sense of just how unfairly they were being treated, even Ranaji said, "Perhaps you can go some other day, without taking our names, and try to help us." Ranaji told me where the kiln owner's home was, and each of his fellow villagers, even the children, pleaded with me to help.

Receiving these earnest requests for assistance from the brick workers near Alwar made me feel extremely powerless and, at some level, even exploitative. I knew that one day I might be writing this story in a book and that very little good would have come to Ranaji and the other bonded laborers who contributed this narrative, other than some faint hope that one day, years from now, things may change for the better as a result of people learning about how they were being mistreated. It did not seem fair, or remotely good enough, given how much they had shared with me and how little I could offer in return.

That night in my hotel room back in Alwar, I deliberated on what to do. I had been asked by the people I interviewed to help many times before, and even when I was not asked, I had always felt the impulse to intervene during my research. One of the most difficult instances of this was with a victim of sex trafficking named Sunee, whom I met almost five years earlier in a Thai massage parlor not more than a thirty-minute drive from my home in Los Angeles.[3] In that case, I reluctantly decided not to alert the authorities at Sunee's request, because of the credible risk of punishment of her parents. She was willing to endure extreme suffering rather than have any harm at all come to her family. There had been so many encounters like that one (but none so close to my home), and where I perceived any risk of accidentally doing more harm than good, I chose inaction. It seemed the wisest policy to maintain in the long run, but it was also very dissatisfying, particularly at that moment, when the people who were suffering were also risking their safety to share their stories with me—and asking me for help.

Perhaps I did not exercise the same wisdom in the case near Alwar as I had done in many other moments. Perhaps I remembered all the other brick kiln owners that I could have confronted and chose not too, or perhaps I was just so frustrated at hearing (and benefiting from) so many stories of desperation from people in anguish that I decided that night in Alwar, I would speak to the owner of Ranaji's brick kiln.

ENCOUNTER WITH THE OWNER OF A BRICK KILN

I have met more than my share of slave exploiters and human traffickers across several years of research into contemporary slavery. This experience base, as well as being in a country in which I possessed considerable connections and knowledge about how things work, helped me feel relatively relaxed as my driver approached the brick owner's compound the morning after I met Ranaji. Once we spotted the owner's three-story whitewashed mansion in the distance, I asked the driver to stop the vehicle, and I continued the rest of the way on foot.

As I approached the owner's palatial residence, I could not help but think that one hundred of the huts in which Ranaji and his fellow villagers lived could easily fit inside it. Not satisfied with the home's immensity, the owner, Mr. Singh, appeared to be adding to his residence: six men, nine women, and eight children were in front of the mansion working with metal pipes and concrete. There were no guards present, so I told one of the women that I wanted to speak with Mr. Singh. She directed me to the front door, where I was eventually greeted by a male member of his staff. I explained that I was a researcher from the United States and that I wanted to speak with Mr. Singh about his brickmaking business. I was first told Mr. Singh was busy. When I said that I would wait, I was told he was not at home and would be back the next day. When I asked at what time, I was told no one knew. This fencing went on for quite some time before I was eventually brought in to meet Mr. Singh.

After another twenty-minute wait in an ornately decorated sitting room, Mr. Singh appeared. He was bearded, in his late fifties, and slightly hefty for his frame. I knew that I was running a fool's errand and that the best I could do was conduct my conversation without raising any issues that could adversely affect any of his laborers, bonded, child, or otherwise. He offered me tea and Parlé biscuits, and we spoke for more than an hour. I told Mr. Singh I was trying to understand rural economies in India so that I could make recommendations on how to boost competitiveness. This approach must have appealed to him, and he freely opened up about his businesses. He told me he owned four brick kilns in the area as well as several hundred acres of agricultural fields. He spoke at length about pressures on his brick kiln's profit margins as a result of the increasing prices of coal, as well as higher taxes, which were not offset by increases in wholesale prices for the bricks, as a result of competitive pressures within India and abroad. He said that as a result he was looking into new technologies to help boost productivity. I took this occasion to explain very carefully that other brick kiln owners I had interviewed had expressed similar concerns about cost and competitive pressures to me and that I had heard that many laborers were being underpaid their wages as a result. "My workers are paid fairly," Mr. Singh assured me. "But yes, some owners may not pay full wages."

I calculated my next sentence very carefully. "I have heard that there is a high prevalence of child labor and bonded labor in many brick kilns in India, and I wonder what you feel can be done to tackle this problem." I knew it did not escape Mr. Singh that I might be suggesting there could be labor issues at his kilns. Without missing a beat, he responded:

You must understand something. Conditions in this area are not like America. Here, we have many poor laborers, and we do our best to give them shelter, food, and a good wage. When they need to borrow money, I am the only one who will lend it to them. The better they work, the more money I am willing to lend. They should be grateful for our assistance, but sometimes they are greedy and make allegations of wrongdoing. Many of them are lazy or take to gambling and drinking alcohol. When they squander their money, they must borrow again and put their children and wives to work. You tell me, is this a good way to behave? I try to teach them to be responsible and to work hard, just as I have. This is the only way to make the country strong.

I nodded at Mr. Singh and finished my last sip of tea. This was his version of the world and the nature of relations between people like him and

Photo 3.2. Child bonded laborer at a brick kiln in Bihar, India.

peasants like Ranaji, and I was not about to challenge him on any of these issues. We spoke a few more minutes about banalities relating to America and some of the cities Mr. Singh had visited, such as Washington and Miami. I thanked Mr. Singh for his time and took my leave. I knew there was little more I could do. Even if I were to go to the police or ask an NGO to intervene, I could reasonably assume that Mr. Singh was in complete control of his land—police, revenue collectors, judges, everyone—and little would come of such interventions other than harm to the laborers. The level of control kiln owners such as Mr. Singh have over their surrounding environments is as strong as any sector I researched—from India, to Bangladesh, to Nepal, to Pakistan. The Human Rights Commission of Pakistan made the point clearly:

> In 2009, there were 13,000 brick kilns in the country where one million labourers, including women and children, were estimated to be employed. A very large number of them were bonded labourers through an

illegal advance payment system. Influential politicians and their relatives owned most of these brick kilns. It was common knowledge that the kiln owners, in collaboration with corrupt police officials, often got criminal cases registered against the labourers to keep them under their control.[4]

So long as brick kiln owners are able to maintain a high level of control over local police, law enforcement, and even members of the government, efforts to intervene in the labor exploitation at brick kilns will face significant challenges. Bricks are big business in South Asia, and to tackle it more effectively, one must first understand exactly how the business of bricks actually works.

THE BUSINESS OF BRICKS

By my calculation, there are anywhere between 55,000 and 65,000 brick kilns in South Asia, approximately 70 percent of which are in India.[5] Pakistan has between 11,000 and 14,000 kilns, Bangladesh has five thousand to six thousand, and Nepal has around 1,500. In aggregate, these kilns produce between 330 and 380 billion bricks per year, worth approximately $13.3 to $15.2 billion. In certain parts of northern India, one can gaze upon dozens of brick kilns in any direction one looks. Brick kilns can be seen spanning the countryside as one flies into Kathmandu or Dhaka, and the Sindh and Punjab provinces of Pakistan are peppered with thousands of kilns. Approximately 4.4 to 5.2 million individuals in South Asia work at these kilns, including unofficial laborers such as the children and wives of male bonded laborers. My best estimate is that approximately 60 to 68 percent of these laborers are caught in some form of bonded, forced, or child labor, which is the highest ratio of any industry I have investigated in South Asia.

The structure of the brickmaking business is fairly simple. It begins with the recruitment of the workers. Recruitment is highly organized and surprisingly similar across South Asia. Kiln owners hire *jamadars* to staff the kilns each season. The *jamadars* recruit workers from rural areas with offers of advances for the season, promises of transport to and from the kiln, and guarantees of minimum wages, food, and shelter. Some agreements are verbal, though most are provided in some degree of written form, which the laborers sign with a thumbprint, since most of them are illiterate. Advances are provided to male workers in all labor categories (see below), and the wives and children of the males who accept the advance are typically included in the bargain (though not on the official muster rolls of the kilns) in order to meet the owner's output demands. The size of the advances varies considerably, depending on the size of the family, the purpose of the advance, and the perceived working ability of the laborer. The cases I documented ranged from $33 to $444 in advances per season. Most of the workers who accept the advances are landless peasants, and 71 percent of all the laborers at the kilns I documented were migrants. Some traveled a hundred kilometers or less from their homes to the kilns; others traveled across international borders. Roughly 20 percent of the brick kiln workers in Nepal I sampled were from Bihar (most working in brick molding), and I also documented Indian migrants at kilns in Bangladesh. Despite this international migration for brickwork, most of the migration in the sector is from rural areas to destinations within the same country, be it rural Bangladesh to the kilns north of Dhaka or rural Punjab and Sindh province to kilns near Lahore and Hyderabad. Though the *jamadars* are tasked with managing the overall advances and wages of the laborers they have recruited, everyone knows that the loans come from the owner. From the owner's perspective, the system of advances is crucial, as it ensnares a captive labor force for the entire brickmaking season each year, which is especially important given the dangers associated with brickmaking work. Coercing debt repayment under deeply unfavorable terms also keeps wages heavily depressed and helps avoid wage competition among kiln owners. These forces in turn boost profits and competitiveness.

Once the workers are recruited, the *jamadars* typically use buses and trains to transport the migrants from their home areas to the kilns. One woman from Bihar, named Deepali, whom I met at a kiln outside Ludhiana in Punjab (India), told me, "The *jamadar* arranged five buses that took all of us from Araria to Ludhiana. More than two hundred of us come from our villages to these kilns each year." The migration typically takes place at the end of the monsoons, usually in September. The brickmaking season then lasts seven to eight months, until the monsoons start again.[6] A medium-sized brick kiln will employ approximately fifty to one hundred laborers. A kiln with fifty laborers is capable of molding, drying, and baking four hundred thousand to six hundred thousand bricks in a single month. Smaller kilns might achieve half this amount, and larger kilns several times more. At a medium-sized kiln like Gaurav's, the steps of the brickmaking process are divided among fifty laborers, with the following roles:[7]

1. *Brick molder* (*pathera*): twenty-four individuals (usually full families) who dig the pits, make the clay by continuously sprinkling water brought in buckets (or pumped) from a local well or canal, and shape the rounds of clay into the brick molds. The molds usually have the name of the owner engraved in them. After the bricks are molded, women and children lay them out to dry in the sun. They regularly rotate the bricks so they can be evenly dried. This process typically takes two to three days, depending on the time of year. *Patheras* are always paid on a piece-rate basis.

2. *Loader* (*kumhar*): six individuals who carry the unbaked, dry bricks to the kilns. Sometimes donkeys are provided. Women and children rarely perform this role. *Kumhars* are typically paid on a piece-rate basis. In some kilns, the role of *pathera* and *kumhar* may be combined.

3. *Stackers* (*beldar*): four individuals who stack the bricks and coal inside the kiln in alternating layers up to a height of three meters. The top of the stack is covered with sand or coal ash. Women and children rarely perform this role. *Beldars* are typically paid on a piece-rate basis or monthly basis.

4. *Arrangers* (*rapaswala*): four individuals who work alongside the stackers, arranging layers of soil between the bricks before the burning process, then removing them afterward. These layers of soil regulate the amount of oxygen exposed to the bricks, thereby producing different shades of red (more oxygen equals more red). Women and children rarely perform this role. *Rapaswalas* are typically paid on a piece-rate or monthly basis.

5. *Firemen* (*jalaiwala*): six adult males who fire the kiln and watch over it twenty-four hours a day to ensure that the kiln's internal temperature is maintained at approximately one thousand degrees centigrade. The baking process takes fifteen days. Women and children never perform this role. *Jalaiwalas* are typically paid on a monthly salary basis. They are always regarded as being at the top of the brick kiln labor ladder, and sometimes *jamadars* will take this role for periods of time to ensure that the bricks are baked as properly as possible (since they are compensated on a per-brick commission basis).

6. *Unloader* (*nikasiwala*): six individuals who remove the baked bricks at the end of the firing cycle and stack them for transportation. The fired

bricks emerge in different grades—some are high quality, some do not burn as well, and some are cracked or otherwise damaged. The bricks are stacked according to their grade. Better-grade bricks command a top price in India of Rs. 2.5 ($0.05) each; lower-grade bricks are sold for Rs. 1.5 ($0.03) each. The prices in Pakistan, Nepal, and Bangladesh are roughly comparable after adjusting for exchange rates. Women and children rarely perform this role. *Nikasiwalas* are typically paid on a piece-rate basis.

Approximately 19 percent of all the laborers I documented at brick kilns were children under the age of eighteen. The youngest child was six years old. More than 88 percent of the brick kiln bonded laborers I documented in India belonged to Scheduled Castes and Tribes. In Nepal, the low-caste groups prevalent at brick kilns include *tamang, magar, gurung, newar,* and *mahato.* In Bangladesh, *dalits* are the primary laborers found at brick kilns. In Pakistan, the minority groups most often exploited at the lowest rungs of the brick kiln labor ladder are Christians and Afghan refugees.

In addition to the six categories of laborers listed above, a medium-sized brick kiln typically has two to four *jamadars* and *chowkidars* (guards) and one accountant. The *jamadars* and *chowkidars* monitor work, ensure no one steals bricks, and mete out punishment when laborers break the rules or make mistakes. The accountant keeps track of the number of bricks baked and sold at each grade level and manages the debits and credits of the bonded laborers. Payments of wages, excluding deductions, are usually provided every two weeks, though sometimes it can be every month or only once, at the end of the season. Roles cannot be interchanged—molders are molders, stackers are stackers. I did, however, find some flexibility in roles at the kilns in the Kathmandu Valley. In all cases, brick kiln laborers are never allowed to leave the kiln area without permission.

Numerous pieces of equipment are used during the brickmaking process, such as the wooden brick molds, shovels for digging, buckets for carrying water, scales for measurement, scoops to fill the kiln with coal, pumps for water, and lanterns for work at night. Aside from labor, equipment, and an oft-underpaid or unpaid government royalty for land used to dig the clay,[8] the biggest expense for a kiln operator is fuel. Diesel fuel is required to operate a pump that transports water from the nearest well to the dirt pits (when it is not transported by hand in buckets), and immense amounts of expensive coal are required for baking. To maintain an oven with a diameter of four hundred feet at a temperature of one thousand degrees centigrade requires roughly sixty to eighty tons of coal per five hundred thousand bricks. Fuel costs are unavoidable, which is why minimized labor costs help boost profits. One kiln owner in the Daimura district of Bangladesh who owned three kilns each with six hundred workers that produced up to three million bricks per month told me point-blank that the high costs of purchasing and transporting coal from the northeastern town of Sylhet is the main reason why "I must take whatever steps I can to reduce costs for labor." Finally, some kilns I documented also turned to burning rubber and plastic to lessen coal costs.

Brickmaking is highly hazardous, back-breaking work. The difficulty of the work is exacerbated by dangerous living conditions. Several brick kiln workers described fellow laborers who had lost a foot or a hand in the kiln. Some laborers lose their lives. *Jalaiwalas* typically wear nothing more than wooden sandals for protection, and one false step atop a kiln seething at one thousand degrees centigrade results in serious injury or death. The kiln owners also use the heat of the kiln to mete out punishment. If a worker is considered lazy, commits errors, or steps foot off the kiln's territory, owners instruct the *chowkidars* to burn them as punishment. Sexual exploitation of women and children is all too common. Some laborers told me about owners who forcibly took sexual favors from the wives or daughters of bonded laborers as payment for advances of food and clothing during the rainy season. In Bangladesh, one of my colleagues named Mostafa, from an NGO called Shushilan ("working for a better future"), told me that the "abuse of women at brick kilns is a daily occurrence; sometimes these kilns are run like brothels for the owners."

The toxic environment of the kilns also promotes severe illness. The workers either sleep in the open air or in small brick huts, inhaling the smoke and fumes of the kiln twenty-four hours a day. The fumes can be particularly noxious for those kilns that resort to burning rubber instead of coal. There is a high level of dust in the air, and most of the roles at the kiln involve constant lifting, squatting, and carting of heavy loads, which damages knees, legs, and spines. The living conditions are extremely unhygienic, with outdoor toilets and a serious shortage of clean water, which produces many cases of dysentery. Because the kiln workers usually only receive one day of rest every fifteen days, exhaustion runs high, and accidents are common. If a laborer is injured or falls ill, he must pay for the medicines out of his wages, which leads to greater debt. As one laborer in central Bangladesh named Rashid explained, "The main reason we are in debt is because we are injured. Then we must borrow for medicine and we cannot work, so our debt is only growing."

Another factor that leads to injury and ill health among many workers is a serious lack of nourishment. At best, most brick laborers are provided two meals a day of rice and lentils—just enough carbohydrates and protein to keep them alive and working—and they must either purchase the food from the kiln owner at inflated prices or have the cost of the meals deducted from their wages.

When the debts finally get too high or a man becomes too injured or old to work, more extreme measures are taken to settle the accounts. In the worst cases, women and children are sold to *dalals* (traffickers) to recoup the remaining debt. Gaurav poignantly described the sale of his daughter earlier in this chapter, and two years before I met Gaurav I met a young girl, Neela, at a tier B brothel[9] in Sonagachi, the red-light district of Kolkata, who told me that her entire family had been working at a brick kiln in West Bengal for several years when the owner suddenly sold her and two other girls to a *dalal*. "I have been in Sonagachi nine months," Neela told me. "I miss my parents so much. I want to go back to them, but the *gharwali* (madam, house manager) said if I try to leave, the landowner will harm my parents."

As debts are manipulated upward year after year, an overall sense of helplessness overcomes most laborers. While some may have family members forcibly sold to repay their debts, others give up and commit suicide. In Pakistan and parts of northern India, there has been an alarming increase in brick kiln laborers selling kidneys in order to repay their debts, or at least part of the debt. Many of the laborers I met actually knew that the system of advances pursuant to debt bondage was illegal and that they were entitled to receive minimum wages and certain standards of working and living conditions. However, they all felt powerless to enforce their rights. "We know what our wages are supposed to be," a bonded laborer named Ramesh, at a kiln in Punjab (India), told me. "The NGOs tell us these debts are illegal and our wages should not be deducted, but they do not give us any alternative. No one is helping people like us."

At the end of the long and arduous brickmaking season, the laborers are usually given some sort of farcical accounting of their debts. They return home for the monsoon season and attempt to secure casual labor in other sectors, such as agriculture, construction, or carpet weaving, sometimes with the same owner/creditor. When the next brickmaking season commences, they take another advance and return to the kiln for another cycle of kiln work. Some of the laborers I met were in less debt than others; some had a reasonable sense of their accounts, and some had no sense at all. Some maintained that they actually cleared their accounts each season before taking a new advance the following year, while others said they had been trying to work off a single ever-increasing loan for as long as they could remember. Overall, the system of ensnaring a captive, coerced, and severely exploited labor force throughout the brickmaking industry of South Asia is widely prevalent and receives very limited intervention.

Aside from corruption, ignorance, and a general disregard for the destitute laborers who toil in South Asia's brick kilns, I suspect that a large part of the resistance to any meaningful intervention in the system of brickmaking is because this sector provides the highest net profit per laborer of any form of bonded labor in South Asia. Table B.3 in the appendix provides details on brickmaking economics at a medium-sized kiln. The paltry wages paid to the various laborers average out to approximately $1.36 per day and are only paid for the eight-month brickmaking season, for a maximum annual salary of approximately $330, up to half of which is deducted. This number is an outrage compared to the $1,990 in annual net profits generated per year per laborer. It is also an immense return on investment, given the range of advances I documented of $33 to $444. Even the high-end number represents a tremendous ROI. The low level of wages is also a primary driver of the need to take out more loans from the kiln owner during the season, which forces the bonded laborers deeper into debt. To the extent that full taxes are collected, the net profitability of brick kilns would be cut by up to one-half; however, bribes to local tax collectors (*tehsildars*) and "cooked" books allow kiln owners to avoid the bulk of their tax burden. The brick kiln owners do not even have to pay for the costs of transportation from the kiln to construction sites, which are typically borne by the purchaser. The combination of maximum cash profitability compared to any other bonded labor industry, along with the deeply toxic and dangerous working conditions, results in some of the highest levels of physical suffering and exploitation of any sector in South Asia. Brick kiln workers are perhaps the most callously exploited, physically destroyed, and spiritually devastated of all the bonded laborers I met. These individuals are also among the most angry slaves I met, and this presents a potentially significant risk for security in the region.

Photo 3.3. Brick-molding (*patheru*) bonded laborer in Punjab, Pakistan.

A WARNING ON SECURITY

After my first visit to a brick kiln more than a decade ago, I felt utter despondency at the human ruination I witnessed. Skeletons had replaced people; despair had replaced hopes and dreams. Knock-kneed children wobbled under the weight of bricks carted on their heads. Pain and anguish were as thick in the air as the dust and stifling heat. As the years went by, the levels of debt bondage and resulting misery at the brick kilns I documented continued to grow. To this day, I struggle to find the words to capture the true plight of the brick workers I met. One of the most poignant expressions I encountered did not come from any narrative I actually recorded but in a telegram I read as part of the transcript of *Darshan Mashih vs. State*, a 1990 Supreme Court case in Pakistan. The brickmaking bonded laborers in this case sent a telegram to the Supreme Court beseeching their help. This is part of what they wrote:

Chief Justice Supreme Court of Pakistan, Rawalpindi. We plead for protection and bread for our family we are brick kiln bonded labourers. . . .
Our children and women are living in danger. . . . We are hiding like animals without protection or food. We are afraid and hungry. Please help
us. . . . We want to live like human beings. The law gives no protection
to us.[10]

The poignant and tormented language of this letter captured the essence
of all eleven years of my research into bonded labor. Protection, bread, and
the desire to live like a human being—all the bonded laborers I met yearned
for these basic necessities. It is an incontrovertible disgrace that the nations
of South Asia have allowed such levels of caustic exploitation to persist in
any industry, particularly one as pervasive and visible as the baking of
bricks. If shame and ignominy are insufficient to motivate the governments
of South Asia to ameliorate the slavelike conditions at the thousands of
brick kilns across the region, perhaps self-preservation is.

Across the years, I have noted more anger in the brickmaking sector
than any other sector in which bonded laborers are exploited. There is only
so much exploitation people will take before some will find a way to strike
back. Extremists in Pakistan and India know this formula well, and brick
kilns appear to have become prime recruiting grounds for some of the
more militant-minded individuals in South Asia. Like the traffickers and
jamadars, they recruit among those at brick kilns who are suffering the
hellish exploitation with promises of food, security, and a way to fight
back. It should not escape anyone's attention that the lone survivor of the
November 26, 2008, Mumbai attacks—Muhammed Ajmal Kasab—told
authorities in India that his peasant father sold him to the people who
ended up operating the militant madrasa where he was ultimately brain-
washed and trained to execute the mindless attacks in Mumbai. Extremists capitalize on rural poverty, anger, and lack of opportunity, and they
often find new recruits among these people. In some cases, they purchase
children outright to serve their agenda. I am not aware of anyone who has
conducted reliable research into this area, including myself. However, the
anecdotes I have received across the years indicate that brick kilns especially are being targeted by extremists in India and Pakistan for recruitment. During my last two research trips, when I enquired about this practice among laborers at the brick kilns I visited, no one said that extremist
recruiters had come to their kilns, but some said they had heard that this

kind of recruitment was happening at other kilns. In most cases, they heard that recruiters paid off the debts of the bonded laborers as part of the deal and sometimes even offered small advances that the laborers did not have to repay. Though tales of recruitment by extremists at brick kilns remain anecdotal, if these anecdotes are true and the trend expands, the risk to security is not insignificant, and the governments of South Asia must take note. As the great American abolitionist Frederick Douglass once said: "Where justice is denied, where poverty is enforced, where ignorance prevails, and where any one class is made to feel that society is an organized conspiracy to oppress, rob and degrade them, neither persons nor property will be safe."[11]

For my part, after more than eleven years of research and scores of narratives about the torment and anguish at brick kilns, I have come to detest the sight of a brick. The red rectangular block signifies suffering and affliction to me. I always inspect the walls of shops and apartment buildings to see whose name is imprinted in the bricks and whether it might be from one of the kilns I have visited. More than once, I have traced a supply chain from a brick kiln in a rural area to a construction site in a major city. I have often wondered if the multinational corporations know that their glitzy new offices in Bangalore and Hyderabad, Mumbai and Gurgaon may have been built with slave labor bricks. Do the burgeoning middle and upper classes of India know that their new flats and sprawling bungalows may have been built with bricks molded by the tiny hands of a shattered child?

After my penultimate investigation into bricks on my fourth research trip, I was traveling along the highway from Varanasi to Allahabad. Earlier that day, I had met Gaurav. Driving down the road, I gazed out the car window and noticed that thousands of small trees had been planted along the highway to beautify the countryside. Each plant was protected from roving cows and hungry goats by a conical brick lattice cage a few feet high. Rage ignited in my chest. Were these bricks from Gaurav's kiln? Was this the purpose of his immeasurable suffering? I asked the driver to stop the car, and I walked up to one of the lattices. The name Vijay was molded into the bricks. They were not from Gaurav's kiln, but it was possible that the bricks in other lattice cages further down the highway would be. At that moment, each and every tale of brickmaking woe that I heard flooded me in a tidal wave. I wanted to tear down every single brick cage one by one. I wanted to bulldoze every brick kiln I had ever seen and raid the bank accounts of their owners to disburse the funds to the men, women, and children they had brutishly exploited. I wanted to take an hour of prime-time television in every South Asian nation and let them know of the hellish agony that was baked into each and every brick that constituted their offices and homes.

As my anger cooled and I realized the futility of my emotions, I took a moment to count the number of bricks in each cage. There were 390. I climbed back into my car and continued my journey. With Gaurav's story still churning in my mind, I calculated that for each day of his life, he molded enough bricks to construct two of these lattice cages. Maybe in a lifetime he molded enough bricks to build a few upper-class bungalows. Such was the measure of his life. And what did he have to show after a lifetime of toil? No money, no savings, no freedom, no beautiful brick bungalow of his own. A lost daughter, an insurmountable debt, and dark memories of a world that took everything from him. This is the dishonor of a nation: that it would build its future on the broken backs of its most vulnerable and tortured people.

BIDIS IN BENGAL

When Durga told me that the devastation of Hurricane Aila had wiped out entire swaths of the countryside in West Bengal in 2009 (as well as in southern Bangladesh, which we will explore in the next chapter), I was curious to investigate the impact of this environmental disaster on the levels of debt bondage and human trafficking in the region. Just as the destructive monsoon season of 2010 that flooded vast expanses of Pakistan, Nepal, northern India, and Bangladesh directly elevated levels of bondage and human trafficking among devastated peasants, I imagined there might have been a similar outcome after Hurricane Aila one year earlier.

With the help of guides referred to me by the grassroots activist Anuradha Talwar, the president of the Paschim Banga Khet Majoor Samity (West Bengal Agricultural Worker's Union), I traveled by jeep along muddy roads deep into the rural areas in West Bengal where Hurricane Aila had caused the most damage, not far from the border with southwestern Bangladesh. This was also the area where Durga said that numerous villages had been completely destroyed. Landowners subsequently made offers to rebuild homes in exchange for work in various sectors, especially bidi rolling. The offers came through *jamadars*, who descended on the region and recruited heavily among the devastated villagers, capitalizing on their suffering.

Several of the villages I visited throughout West Bengal were Muslim. Most of the villagers had new mud huts, and some of the larger families even had brick homes. In four different villages I toured, ones that had been completely rebuilt by landowners, a total of 2,900 villagers were caught in bonded labor for bidi rolling. In exchange for rebuilding the homes and allowing the villagers to live in them, the landowners required the villagers to work six days a week rolling bidis. They were not allowed to leave the village area nor take any other work. If they broke these rules or did not roll enough bidis, they would be evicted from their homes, and another family would take their place.

Here is how a young woman named Khadija Bibi described the process:

> Every two weeks, the *jamadar* brings the tendu leaf and the tobacco. At this time he also collects the bidis we have rolled. We roll the bidis on Monday to Saturday, usually ten or twelve hours a day. To roll the bidi, we cut the tendu leaf to size with this slide. Each piece must be two inches by one inch. We roll a pinch of the dry tobacco into the leaf, then we tie a thread around one side. Using this thin metal piece, we press the tobacco down, then we fold the bidi closed. Our hands get very sweaty in the heat, so we use ash to keep our fingers dry. The *jamadar* demands that each family complete at least three thousand bidis per day. One person working all day can roll maybe eight hundred bidis, so several people in the family must work. This amount is very difficult, and our fingers are in pain. When the *jamadar* picks up the bidis, he gives us a wage of Rs. 40 ($0.89) for every one thousand bidis. The government minimum wage is Rs. 58 ($1.29), but he says the deduction is for living in these homes and also if we use too much tendu leaf or the bidis are uneven.

More than two dozen other villagers in this area that I interviewed described the system in exactly the same way. The villagers were well aware of their rights to the state-stipulated minimum wage of Rs. 58 per one thousand rolled bidis, but they had no choice but to accept the 30 percent (or more) wage deduction; otherwise, they would have no place to live. The youngest villager I documented rolling bidis was a five-year-old boy, and the eldest was a sixty-six-year-old woman. This same elderly woman,

Photo 3.4. Bidi-rolling bonded laborer in West Bengal, India.

Amina Bibi, described in vivid terms the desperation faced by the villagers after Hurricane Aila:

> The hurricane destroyed everything. All our possessions were lost. Our home was gone, and we were living in the mud for days with no food or water. My grandchildren were starving. They were crying every night. We prayed to God to help us. After so many days, the landowner's men came to this area and told us they could rebuild our homes if we work for them. We knew they would take advantage of us, but we had no choice. We were all suffering so much pain in this place. God favors you that you do not live like us.

The anguish in Amina Bibi's voice was so palpable that I felt as if the hurricane had struck just a few days ago. Though the villagers in this part of West Bengal had very little, losing what little they had was utterly ruinous.

Since that time, Amina Bibi and thousands of villagers like her had no choice but to accept bondage or similarly exploitative conditions. They roll the bidis all year round, and at some point during the year just about every family needs an advance of some kind or another. The *jamadar* offers the advance, and the family is that much more pressured to roll more bidis to repay the loan. In addition, some family members were carted off by the *jamadars* to brick kilns or construction sites to work off the advances. It only took a few minutes to see how terribly monotonous and painful the labor of bidi rolling was. In addition to severely cramped fingers and neck and back ailments, many villagers were suffering from tuberculosis and other respiratory ailments from inhaling raw tobacco ten to twelve hours a day, at least 310 days a year. Tobacco also seeps through the skin on their fingers all day long. One can only imagine a few years down the road how many of them will end up with cancer of some sort and how many of the children will have stunted development and other serious health ailments as a result of the heavy exposure to raw tobacco.

As for the rolled bidis, the *jamadars* arrive every two weeks and transport them to the north of West Bengal, where they are sold to packagers on behalf of the landowners, who then package and distribute them for retail sale. The *jamadars* receive a commission of around $0.22 per thousand bidis rolled. Most or all of the wage deduction they take from the villagers goes back to the landowners. Packaged bidis can be found throughout South Asia for retail sale at dirt-cheap prices of $0.15 to $0.20 for a pack of twenty-five. Table B.4 in the appendix shows just how profitable the wholesale production of bidis through debt bondage can be (typically a pack of twenty-five sells for $0.10), with a per laborer net profit of roughly $590 per year, leaving ample net margin to increase the minimum wage for bidi rolling substantially—as well as pay that wage in full. However, greed and callousness motivate the producers to use debt bondage to extract the cheapest labor possible. India is responsible for just about every bidi produced in South Asia, and approximately 98 percent of the nine hundred billion to one trillion bidis produced in India each year are rolled by hand by more than four million laborers like Khadija Bibi and Amina Bibi.[12] My best estimate is that approximately 47 to 55 percent of the $3.6 to $4.0 billion wholesale bidi market ($5.8 to $6.4 billion at retail)[13] can be attributed to bonded, forced, or child labor.

Beyond the area of West Bengal that was devastated by Hurricane Aila, I also visited villages further inland in which individuals were similarly

Photo 3.5. One day's rolled bidis.

caught in debt bondage for bidi rolling, not because their villages had been devastated but because they were simply landless and impoverished and needed loans in order to survive. Coercion, the threat of eviction, physical punishment, and a simple lack of any alternative consigned these villagers to a life of debt bondage as the only means of survival. I also managed to speak to two *jamadars* in this area. I told them the same thing I told Mr. Singh in Rajasthan: I was an American researcher investigating the nature of rural economies in India, and I made sure that I did not say anything that could lead to any suspicion that the villagers were revealing information that would be problematic for them or their employers. We spoke mostly about the supply chain for bidi manufacturing and overall wage rates, wholesale rates, and other costs built into the system of production. The *jamadars* explained the commission basis of their compensation and that they had both been doing this work for more than ten years. They each chain smoked at least ten bidis while I spoke to them, adding a few more shades of brown to their already mud-colored teeth. I asked if they ever had problems meeting their production quotas, and they both said yes.

"What happens in that case?" I asked the *jamadars*.

"In this case, we have to make a wage deduction. Sometimes we have to find other work for the family."

The *jamadars*, of course, did not know that I had already been told by the villagers that whenever the *jamadars* were displeased with their production levels, they threatened the families with eviction from their homes. In fact, in the same village in which I met the *jamadars*, I was told that four families out of eighty-four had been evicted in the last year.

The *jamadars* claimed they paid the full minimum wages stipulated by the state of West Bengal and that the villagers found the work very easy. "All they have to do is sit on the floor and do this work," one of the *jamadars* explained. "We bring all the materials to them, and we fetch the bidis when they are finished. We must travel so much for our work. We have so many headaches. If the villagers do not work hard enough, we are punished, not them. The life of these villagers is much easier."

The *jamadars* went on to explain how lazy the villagers were and how if they were not forced to work they would not work at all. I knew what "forcing" the villagers to work really meant—threats, evictions, and physical abuse. Eventually, the *jamadars* moved on to the next village to collect more bidis. Whether they truly believed the villagers were lazy and led a comparatively easy life or whether they just said this to me as a way of perpetuating their false version of reality, there is no disputing what I saw with my own eyes, and that was the severe exploitation of the deprived and trampled people of this area for the purpose of rolling bidis at maximum profit. Deducted wages, the threat of eviction, and restrictions on any other form of employment or movement meant that these villagers were rolling bidis in what essentially amounted to outdoor prisons.

Similar to the brickmaking industry, after I saw the destructive, large-scale, and wanton exploitation involved in rolling bidis in West Bengal, it was difficult for me to see bidis the same way again. All across South Asia, every corner shop sells bidis to taxi drivers, students, day laborers, and professionals. Their quick tobacco buzz is enjoyed at the expense of millions of men, women, and children who work in deeply exploitative conditions. Through no fault of their own, consumers puff away, oblivious to the pain endured by their impoverished countrymen. I would like to believe that were they to know more about what it takes to deliver these penny-costing bidis to them, they would demand that bidi producers provide decent treatment, freedom, and fair wages to the laborers at the bottom end of the supply chain. As for those specific producers who capitalized on the environmental disaster of Hurricane Aila to exploit the peasants who were driven to the precipice of absolute destitution—they know full well what they are doing, and I pray there is a special place in hell for scoundrels such as these.

{ 4 }

Shrimp and Tea

Even as the fingers of the two hands are equal, so are human beings equal to one another. No one has any right, nor any preference to claim over another.

—MOHAMMED

SHRIMP IN BANGLADESH: CLIMATE CHANGE AND SLAVERY

Flying into Dhaka during the monsoon season provides a breathtaking vantage of exactly what climatologists mean when they say that Bangladesh is ground zero for climate change. At least half the country appears to be underwater. The country itself sits just five feet above sea level and is located in the estuary of three large rivers—the Ganges, Brahmaputra, and Meghna. In addition to being struck regularly by cyclones, each monsoon season the majority of the water collected by the Himalayas in Nepal, northeastern India, and Bhutan washes through Bangladesh en route to the Bay of Bengal. Half the country is engulfed by rising tides and swelling rivers. Climatologists estimate that a mere one-meter rise in sea levels would put up to one-fifth of Bangladesh underwater and displace up to twenty-five million of the country's 156 million people. In a country with the world's highest population density (excluding city-states such as Monaco), this level of population displacement would be a humanitarian disaster. It would also be a slave exploiter's dream. In fact, rising tides have already had a significant effect on the levels of debt bondage, child labor, and human trafficking throughout southwestern Bangladesh, home to the country's fast-growing shrimp industry. *Chingri* (shrimp) harvesting provides a highly illustrative case study of the very powerful ways in which environmental change can directly contribute to human trafficking and slavelike labor exploitation, especially in the far reaches of the developing world.

Navigating Bangladesh in order to conduct research deep in the country's rural areas is no small feat. In fact, just navigating through Dhaka from the Hazrat Shahjalal International Airport to one's hotel can be an exhausting experience. Dhaka is unlike any city I have visited—it teems with a higher density of people, vehicles, rubbish, beggars, street children, smog, grime, and human filth than almost any other South Asian city. Mumbai and Kolkata come close, but Dhaka stands alone as the apotheosis of urban bedlam. I have a good friend from Bangladesh, and I often tease him for appearing confused, spaced out, or generally off kilter. After my first few days in Dhaka, I wrote him an e-mail that said, "I understand."

Small hurdles abound when navigating Bangladesh. First, my taxi broke down on the way to the hotel from the airport. We waited in the middle of a major road overrun with vehicles and carbon monoxide fumes for almost an hour before the driver's uncle arrived with another vehicle to complete the journey. On arrival at my hotel, there was no electricity, because earlier that day a "big rat" went into the "electricity box," chewed some wires, and short-circuited the entire building. After a dark, sweat-drenched night, the next morning I hired a driver with an air-conditioned car to take me to a few meetings in Dhaka, but the driver showed up in a car without air conditioning and said that the other car could come for twice the agreed price. I opted for a different driver whose car had air conditioning, but as fate would have it his car broke down in the middle of the street halfway through the day. The next day, another driver just disappeared on me while I was in meetings at Dhaka University. There are not many taxis to be hailed in Dhaka, so I ended up walking about a mile before I managed to find a bicycle rickshaw that was willing to take me to my next destination. After a few days of similar chaos in Dhaka, I was exhausted. I began to worry about what might lie in store for me once I traveled farther off the beaten path. The night before I was meant to commence my journey to the southwest of the country, I was returning from a long day of researching child labor[1] throughout Dhaka (begging, garbage collecting, shoe repair) when I noticed that suddenly all the disarray of Dhaka had settled down and that people were gathering in mosques and sidewalks all over the city. A collective calm completely overcame Dhaka, as if everyone were in a trance. I asked my driver what was going on, and he said, "In one hour it will be *sab-e-barat* (night for fortune). Tonight the Almighty will determine each and everyone's fortune for the next year. The prayers will start at seven and will continue until six tomorrow morning."

Struggling as I was with the heat and disorder of Bangladesh, that night I prayed for a safe and productive journey throughout the country, especially since this was the only visit I had planned. I knew that millions of Bangladeshis would be praying for blessings much more essential—food, income, security, and good health. Fortunately, my prayers were answered, as I did in fact benefit from a safe and productive research trip across Bangladesh after *sab-e-barat*. Given that my relatively mundane request had been granted, I hoped that the far more important prayers of Bangladesh's poor and needy had been as well.

ON THE TRAIL OF *CHINGRI*

To research the shrimp industry of Bangladesh requires a journey south, far south. There are four stages involved in Bangladesh's shrimp industry supply chain: (1) shrimp fry (baby shrimp) collection, (2) shrimp farming, (3) distribution to processors, and (4) shrimp processing.[2] The first three stages take place in the southwestern portion of the country, primarily in the Khulna Division, which borders West Bengal to the west and is north of the world's largest mangrove forest, the Sundarban ("beautiful forest"), home of the majestic Bengal tiger. Most shrimp processors are also in the Khulna Division, though some are further north, near Dhaka.

I boarded a 6 A.M. bus from the Shohag bus company for the nine-hour road and ferry journey to the city of Khulna. The bus was comfortable enough, except for the driver's penchant to blare his horn at a rate that exceeded even the most maniacal South Asian driver. Crossing the mud-colored Januma River was another story. The rusted, ancient ferryboat looked barely able to float. The papers in Bangladesh regularly contain stories of capsized ferries, especially during the monsoon season, when the swollen rivers behave more like angry beasts than waterways. Two people vomited during the crossing, but we arrived on the other side safely. By afternoon, I met my guide at the dusty Khulna bus station, where we continued southwest by car for another three hours along narrow roads covered for miles in drying jute. Dodging a frenetic mix of goats, children, motorbikes, and trucks, we arrived at the absolute southern tip of the inhabited portion of Bangladesh, a village called Munshiganj.

Step 1: Shrimp Fry Collection

Munshiganj is a gray, muddy, soggy village. It is also home to the first two steps in the shrimp supply chain: shrimp fry collection and shrimp farming for saline species of shrimp. Freshwater shrimp are farmed further north, near the towns of Khulna and Satkhira, which I explored after Munshiganj. Aside from being the last inhabited outpost before the majestic Sundarban begins, Munshiganj is also ground zero for the devastation caused by Hurricane Aila in 2009.

My guides in Munshiganj were Satu and Zakir, both of whom work for an NGO called Shushilan. Shushilan operates throughout southwestern Bangladesh on a variety of rural development projects, and they were indispensable to me in navigating this remote area. The first question I asked my guides related to an island called Dublar Char, about a fourteen-hour boat ride south of Munshiganj, at the far tip of the Sundarban. Dublar Char is supposed to be replete with slave labor in the fishing industry. Tales of beatings, torture, and outright murder are not uncommon. When I enquired about the possibility of researching the island to verify these stories, my guides told me, "This is the monsoon season—Dublar Char is under water!" Dublar Char is a few kilometers across, so for the entire island (or most of it) to be underwater gives a sense of the immense level of flooding caused by the monsoons in Bangladesh. Though I was not able to explore the island of Dublar Char, later in my trip I did manage to visit another infamous fishing island called Nijhum Dwip, which is an overnight ferry ride from Dhaka. There was little fishing activity at the time of my visit, because of the dangerous monsoon waters. A few local villagers described stories of beatings and under- or unpaid wages during the season. Some also said that many Bangladeshi fishermen from this and other islands migrated during the monsoon season with agents to other countries in Southeast Asia, especially Thailand, for work in the fishing sector abroad. Most returned with meager wages, and others did not return for several years, if ever. Back in 2005 when I was in Thailand, Police Lieutenant Colonel Suchai Chindavanich of the Crime Against Child, Juvenile,

Photo 4.1. Children in boats catching baby shrimp at three rivers' convergence in south-western Bangladesh.

and Woman Suppression Division in Bangkok told me stories of Cambodian, Laotian, and Bangladeshi fishermen who were often taken onto Thai fishing ships for the fishing season—and then shot and thrown into the sea.[3] The fishermen I met at Nijhum Dwip knew of these stories, but as a frail fisherman named Imran told me, "We must take any opportunity we can find."

With Dublar Char underwater and out of the question, I focused on my shrimp explorations. Early the following morning, I hired a rickety boat by the banks of the Kholpetua River, where shrimp fry collection was in full swing by 7 A.M. In the pouring rain, we made our way thirty minutes downstream, where a group of small wooden boats slowly emerged on the horizon at the intersection of three rivers—the Kholpetua, Kalagacha, and Malaneha. I estimated close to five hundred boats, and by random sample, roughly seven out of ten were manned by children. Satu told me that during the peak season in March and April, this same intersection of rivers would have over two thousand boats. In order to catch the baby shrimp, the children huddle under plastic tarps to keep out of the rain, waiting all morning for the current to wash as many baby shrimp as possible into their small, blue nets. Boys and girls were present in equal numbers, from ages ten to the upper teens. One young boy named Mohammad explained the process to me:

Each morning we take the boats in this area. This is the best area to catch the shrimp because the current is strong. During the peak season we catch hundreds of shrimp each day, but now we can catch one hundred or two hundred if we are lucky. After three or four hours, we take the shrimp we have collected to Munshiganj, where we sell them to the farmers. The sale price is higher now, since it is not the peak season. These days we can get BTK 70 ($1.00) for one hundred shrimp. During the peak season the price is BTK 30 ($0.43) for one hundred.

I asked Mohammed if he went to school or if there was any other work for him to do.

None of us are in school. I wish I could be in school, but I must do this work or else we cannot earn enough money. My father left three years ago to find work in India. Sometimes he sends money, but it is not much. My two sisters do shrimp collection with me sometimes, especially in the peak season. My mother tends the home, and each day she has to walk two hours to get water. This entire area is for shrimp farming, so there is no other work for us.

More than twenty other children I spoke with echoed Mohammad's story. The only work available for miles around was to catch baby shrimp or to grow the fry into adult shrimp at a farm. The poorest of the poor had no access to land or any ability to take loans for shrimp farming, so they were consigned to collecting the baby shrimp. In fact, most of them did not even have boats like Mohammad and attempted to catch the shrimp along the muddy riverbanks. After Hurricane Aila, relief organizations such as UNICEF, USAID, OXFAM, Christian Aid, and Islamic Relief (all of which have prominent signs at the dock in Munshiganj) helped rebuild some homes and provided fishing boats for some of the families. Those families who received the boats use them to collect shrimp. Those who did not receive

Photo 4.2. Children catching baby shrimp by the muddy riverbanks.

boats send their children through the knee-deep mud into the parasite-infested river waters to collect as many baby shrimp as they can. Children wade neck deep in the strong currents and eventually emerge with twenty or thirty baby shrimp in their nets. Infections and illness are common, and, on occasion, a child is swept downstream and drowns.

When I spoke to some of these families in their muddy, riverside huts, their stories were remarkably similar. Men regularly left with offers from agents for work in India, Singapore, Malaysia, and even the Middle East—almost always after first entering into considerable debt because of the fees required by the agents. Some of these men eventually managed to send small amounts of money back to their families; others were never heard from again. In September 2011, I documented a few Bangladeshi construction workers in Singapore with the help of an organization called the Cuff Road Project, and these workers described a shocking array of coercive labor conditions ranging from unpaid wages to beatings in broad daylight. The women and children these men left behind turned to the only vocation available to them—catching baby shrimp for a dollar or so a day. But this vocation only serves a small portion of the individuals living in the area; the remainder are completely destitute and lack almost any source of income. I spent most of the next day touring through the Kholpetua River to the most remote, hurricane-wrecked villages beyond Munshiganj. The half-destroyed huts were barely above water, and everyone lived in knee-deep mud. These people were exceedingly desperate and caught in the worst extremes of abject poverty. Their afflicted existences gave new meaning to Gandhi's proclamation: "Poverty is the worst form of violence." Pain after pain was piled upon these people. Absolute deprivation was like a club that bludgeoned their bodies and spirits with misfortune each and every day. The more time I spent in these nether regions of Bangladesh, the more I struggled to find even one point of similarity between someone like me and someone like them. I could not comprehend how such extremes of existence could be found on the same planet. One woman, Sumaiya, told me a story that haunts me to this day:

> Do you know what life is like for people like us? I watch my family die all around me. My father was killed in Hurricane Aila. Two years ago, my son was kidnapped, and they demanded ransom to return him. What ransom can we pay? They sent my son to India and said they will return him after one year. We hear stories of how our children are slaves in India. We hear stories that they are beaten and made to work all day and all night until they collapse. I pray every night that my son will return. You cannot imagine how much I cry. I wish I could hold my child again. I tell Allah to take my life so long as my son will be safe. You tell me why something like this happens to people like us!

I had no answer to Sumaiya's question. I did not understand why the people who had the least often suffered the most. It is the question that has plagued me the most throughout my journeys, and on that day when I saw the ruinous pain in Sumaiya's eyes, I felt like giving up. I had only seen pain like that a few times in my life. Once in India, in the eyes of Shama. Once in Moldova, in the eyes of Olga. Once in Nigeria, in the eyes of Comfort. Each time it was a mother desperately yearning for the safe return of her child. I felt paralyzed before Sumaiya. What on earth was I ever going to do that would be of any benefit to someone like her? She and the appallingly destitute villagers I met in the rivers beyond Munshiganj needed a stroke of good fortune from the world, not some transient researcher who would never return. They certainly did not need the immensity of misfortune that continued to torment their meager existences—hurricanes, floods, illness, and, to top it off—human traffickers stealing their precious children. Poverty was unleashing a daily violence against these people that was too painful to bear, and the body count was mounting.

Step 2: Shrimp Farming

Munshiganj is a gray and barren place. Elders tell me it was once green and filled with crops and grazing animals. The reason for the radical degeneration of the environment becomes abundantly clear the moment one begins to investigate the second stage of the shrimp supply chain: shrimp farming. I documented ten different shrimp farming families in the area. I stumbled upon the first family, headed by an elderly man named Aziz, by accident. Satu, Zakir, and I were walking down a dirt road surveying the countryside. As far as the eye could see, the land was divided into neat rectangles of brackish water three to five feet deep, with narrow strips of mud forming the perimeters between each rectangle. These were the shrimp *ghers* (farms) in which during the July to March season the fry were growing into adult shrimp. As we continued our walk through the area, a torrential rainstorm suddenly erupted. There was a hut in the distance, so we raced toward it. The elderly Aziz invited us in.

Aziz had been a *hari* sharecropper (the same system as in the Sindh province of Pakistan) for most of his life. When in the 1990s shrimp aquaculture began to replace traditional agriculture in the area, Aziz told me that thousands of *hari* sharecroppers like him were displaced. This is because a giant shrimp *gher* only requires a few people to tend and harvest, as opposed to an agricultural field of equal size, which is much more labor intensive. Whereas numerous people and countless hours of work are required to plant, cultivate, and harvest ten hectares of rice, it only takes a handful of people a relatively minor number of hours to fill an equivalently sized shrimp farm with baby shrimp, watch them grow for three months, and then harvest them in nets. Fully aware of the advantageous economics associated with shrimp aquaculture, wealthy landowners and corporate interests swooped into the area during the 1990s and took title of whatever land was not theirs already, then forcibly evicted the superfluous peasants

Photo 4.3 Saltwater shrimp farms near Munshiganj.

who had been living on the land for generations. Ejected from their land, most peasants migrated to find work. Many were trafficked to India, Southeast Asia, or the Middle East, and many more were left homeless, penniless, and struggling to survive. Simultaneously, the commercial interests that acquired the land transformed the verdant agricultural fields throughout the area into saline farms for black tiger shrimp, the most prized product of the Bangladesh shrimp industry.[4] The saline black tiger shrimp is the most valued because of its immense size, of up to twenty-five centimeters in length, with a weight of .29 to .31 kilograms. Since its head is smaller than its freshwater black tiger cousin, more weight (and thus more money) is left over after the shrimp are beheaded. This is the most common type of shrimp that is exported abroad.

The reason for the sudden and relatively recent shift from agriculture to aquaculture in southwestern Bangladesh is primarily a result of climate change. Beginning in the 1990s, farmers began to notice more and more saline shrimp in their irrigation channels during the monsoon season, as a result of rising sea levels. Bangladesh is within close proximity of several multi-billion-dollar shrimp exporting nations such as Thailand, India, and Vietnam, so landowners quickly did the math and realized that low-intensity saline shrimp would generate far more profit than rice or potatoes ever would. They rapidly transformed the area from freshwater agriculture to saline aquaculture. Now the saltwater *ghers* span the horizon; there are more than 170,000 hectares of saline shrimp farming land along the southwestern coast.[5] Nothing else can grow here, and no animals can graze. "Our children have no vegetables to eat, no fresh water, and no milk," Aziz told me. "It is terrible here, but we have no choice. We are lucky to have this *gher*; otherwise what would we do?"

Those few *hari* sharecroppers like Aziz who managed to secure deals from the new landowners became shrimp farming bonded laborers overnight. After almost twenty years as a shrimp farmer, Aziz described the system in detail:

Each season I take a loan from the landowner of BTK 4,500 ($64.30) to lease each thirty-three decimals[6] of land. I buy the shrimp fry from Munshiganj at the rate of BTK 900 to BTK 1,000 per thirty-three decimals. My total farm area is 2,465 decimals. Sometimes I send my children to the river to catch the fry, so that I can save this expense. The shrimp take three or four months to grow. The water channel brings water into the *gher* at high tide each day and provides aeration. We harvest the mature shrimp with our nets during the black moon and the full moon. The yield is only 10 percent, because we do not have funds for food or medicine. I sell the shrimp to the distributors depending on the grade, but the average is BTK 300 ($4.29) per kilogram. Based on this income, I must pay back my loan to the landowner. Even when the harvest is good, I do not have enough money. If there is a season with an infection, or if the entire harvest is ruined, as it was in 2007 with Hurricane Sidr and in 2009 with Hurricane Aila, then I have no income and I must borrow more money. Oh, I should tell you, when we borrow extra money, the landowner also charges interest, sometimes 50 percent, sometimes 100 percent. This makes it more difficult to pay the money back. My wife is able to get small microcredit loans from BRAC[7] for 12.5 percent interest, but this is only enough for small purchases for the family or for calcium carbonate for the shrimp. Since the beginning, I have been in debt with no income at the end of the season. I do not even try to keep my accounts.

I spoke with Aziz until the rain let up, almost an hour later. During that time, his children and grandchildren gathered, as well as people from nearby shrimp farms, some of whom I interviewed next. They all described similar systems of debt bondage, from which there seemed little escape. Not all the shrimp farmers in this area were bonded laborers. Many were family members of the landowners or small farmers taking advantage of the opportunity to farm shrimp. However, those who were in debt bondage eked out a dreary existence at the whims of storms, infections, and other calamities.

Further north, in and around the towns of Satkhira and Khulna, I researched the freshwater shrimp farming sector, which has expanded to occupy more than four hundred thousand hectares of land across the region.[8] The *ghers* are freshwater ones in this area, because it is too far north for the tidal surges to bring salt water over the land. The advantages of freshwater shrimp farming are that the farms do not ruin the land for agriculture during the off season. The disadvantage is that the freshwater tiger shrimp is smaller and has a bigger head than its saltwater cousin, so once beheaded there is considerably less weight left over, which means much less revenue. Other freshwater shrimp species are also generally smaller than saltwater species.

I hiked deep into the countryside to dozens of shrimp *ghers* in this area. Just as in the south, the land was neatly divided into rectangles of water, with narrow strips of land forming the perimeters. Unlike the south, the land here also had green palm trees swaying in the breeze, grass and grazing animals, and a general abundance of life. There were even birds flying in the sky. Once I spoke to a few of the shrimp farmers, I noticed a few other differences as well. The lease rates were slightly higher (BTK 5,000 per thirty-three decimals, instead of 4,500), which I attributed to the higher price of land in general, offset slightly by the lower economic return of freshwater shrimp. The cost of the shrimp fry was also slightly higher than in the south, which I attributed to the fact that they had to be captured and transported from rivers slightly farther away from the *ghers* and also because many farms purchased their fry from the small number of baby shrimp hatcheries in the area. There was also security required, in the form of thatched shacks placed at the intersection of every four to six *ghers*, each manned by guards who monitored the *ghers* twenty-four hours a day. Armed guards were necessary because the freshwater *ghers* were much closer to large towns such as Khulna and Satkhira, where most of the shrimp distributors (and many processors) were based. As a result, many impoverished, displaced, or otherwise desperate villagers regularly attempted to steal shrimp out of the *ghers* and sell them to distributors as a way to make money. As my local guide from Sushilan explained, "Every week or two we hear of a villager being shot in the night when he tries to steal the shrimp. People are so desperate here, and with so many *ghers* there is very little land to do anything else."

There is also a small amount of investment in food and fertilizer in the freshwater *ghers*, which leads to slightly higher yields in the north versus the south, but this is somewhat offset by less aeration, since there is no natural ebb and flow of the tide in the area. In fact, as I walked through the strips of land between the *ghers* deeper and deeper into the countryside, I noticed numerous dead shrimp and fish floating at the surface, something I did not see as much in the south. Finally, I noticed that more of the land in the north was owned and operated by the actual landowners than in the south, but there were still plenty of independent farmers caught in debt bondage.

When I ran the numbers on shrimp farming debt bondage throughout southwestern Bangladesh, it was striking to see that the lease rates were just slightly higher than the average gross profit from shrimp farming. Table B.5 in the appendix shows the average economics of a ten hectare freshwater *gher*, for which the lease rate would be $5,337 and for which the average expected gross profit would be $5,070. This means that on average, shrimp farmers can expect to have a small carryover of debt (roughly 5 percent of the original loan amount) to the following season, be they freshwater or saltwater farmers. Any sort of systemic infection or natural disaster that obliterates a single season of shrimp obviously places them in a debt hole from which it would be virtually impossible to escape. From one season to the next, any single farmer may show a slight profit instead of a slight loss, but overall, the economics of the system were clearly designed to ensure the persistence of debt bondage for many of the eight hundred thousand to one million shrimp farmers in Bangladesh.

Step 3: Shrimp Distribution

The third step in the shrimp supply chain also takes place in the Khulna-Satkhira area. This step involves distribution of the harvested shrimp from the *ghers* to the processors. On the face of it, it seemed like an inefficient intermediate step, but when I visited a few distributors and understood the sheer volume of shrimp being sorted and distributed, it was clear that the average farmer could not handle this process, let alone subsequently transport the sorted shrimp in refrigerated cars to the processors, be they nearby in Khula or farther away in Dhaka.

A few farmers do manage to transport their shrimp to the distributors immediately after harvest, but most pay "commission agents" to transport the shrimp to the distributors for a small commission of BTK 2 to BTK 3 ($0.03 to $0.04) per kilogram, regardless of the grade of shrimp. The distributors then sort the shrimp into ten different grades determined by size and weight and pay out fees accordingly. A kilogram of top-grade black tiger shrimp (twelve to sixteen shrimp) will sell to a distributor for around BTK 900 ($12.85), and the bottom-grade black tiger shrimp (100+ shrimp) will sell for around BTK 200 ($2.85) per kilogram. The distributor then packs the shrimp into refrigerated cars, transports them to the processors, and sells them for a 2 to 3 percent markup on the purchase price.

I investigated several distributors of various sizes throughout Khulna district. Some handled a few hundred kilograms of shrimp per month; others handled thousands of kilograms. There was a wide variance in working conditions, from fair and reasonable to outright forced labor. In an area called Nutan Bazar in Khulna, I investigated three midsize distributors where conditions were particularly worrisome. Each had a foreman who made around $100 per month, one or two guards who made about half this amount, and fifteen to twenty workers who made around BTK 10 ($0.14) per hour.

While the foremen were generally willing to discuss how they sorted and distributed shrimp, they all refused to let me speak to their workers. I waited outside these distributors for several hours on a few separate days and managed to secure several conversations with the workers during their breaks. Most of them described the work conditions in detail. They were primarily migrants from rural areas who had traveled to Khulna for the shrimp season. Some had taken advances to do so, but more than half had not. Those who took advances were paid almost nothing, because of the debt repayments deducted from their wages. The foremen and guards used force to confine the workers to the premises for eighteen- to twenty-four-hour shifts, after which they were allowed take a short break to eat and sleep on cots in the back of the buildings. The living quarters were described as cramped, filthy, and perpetually damp. "We are never allowed to leave the building without permission," a worker named Manik told me. "And we cannot leave this area until the end of the season." Manik explained that he and other workers were usually paid monthly, though sometimes they were only paid at the end of the season.

Only a few of the workers described harsh physical abuse, but all of them stated that they were not allowed to leave the processors or pursue any other work options. If they tried to, the penalties included beatings or being forced to work without wages for a few days. At the end of the season, most returned back to their home villages and searched for casual labor, which was always difficult to find.

Step 4: Shrimp Processing

As secretive as some of the distributors were about their operations, the industrial shrimp processors were even more so. I heard numerous anecdotes about severe forms of forced and child labor in the processors. When I attempted to research any of the processors in the Khulna-Satkhira area, I was angrily turned away from the front gates by armed guards. It did not matter what I said or how often I tried—there was no getting in. I imagined there was not much in the way of trade secrets to protect, so it was difficult to ascertain exactly why the processors were so aggressive about maintaining their secrecy.

One processor, however, finally did invite me in. Khondoker Aynul Islam, the managing director of Southfield Fisheries, arranged a comprehensive tour of his facilities, then sat with me for over an hour and described just about every aspect of the shrimp processing industry in detail. I found nothing in the way of severe labor exploitation taking place among his two hundred workers, other than the fairly low wages of $1.42 to $2.85 per day. Shrimp processing is a highly industrial and capital-intensive business, which is why it is primarily conducted by large businesses with access to capital and distribution networks. Here, briefly, is how the business works.

Shrimp are purchased by grade from the distributors and are deposited in a "reception room." Next, they are passed to the beheading room, where 25 to 30 percent are beheaded. This results in an average 35 percent loss in weight. Peeling the shrimp results in another 15 percent loss in weight. Next, the shrimp are passed to a processing room, where they are processed into one of seven categories: head on, headless, peeled, peeled tail on, peeled but not deveined, peeled deveined, and peeled deveined with tail on. The freezing room comes next, where the shrimp are frozen either through contact plate freezing or individual quick freezing. Finally, the frozen shrimp are taken to an "anteroom," where they are packaged and placed in cold storage between –18 and –22 degrees centigrade.[9] Upon order from wholesalers, the frozen shrimp are transported to one of the two seaports in Bangladesh—Mongla or Chittagong—where they are loaded into forty-foot-long refrigerated containers holding 18,000 kilograms of shrimp each. Shipping is the most expensive component of the processors' business (around 25 percent of the total expenses). Shipping to the European Union costs $4,500 to $6,000 per container, to the United States $6,000 to $7,000 per container, and to Japan around $4,000 to $5,000 per container. After wages (roughly 5 percent of expenses), electricity (roughly 4 percent of expenses), and debt repayment, shrimp processors like Southfield Fisheries typically operate on a thin net profit margin of around 1.5 percent. The primary disadvantage to shrimp processing is that prices are determined by weight. Although the processors must purchase shrimp with the heads and scales still attached, they must sell half or more of the shrimp without heads and scales. A government incentive of 10 percent of sales helps offset some of this disadvantage.

The razor-thin margins of the processing business are the primary catalyst for issues that arise with labor exploitation. Wages are barely 5 percent of expenses, but this 5 percent can mean the difference between turning a profit or a loss on a 1.5 percent net profit margin. Because of the global economic downturn during 2008 and 2009, consumer demand for shrimp dropped by 10 to 15 percent worldwide. This meant that just about every processor in Bangladesh was faced with turning a significant loss during those years. Also, most processors have heavy debt loads, because of the high capital expenses associated with the expensive equipment used to behead, peel, devein, freeze, and store the shrimp. Debt repayments cannot be halted during periods of adverse market conditions, and other expenses such as shipping, packaging, and electricity are not very elastic. This leaves wages as the only expense that can be manipulated. Several colleagues pointed to the recent adverse market conditions for shrimp as a primary driver of the increase in the harsh exploitation of child and forced labor that may be occurring at the processors. These same forces in turn place pressure to minimize costs down the supply chain, by exploiting labor at the distributor, farming, and fry collection stages. Minimizing wages by extracting forced or bonded labor from distributor workers and shrimp farmers is the primary mode of doing so. Mr. Islam informed me that he had absorbed two very negative years of business by taking out more loans and that he desperately needed 2010 and 2011 to be much more profitable years. It appeared that other processors may not be as decent as him, given the stories I heard about forced labor exploitation at the processors. Despite my best efforts, I was unable to verify the anecdotes of forced and child labor exploitation in the shrimp processing facilities directly. I hope additional efforts can be made to investigate the labor conditions in Bangladesh's shrimp processors soon, particularly during times of global economic slowdown or downward fluctuations in global consumer demand for shrimp.

WHAT ABOUT YOUR SHRIMP COCKTAIL?

Billions of shrimp are consumed around the world each year, helping shrimp to become the largest commodity in the global seafood industry (tuna is second). Having only commenced a little more than thirty years ago, shrimp aquaculture has quickly grown to become the dominant mode of shrimp production. Overall, global aquaculture production (excluding aquatic plants) exceeded fifty-three million tons in 2009, with a value of $102 billion, which is double the market size of ten years earlier. This rapid growth rate from 1999 to 2009 was three times that of meat production during the same period. Asia is by far the world leader in aquaculture, responsible for 88 percent of the global market in 2009. China alone produced 62.3 percent in 2009.[10] Bangladesh was responsible for a relatively modest one million tons of aquaculture in 2009, but it has been growing at a brisk pace of 10 percent per year since 1990.

The United States is the largest importer of frozen shrimp in the world, and U.S. consumer demand for low-cost shrimp has been a key driver of the growth among Asian nations in shrimp aquaculture. Seven of the ten largest shrimp producers in the world are in Asia (China, India, Indonesia, Thailand, Vietnam, Malaysia, and the Philippines). Bangladesh is a small producer by Asian standards, but it produced more than thirty-two million kilograms of shrimp in 2010, worth $353 million,[11] representing 2.5 percent of the global shrimp and prawn export market of $14.2 billion. More than 26 percent of these shrimp were exported to the United States, followed by 42 percent to the European Union.[12] Another $101 million in fish—often caught and processed under forced labor conditions in places like Dublar Char and Nijhum Dwip—were exported by Bangladesh in 2010. This makes the fast-growing fish and shrimp sector Bangladesh's third largest export, responsible for 5 percent of GDP.[13]

So what exactly do these numbers suggest in terms of the shrimp you eat at your cocktail parties or the local all-you-can-eat shrimp specials? Labor conditions in most Asian countries exporting shrimp to the United States and European Union are generally problematic, be it child labor, low-wage labor, or outright slave labor. This is how costs of production are kept low, which helps keep prices low, which in turn stimulates consumer demand to eat more shrimp. Countries like Thailand and Vietnam generally seem to have a better profile than India or Bangladesh, and it is unclear what the conditions are in China. Bangladesh occupies the unique position of being a relatively new and aggressive entrant into the shrimp aquaculture sector, but as a result of its very small amount of investment in production technology it achieves some of the lowest yields among Asian producers. Being cyclone prone, entire seasons can also be devastated. Underregulation also promotes labor exploitation. Above all, the rapid transformation of 570,000 hectares of precious agricultural land into shrimp farms has displaced millions of people and led to an industry replete with various forms of labor abuses. Just as agriculture has been a historic home to bonded labor, forced labor, and child labor, aquaculture has become the marine version of its terrestrial cousin.

Taking the small slice of Bangladesh's shrimp sector, I conservatively estimate that approximately 69 to 72 percent of all frozen shrimp exported from Bangladesh is tainted by child, forced, or bonded labor.[14] This implies than one out of every fifty-six to fifty-seven frozen shrimp in the world is produced by contemporary forms of slavery or child labor in Bangladesh alone. This may not seem like much, but consider that each person in the United States consumes almost two kilograms of shrimp per year (double the rate from 1990),[15] which represents anywhere between sixty to two hundred pieces of shrimp. This implies that each shrimp eater in the United States will consume a few pieces of shrimp per year that are produced through child, forced, or bonded labor from Bangladesh alone. Adding other shrimp-producing nations to the list would only increase the ratio. So, the next time you dip a shrimp into the vermillion cocktail sauce and bite down into its fleshy texture, try to imagine that shrimp being caught, farmed, distributed, and processed by a child, forced, or bonded laborer in Bangladesh or somewhere else in the world. Doing so is the starting point in demanding that the companies that deliver these shrimp to our local groceries and restaurants ensure that their supply chains are untainted by slavelike labor abuses. The forces of economic globalization have brought an unprecedented bounty of inexpensive products to us from all corners of the globe, but they often come with a level of violence and predation that makes the lives of the producers of these products much worse. This violence must not stand, even if it means paying a little more for these products or foregoing them all together.

INSIDE A CUP OF TEA

In chapter 1, I discussed how land and tax policy under the British East India Company, beginning with the Permanent Settlement of 1793, catalyzed the mass trafficking of newly landless peasants from Orissa and Bihar to the tea plantations of Assam and Bengal during the early and mid-1800s. On arrival, these workers were met with outright slavery in the form of debt bondage that eventually became legally enforceable under the Workman's Breach of Contract Act, 1859. More than 150 years later, I traveled to the historic Bengal tea plantations in Bangladesh near Sylhet and Srimangal, just on the other side of the border from Assam.[16] What I saw was a sobering example of the bleak fates faced by former slaves after several generations during which virtually no rehabilitation, reempowerment, social integration, or economic development had been provided. In short, the descendants of these trafficked slave laborers were still eking out deeply impoverished and isolated existences, and many of them remained ensnared in forced and bonded labor in the tea industry.

Each and every tea worker I met in northeastern Bangladesh told me they were descendants of tea plantation migrants from Bihar and Orissa from 150 years earlier. It was surprising to me that they could trace their ancestry back that far, but their ability to do so was a testament to how isolated they remained even after so many decades. Across generations, the tea plantation workforce remained almost entirely the descendents of these trafficked workers, with few new workers entering the plantations—and almost none leaving.

Speaking to the tea workers and documenting their stories was no easy task. I visited six different tea plantations in northeastern Bangladesh, and they were almost as secretive as their shrimp processing cousins in the southwest. Each plantation consisted of an endless expanse of verdant tea fields. The central processing facilities were always gated and guarded, though this did not prevent the intoxicating scent of freshly ground tea leaves from suffusing the air in every direction. While one set of workers cultivated and harvested the plants in the tea fields, another set of workers processed the harvested tea leaves in facilities that used machines so old they seemed to have been held over from colonial times. Whenever I attempted to speak to anyone in a tea field, the nearest foreman quickly intervened and told me to be on my way. Whenever I tried to gain entry to the processing plants to speak to the workers inside, the guards at the front gate pointed to a painted sign that said "Unauthorized Entry Is Liable for Prosecution" or words to that effect. If I did not leave quickly enough, they forcibly escorted me away from the front gates. Many of these guards were

Photo 4.4. Not allowed in a tea processing plant near Srimangal, Bangladesh.

armed, which left little room for debate. However, sometimes they were not, and on those occasions, I pushed a little harder.

The conversations that ensued were among the most absurd I had during any of my research trips. Eventually, after I refused to walk away, an angry guard would fetch a foreman to handle my request. On all three occasions, the conversations went something like this:

FOREMAN: We are very busy. No one is allowed inside.

ME: I won't take long. I would just like to see how the tea is made.

FOREMAN: I cannot let you in. Please write a letter to the main office in Chittagong to ask for permission.

ME: That will take too long. Can't you ask your manager to give me permission?

FOREMAN: The manager is not here.

ME: Where is he?

FOREMAN: I don't know.

ME: You don't know where your manager is?

FOREMAN: No.

ME: So call him on his mobile phone.

FOREMAN: He does not have a mobile phone.

ME: The manager of this tea plantation does not have a mobile phone?

FOREMAN: No.

ME: How do you contact him in an emergency?

FOREMAN: I don't know. Please go away.

ME: I will not go away until I see the inside of that plant.

FOREMAN (frustrated): Just wait here . . .

Twenty minutes later, the foreman returned to the front gate.

FOREMAN: I cannot let you in. Please go away. Someone will be here soon, and I will get in trouble.

ME: Who will be here?

FOREMAN: Someone important. We have a guest today. I will get in trouble if he sees you here. Please go away.

ME: Now I am concerned that you have something to hide. Maybe there are labor violations going on? Maybe that is why you don't want me to come in?

FOREMAN: Wait here.

Twenty minutes later, the manager, who was supposed to be far away with no mobile phone, arrived at the front gate.

MANAGER: Okay, you can come back tomorrow and see the plant.
ME: No, I would like to see it now. I believe you might be hiding something you don't want me to see. Maybe you are not treating your workers properly.
MANAGER: Okay, there must be a misunderstanding. I did not realize what you were saying. There is no problem with the workers. Please come inside for a few minutes and we can give you a tour . . . but you must not take any photos!

I managed to inspect three tea processing facilities in Bangladesh after three conversations almost exactly like this. Two of the plants processed black tea; the other processed green tea.[17] During my inspections, I was followed closely by the managers, who were all in mortal fear of some guest who might see me in the plant. I surmised this was probably the head of the plantation, who most likely had given strict orders that no one should ever see what was happening inside. If I was right, the managers had good reason to be afraid, because the conditions inside the processing facilities were worrisome. Apart from the ancient machinery, the conditions were extremely unhygienic. The workers' skin and hair were covered in thick layers of tea dust, and they were breathing humid, stagnant air twenty-four hours a day. The air was so dense with particulate matter that I was coughing within minutes of being inside the plants. Some of the workers I managed to speak with told me they were forced to work two or three eight-hour shifts in a row to ensure that the plants were running around the clock, and that when they were not being forced to work multiple shifts inside the plants they were confined to the residential areas provided by the plantation company and could only leave the premises on rare occasions. Some workers were so exhausted they fell asleep right on top of piles of tea leaves. Others had not eaten in over a day, and still others were coerced to work no matter how ill or exhausted they were. My conversations in the plants were brief, and I only managed to speak to some of the workers by using my rickshaw driver as a decoy to distract the manager while my guide and I swiftly moved around the plant and asked as many questions as we could. The workers were timid and frightened, especially the women, though they spoke just enough for me to piece together what was going in inside the tea

Photo 4.5. Two laborers after working three consecutive shifts at a tea processing plant, to the point of exhaustion.

processing facilities. Each of the plantations I visited exported tea to South Asia, Russia, the European Union, and the United States.

Working backward through the tea processing supply chain, I returned in the evenings to some of the residential areas in which the tea workers lived. Guards patrolled the front gates, but the residential areas were a distance away, and I easily hopped the fence and managed to have several extensive conversations with the plantation workers in their small, mud-hut homes. The workers were all paid BTK 40 to BTK 48 per day ($0.57 to $0.69) for work in the plant, no matter how many eight-hour shifts in a row they were forced to work. If they were ill and did not work, they were not paid. If they did not want to work three shifts in a row, they might be evicted from their homes. More experienced workers might be paid a weekly salary of BTK 350 ($5.00), and the foremen and managers were paid BTK 5,000 to BTK 10,000 ($71.43 to $142.85) per month. The workers were all Hindus from Bihar and Orissa and were completely ostracized from mainstream Bangladeshi society. Most were provided tiny huts on the plantation as part of their compensation, but they were typically not allowed to leave or to pursue other work. Some workers said they could leave the plantation now and again, but no one else would hire them because they were known to be tea plantation workers (which meant they were lower class and unfit to do anything else), so they had no choice but to work at the tea plantations. They lived in acute deprivation and had barely enough income for basic provisions, which were sold to them by the plantations on the premises. Most of the workers were illiterate, many were ill with lung and skin ailments, and none of them had any other possibilities other than working in severely exploitative conditions in the tea plantations (low-wage, forced, or bonded labor). Of course, not every plantation in Bangladesh will be exactly the same as the three I visited, but it is reasonable to assume that there would be similarities. As one of the workers explained while eating rice in the darkness of his dusty, lizard-infested hut:

> All the plantations are like this. We work all year until we are so tired we cannot stand. Even if we leave this place, they take one look at us and know we are tea workers. No one will give us work. No one will take our children in school. I have been working here for thirty-five years. I have no savings, and even this home can be taken from me if I displease the owners.

I asked several of the workers if they ever had to take loans for expenses, and, as expected, many did. Most said that after taking these loans they were cajoled into working one or two extra shifts in a row with no extra pay, though others said that they had to do this even without taking loans. Overall, the conditions for the workers inside the processing facilities ran the spectrum from exploitative to hazardous to slavelike, and more research must be done in other tea processing facilities to ascertain just how extensive these problematic conditions are.

Continuing my research up the tea industry supply chain, the first step ended up being the last one I researched—harvesting tea leaves. Though I was forbidden entry to the plantations at the front gates (and even though guards patrol the fields as the workers pick the tea leaves), most of the plantations cover thousands of hectares, and there is absolutely no way to patrol all of them. One afternoon I hired a rickshaw, and we drove four kilometers down a narrow and bumpy dirt path deep into the tea fields of one of the largest plantations near Srimangal. Far in the fields, we came across scores of women (and a small number of children) picking tea leaves. They picked two leaves and one bud at a time, placing them in large burlap sacks holding up to twenty kilograms when full. It was oppressively hot and humid, and a man with a pole on his shoulders that held two water buckets on either end roamed the hills and delivered water to the tea pickers.

Once or twice a day, a foreman who makes BTK 100 ($1.43) per day drives down the same dirt path in a small tractor and collects the accumulated tea leaves. Women hear him coming, tie up their burlap sacks, and cart them on their heads to the meeting point. It was quite a sight to see forty or fifty women with sacks bursting with tea leaves atop their heads walking down the hillside to meet the foreman. Each bag was weighed on a scale, and the foreman announced the weight and recorded it next to the workers' names in a ledger. The leaves were loaded into the tractor and driven back to the plant for processing.

Much to my consternation, I noticed that the scale was set at 0.5 kilograms below zero and that the weight the foreman announced was always rounded down another kilogram or so from the number I read on the scale. The women are paid BTK 2 ($0.03) per kilogram, and on their best day they can pick forty kilograms. Because they were being cheated on the actual weight, they were typically being paid for about thirty kilograms of tea leaves, or maybe a maximum of $0.86 per day. They did not eat at all during their twelve- to fourteen-hour shifts, and they had to walk several kilometers both directions to and from the plantation huts, which contributed to very long work days, six to seven days a week. When I asked the foreman why the scale was set below zero and why he deducted from the actual weights in his ledger, he said, "The company tells me to do this." The women never contested the numbers and carried on working after the foreman left. When I asked them about the weight, a few said they knew the scale was set low and that their actual weights were reduced in the ledger. "We cannot say anything," one woman explained. "If we make trouble, we will be told not to work anymore, or they may send our entire family from the home." I surveyed a few other tea fields near Srimangal and Sylhet, and the system was exactly the same. All the tea pickers were women, all were being shortchanged on their wages, all worked exceedingly long hours with little or no food, and no one protested for fear of losing the only source of income and shelter available to them.

Photo 4.6. Coming to weigh the day's collection.

Photo 4.7. Tea scale calibrated unfairly.

At every stage of the tea supply chain, labor was being coerced to submit to deeply exploitative conditions. Tea laborers were provided homes but threatened with eviction if they did not accept unlawfully deducted wages. They were coerced to work two and three eight-hour shifts in a row at a single day's wage. They were shortchanged on wages, and they were kept isolated so that they had no chance of cultivating any other opportunities. In aggregate, the tea plantations in Bangladesh produce approximately sixty million kilograms of tea annually, worth $140 million at wholesale. Though it was difficult to calculate, because I was unable to access more of the tea plantations and processing facilities in northeastern Bangladesh, I conservatively estimate that approximately 30 to 45 percent of the industry is tainted by bonded, forced, or child labor.[18]

Perhaps the most critical point of my investigations into the tea industry of Bangladesh is that the sector provides a stark example of the importance of empowering the lives of those who are trafficked into slavelike conditions or who may be descended from those who were trafficked. Even though the colonial forces that led to the coerced and bonded labor of the trafficked tea plantation workers from generations ago have long ago disappeared, the unremediated legacies of that exploitation have persisted far longer than they should have. After 150 years, the tea laborers in Bangladesh remain an isolated and harshly exploited subpopulation in their host country. As a result, they have not managed to move one foot beyond the plantations to which their forefathers were trafficked generations before. Individuals who are trafficked or who have migrated under desperate circumstances invariably face a future of deep segregation and lack of opportunity. In the worst cases, they also face racism, xenophobia, and violence. A few of the elder tea workers I met described facing such conditions in the most extreme way when they were specifically targeted for genocide by Pakistani military forces during Bangladesh's Liberation War from West Pakistan in 1971, because they were Hindus originally from India.[19] It is imperative that once trafficked slaves or exploited migrant workers are freed from coercive labor conditions, sustained efforts must be made to help them empower their lives. In the absence of appropriate and sustained care for trafficked or similarly exploited laborers, they will all suffer fates similar to the disheartening outcome of the tea plantation workers in Bangladesh. These workers provide a glimpse at the fates that could be faced by millions of today's trafficked slaves, unless they are integrated into their host countries and receive reasonable educational and economic opportunities.

Without sufficient human-rights care for victims of modern-day human trafficking, all countries will possess a growing underclass of formerly trafficked slaves and their descendents, who will be consigned to live in virtual prisons of persistent exploitation and hardship long after their obvious servitude has ended. No good can come of a world that adds yet another subclass of oppressed individuals to the already immense roster of expendable people.

As one final note to this chapter, I must stress that even though I was able to gather comprehensive data in the agricultural, brickmaking, and other sectors in Bangladesh, the secrecy at the shrimp and tea processing plants is deeply concerning. These industries must be more transparent in the concluding steps of their respective supply chains to ensure that the worst anecdotes and rumors of forced, bonded, and child labor are not true. Much more research must be conducted in these sectors, and I hope that others will have more success at undertaking this research soon. The lives of millions of workers in Bangladesh depend on it.

{ 5 }

Construction and Stone Breaking

It has always been a mystery to me how men can feel honored by the humiliation of their fellow beings.

—GANDHI

BUILDING NATIONS ON THE BACKS OF SLAVES

The Commonwealth Games

In 1982, New Delhi was gearing up to host the Asian Games, an Olympics-style athletic competition for nations across Asia.[1] Several large construction projects were undertaken to erect new athletic and tourist facilities for the event. The manner in which a portion of this construction was achieved became the subject of one of the landmark Supreme Court cases in India relating to bonded labor: *People's Union for Democratic Rights vs. Union of India and Others*, 1982. This case, also referred to as the "Asiad Workers" case, will be discussed in more detail in chapter 7, but the basic list of complaints from some of the workers involved with the Asian Games construction projects included wage deductions for commissions to *jamadars*, the exploitation of child labor, severely subhuman living conditions in the work areas (lack of clean water, toilets, adequate shelter), unpaid wages, restrictions on movement, and other infractions that were deemed to be violations of Article 23 of the Constitution of India (the prohibition against forced labor) as well as India's then recently passed Bonded Labour System (Abolition) Act, 1976.

Reading the list of complaints from this case is like reading a list of violations that I documented almost three decades later, in New Delhi, for construction relating to yet another international sporting event—the Commonwealth Games 2010. The fact that a virtually identical scene played out in New Delhi three decades after the PUDR, 1982, case—in exactly the same circumstances, involving construction for an international sporting event—is a baffling and disappointing testament to the failures of the Indian government to eliminate labor exploitation and uphold the law. It is also a blistering indictment of the corruption and exploitation inherent in the *jamadar* system of labor subcontracting.

In the summer of 2010, I documented numerous violations of Indian labor laws relating to construction for the Commonwealth Games. Some of the specific laws that were violated include the Bonded Labour System (Abolition) Act, 1976; the Building and Other Construction Workers (Regulation of Employment and Condition of Service) Act, 1996; the Child Labour (Prohibition and Regulation) Act, 1986; the Contract Labour (Regulation and Abolition) Act, 1970; the Inter-State Migrant Workmen (Regulation of Employment and Condition of Service) Act, 1979; the Equal Remuneration Act, 1976; and the Minimum Wages Act, 1948. In addition, Articles 23, 24, and 43 of the Constitution of India were also being violated.[2]

After more than eleven years of research in the region, I can say without hesitation that the construction sector in South Asia is more extensively and consistently in violation of more labor laws and prohibitions against bonded, forced, and child labor than any other sector I have documented. This is particularly the case when one includes basic inputs into the construction sector, such as bricks (discussed in the previous chapter) and stones (discussed later in this chapter). The Commonwealth Games 2010 of New Delhi were no exception.

I spent two weeks driving, hiking, and pressing through the blazing heat and dust of New Delhi in July 2010 in order to document the labor conditions leading up to the October 2010 Commonwealth Games. The most helpful organization to me during this period was the People's Rights and Social Research Centre (PRASAR), led by the courageous activist and advocate for worker's rights S. A. Azad. As exhausted and drenched in sweat as I was battling the congested, polluted, baking city at every turn, the workers who were toiling up to eighteen or more hours a day in forty degrees centigrade heat or higher, seven days a week, in the mad rush to finish the faltering construction projects on time were literally on the verge of collapse. Local newspapers at the time were brimming with stories of crumbling structures, dangerous work areas that resulted in injury or death to laborers as well as civilians, and ongoing accusations of graft among the bureaucrats overseeing the construction.[3] At the bottom of the fiasco, the construction workers who had been trafficked to Delhi from villages throughout Uttar Pradesh, Bihar, Haryana, and West Bengal were tasked with building the stadiums and other sporting facilities, as well as "beautifying" New Delhi for the international exposé to come, at any and all human cost.

Here is how Vishnu, a trafficked worker from Bihar who was working outside the impressive Indira Gandhi National Sports Stadium, described the situation:

> The *jamadar* came to our village and made an offer for work in Delhi for the Commonwealth Games for very good wages. He said my family can work here and he will provide us wages of Rs. 120 ($2.67) per day for skilled work and Rs. 80 ($1.78) per day for unskilled work. He said my children will be paid half this wage if they also work. He described the work in detail, and he promised we will have huts to live in and sufficient food and water. He said we will work eight hours each day and only six days each week and that we will be paid our wages every two weeks. He arranged our transport to Delhi by train. We have all five been working here for four months since that time. I think this same *jamadar* brought at least one hundred people from my village and one other village also. Nothing is what he promised. We sleep under a plastic sheet on the side of the road. We must work seventeen or eighteen hours each day, seven days a week. We use the toilet outside, and we are given only bad food and water. We have not been paid any wages in four months. We have so many injuries, and we must borrow money from the *jamadar* for medicine. When I crushed this finger here, I could not work for five days. The *jamadar* said we will not have any wages for this time, even though my wife and children were working. The *jamadar* says we must keep working to pay off these loans; only then will he pay our wages. I wish I could go back to my home, but the *jamadar*'s men keep us working. Sometimes I try to sleep under that tractor there, but the *jamadar*'s men kick me and make me work. They also wake the children when they sleep. My

children work until they cry. I do not know how much longer we will survive like this. I will only have rest when I die.

During the course of my research in New Delhi that summer, the streets were filled with thousands of migrant, trafficked, and local construction laborers like Vishnu who were working day and night on countless construction projects throughout the city—new residential buildings, extensions of the Delhi Metro, a gargantuan upgrade of Delhi's international airport, new dormitory facilities for the India Institute of Technology (IIT) campus in Delhi, and a comprehensive facelift for the historic shopping center Connaught Place. At Connaught Place, I even came across a pile of bricks being used for construction with the initials MBK molded into each brick. On a previous research trip, I had gathered data from a brick kiln with more than seventy bonded and child laborers called MBK in rural Uttar Pradesh, not far from the town of Ayodhya. The construction workers eating rice and daal in the dirt near the pile of bricks were not sure where the bricks came from, but in all my years researching brick kilns in South Asia, I had never encountered two kilns that had the same name. In addition to the heavy construction for new buildings and stadiums, bonded laborers like Vishnu were busy at work on numerous "beautification" projects. Cratered and uneven sidewalks were being refurbished across the city and suburbs, traffic medians were being upgraded with new grass and small trees, and outside the main stadiums and political buildings, beautiful lion statues and clay lamps were being set down every ten meters along the roads in groups of three.

As I continued to conduct interviews with men, women, and children involved in the construction work throughout New Delhi, it became clear that each and every one of them had been recruited by a *jamadar* who promised fair wages and decent living conditions. They were told they would be paid regularly and could leave at any time. On arrival, they were forced to live in subhuman slums or filthy huts near roadsides, on dirt-filled medians between roads, or in the open air of the construction sites. Slums for construction workers popped up right next to major stadiums, with open sewers and rusty steel pipes and nails strewn everywhere. Garbage was piled several feet high, stray electrical wires electrocuted workers as well as playing children, and a host of other dangerous and unhygienic conditions made the entire area look like a war zone. In the midst of it all, I reliably documented forty-four cases of bonded, forced, and child labor in New Delhi in the span of two weeks, and I anecdotally documented scores of additional cases. Wages were completely unpaid or severely underpaid. Food, water, and medicine were provided as loans, which the workers had to repay through debt bondage. To top it off, the water that was provided was rarely more than two or three brackish liters per family per day, and the food consisted of little more than meager portions of rice and daal, infested with swarming flies and vermin. Filth-covered children worked as much as possible, because many *jamadars* promised half wages for their labor. Many workers were moved from one site to another every two to three months to keep them disconnected and unable to form ties or get too familiar with their surroundings. All around them, life in Delhi continued with as much normalcy as possible (though true normalcy for everyday Delhi citizens during the madness of the Commonwealth Games construction was hardly an option). Sometimes I sat on the sidewalk for an hour and watched as common citizens made their way from work to play by walking around piles of bricks with the same nonchalance as they circumnavigated child laborers and sleeping peasants, as if they were all equally annoying obstacles in the road. I am not suggesting that everyone in Delhi was oblivious to the labor exploitation that was happening front and center all around them; on the contrary, many everyday citizens and NGOs decried these abuses. However, in general, there was a systemic acceptance that these bonded and child laborers could be worked to the bone in order to finish the construction projects on time. That was the way things worked in India. The bonded and child laborers were part of a system that had functioned in much the same way for centuries, and there was hardly any sort of overwhelming social movement that was succeeding in altering that system, even as it violated the mandates of a thirty-year-old landmark Indian Supreme Court case by duplicating many of the same abuses in the same context.

Delhi's main red-light area on G. B. Road was also getting a facelift during the lead-up to the Commonwealth Games. I researched this area several years earlier for *Sex Trafficking*, but my results were not as extensive as they were in other major cities like Mumbai and Kolkata. I only managed a few brief conversations inside the *kothas* (brothels) on G. B. Road during previous trips, but I still saw and heard enough to know that a large number of trafficked women and children were being raped and abused with a barbarity that left searing scars in my memory. I had little appetite for a

Photo 5.1. Child laborer for the 2010 Commonwealth Games construction.

return to this area, but with my driver, Srijeet, by my side, I visited some of the *kothas* and managed to speak with a few women and girls living in the brothels. One of the women, Leela, who had been working on G. B. Road for more than ten years, told me that *kothawalis* (madam or brothel manager) had been injecting the younger girls with steroids to plump them up for Western tourists who would be attending the Commonwealth Games. As I walked through some of *kothas*, I also noticed that they were not as grimy and dilapidated as I remembered them. Air conditioners had been installed in many of the caged windows, rooms were being repainted, new sheets were fitted on the beds, and the girls were being taught English phrases like "Yes, sir" and "Thank you, sir" for English-speaking customers. There were still plenty of very young children playing in the halls, along with a heavy amount of alcohol and drug use. Ruchira Gupta, the courageous founder of the antitrafficking NGO Apne Aap International, later told me that she and her colleagues had noticed a considerable increase in recent weeks in the number of women from other states in India, as well as from Nepal and Bangladesh, who were arriving at G. B. Road leading up to the Commonwealth Games. I can only assume based on experience that the majority of these women and girls were trafficked and that the elevated numbers were intended to ensure a selection for the increase in international male sex consumers around the Commonwealth Games. I also asked Ruchira about Leela's report of steroid injections, and she said that she and her colleagues had also documented this and that the steroids being used were primarily bovine. There was no telling what the long-term side effects of these injections on the young girls would be, assuming they survived long enough to find out. Beyond G. B. Road, there were also anecdotes of certain hotels in Delhi being taken over by East European organized crime groups who were trafficking women from countries such as Romania, Poland, Russia, and the Ukraine in the months leading up to the Commonwealth Games, but I was not able to verify these rumors.

All around Delhi, a city was being reborn in the summer of 2010 as a showcase to the world. However, that rebirth was occurring at the expense of thousands of the country's poorest and most disposable and exploitable citizens. I attempted several times to contact the Ministry of Labour and Employment in New Delhi to discuss my findings, but I received no reply. I did the same with the chief minister of New Delhi, Sheila Dikshit, but again I received no reply. Eventually, some of my colleagues at CNN International, from the show *Connect the World* and who were following my research that summer, approached Ms. Dikshit separately with my findings, and two months after their initial contact she responded that she was unaware of any labor violations but that if they had been brought to her attention previously she would have investigated the matter. Ms. Dikshit was later indicted for corrupt practices relating to the Commonwealth Games in an August 2011 report issued by the comptroller and auditor-general (CAG) of India.[4]

The brutish realities that I documented of the horrid exploitation behind Delhi's rebirth for the Commonwealth Games was beyond anything I anticipated. It also became increasingly difficult to reconcile these abuses with the kind of language found on the official Commonwealth Games Web site:

Hosting a sporting event at a scale such as the Commonwealth Games is a matter of international prestige for the country, and is bound to boost brand India. The country is heralded as the next world economic super-

power and the Games will be another opportunity to project the nation on the world Stage. Delhi too, as the host city, will get the chance to exhibit a new image for itself—that of a world class city with international standards. . . . The historic city of Delhi will look its best for visitors of the XIX Commonwealth Games 2010 Delhi. One of the legacies of the event will be that it will leave behind a city much more beautiful and charming than it currently is.
(www.cwgdelhi2010.org)

In the end, Delhi did indeed look its best when the games opened on October 3, 2010. Dignitaries proudly introduced this "new" New Delhi and its heralding of India as the next world superpower. However, they did not reveal that this reborn Delhi had been built on the backs of the country's downtrodden and oppressed masses. This was neither the brand nor the international standards that the dignitaries wanted to show the world. It is difficult to see how any country can become a legitimate superpower so long as it allows its poorest citizens to be subjugated and exploited without consequence. From an initial budget of $360 million to a final expense ranging from $10 to $13 billion spent preparing for the Commonwealth Games (in a country in which approximately nine hundred million people live on less than two dollars per day), it is difficult to understand how there was not enough money available to provide decent work standards and wages for the poor laborers toiling day and night to make this proud day possible for their country. To those countless workers like Vishnu, it is a painful irony that the Commonwealth Games appeared to provide little common wealth at all.

A System Designed to Exploit

The Commonwealth Games are far from the first or the last construction venture in South Asia systematically to exploit forced, bonded, trafficked, and child labor. From Indian cities including Mumbai, New Delhi, Kolkata, Chennai, Bangalore, and Patna to other South Asian cities such as Dhaka and Kathmandu, I documented nearly identical systems of *jamadar*-managed labor exploitation relating to construction of everything from office buildings to street overpasses. The same system is also prevalent throughout Pakistan as well as Sri Lanka and Afghanistan. Indeed, the entire construction sector across South Asia is a poorly regulated system designed to exploit low-end laborers, in which one step in the business chain pays little regard to the actions or infractions of the others. In its most basic form, the construction business chain consists of the following:

- Step 1: Major construction ventures or government agencies commission a real estate or infrastructure project
- Step 2: Smaller construction companies offer competitive bids (and bribes) for various pieces of the overall project
- Step 3: The winning bidders hire *jamadars* to staff the project
- Step 4: *Jamadars* recruit labor and oversee the work while also disbursing wages and managing labor conditions

The primary breakdowns that lead to numerous forms of labor exploitation in the construction industry occur at step 4, at the *jamadar* level, where an entire subclass of vulnerable South Asians belonging to minority ethnicities and castes are regularly conscripted into slavelike exploitation to maximize profit and line the pockets of greedy contractors, construction company directors, and government bureaucrats. The limited scope and enforcement of vicarious liability laws, which do not include the relationship between employers and *jamadars*, as well as the lack of any semblance of rule of law, provide an impenetrable wall of impunity between the actions of the *jamadar* and any parties higher up the business chain. (I discuss this point in more detail as part of my recommendations in chapter 8.) The fact that there can be several layers of *jamadars* who subcontract to yet more *jamadars* who eventually hire and manage labor further complicates the situation and makes it exceedingly difficult to trace any sort of culpability.

I spoke with a handful of construction company directors and several *jamadars* to get a more detailed sense of exactly how the system works. Most of the construction company directors I approached were involved in various degrees of labor exploitation, and they typically refused to speak with me. "Go away" or "get off this property immediately" were the usual responses. On one occasion, at the new dormitory construction site for the IIT campus in New Delhi, the director had some of his foremen try to take my camera and notebook from me by force. I tried to reason with them calmly, but they were aggressive from the outset. There was a tussle and raised voices, but fortunately my driver was parked on the other side of a wall just outside the main construction site. He heard the commotion and rushed over with a crowbar, which allowed us to escape with our property and bodies intact.

Beyond a handful of short conversations and aborted encounters with the more dubious construction company directors I met, there was one director who took the better part of a day to describe the system to me in detail. Krishnendu Ghosh, the managing director of the Basumati Construction Company, is one of the good ones. We met in his office on a rainy day in Kolkata, where he talked to me at length about the modern business of construction.

Mr. Ghosh was primarily involved in construction projects for the Catholic Church in and around Kolkata. He had a picture of Mother Theresa on his desk, and he proudly explained that he trained all *jamadars* he hired to maintain legal standards of conduct, including full payment of wages, medicine for illness or injury, and decent working and living conditions. He was also proud to tell me that he sent the children of the families at his construction sites to school at his expense. "Not everyone is like me," Mr. Ghosh explained. "This industry is filled with goons and musclemen. Twenty-five percent of the customers in Sonagachi are *jamadars*. The raw section of society has taken over this business."

Mr. Ghosh outlined how the typical construction project works. He explained that at the commencement of any project, the contracting company or government agency that is requesting the project provides the construction company with a detailed outline of the desired construction, timelines, technical specifications, overall budget, payment schedule, and other terms and conditions. There are always terms for steep fines (1 to 2 percent of the contract value per week) for any delay, cost overrun, or other material breach. "Once we receive the contract," Ghosh explained, "we use our subcontractors to fill the labor requirements."

There are a handful of specific steps in most construction projects for buildings and residences that require particular skill sets from the laborers: foundation and cement, steel work, woodwork, electricity, paint, fabrication, shuttering, and plumbing. There are numerous substeps to these steps, which may require further specialization. The greater the training required, the higher the wages—up to $2.00 per day for unskilled work, up to $5.00 per day for skilled work. A fixed portion of the project budget is allocated for labor (wages, medicine and first aid, safety equipment, proper living environment, etc.), and this sum is provided to the *jamadar*, who then bears the responsibility of staffing the project, disbursing wages, and ensuring the work gets done to specifications. A pot-bellied *jamadar* named Mustafa explained how he typically works:

> Once I receive the contract, I go to the villages I know or to shantytowns and talk to people about a job. We bargain for some time, then we finalize an agreement. I arrange the travel of the worker and his family to the construction site, and I come each day to ensure the work is completed. If the work is not completed properly, then my compensation can be reduced by the construction company. Often times I must discipline the workers if they make mistakes or try to leave without finishing their work.

The hitch in the system is that most *jamadars* take the labor budget from the construction company, staff the project, and then exploit the labor with underpaid or unpaid wages, no medicines, bare minimum food and water, debt bondage, and other tactics that allow them to pocket the difference between what is allocated to them and what they disburse. This process may be confined to a few months for a single project or range across several projects lasting years before workers are ultimately discarded. Along the way, as part of the overall racket, a portion of the funds the *jamadars* pocket is kicked back to the construction company that hired them. The construction company is pressed to recoup these funds because, as Mr. Ghosh explained:

> We must pay bribes at every step of the way. We must pay bribes to get the permits for the construction, we must bribe the police not to harass us, and we must pay bribes to the client to get the project in the first place. Because of this, many companies exploit the labor in order to make some profit. The system is designed this way, and the workers suffer.

Mr. Ghosh told me that roughly 90 percent of *jamadars* deduct wages or extract free labor through debt bondage, but he did not absolve labor completely. "Laborers also take the money and waste it. They take loans and get into bonded labor. Many times, they waste their money on alcohol and gambling." Most construction company directors with whom I spoke were not nearly as charitable as Mr. Ghosh when it came to the individuals who worked for them. In fact, each one of them justified their exploitation with arguments that the workers were deficient and unethical. Time and again, I was told:

"Laborers have no self-respect, so why must we respect them?"

"They must be treated like animals because they act this way."

"These workers are lazy and dishonest. They want money without work."

"The workers must be restricted from leaving or else they will leave after they are given their wages."

No matter how many times I asked the construction companies about their use of exploitative *jamadars*, they all responded, "We cannot be held responsible for how the *jamadar* acts. We tell them to uphold proper standards, but if they do not, what are we to do?" When I suggested that they do more than just tell the *jamadars* to uphold proper standards, they looked at me as if I were a fool. "If you care so much, why don't you make them behave the way you like?" one construction director snidely told me.

The remarks of these callous and bigoted exploiters reminded me of the self-serving logic of the brick kiln owner Mr. Singh near Alwar. Like him, these exploiters looked down upon the workers they "employed" as subhuman. Given this outlook, it should be no surprise that this is exactly how they treated the men, women, and children who worked for them. Numerous construction workers I met stated time and again that they were treated as if their lives had little to no value at all.

One man named Sheik from Musirabad told me, "We live like animals on the construction sites. We sleep under a tarp. We have little food or water. We do this work because we have no choice." Another worker named Prasad from Dhaka told me, "We are ever hungry. When we borrow money from the contractor for food, we must pay this money back with interest by working for no wages. If we dare ask for a scrap of food, we are beaten." Sanjay from Mumbai told me, "The *jamadar* mocks us and beats us. Sometimes they leave at the end of the project and we are paid nothing. Every day, we are mistreated. We cannot live long doing this work." Finally, a man named Ram from Kathmandu echoed the near-universal desire among the poor in South Asia to have access to some form of credit other than exploitative moneylenders and *jamadars*: "We all have a desire for capital so we can do some other work. We cannot find any loans, so we have no other option than to do this work. If we need a loan, our only option is to take it from people who treat us like slaves."

Right under the noses of every law enforcement official, government minister, lawyer, judge, and ordinary citizen in South Asia, millions of the poorest citizens in the region are working in broad daylight in a system whose economic model directly promotes slavelike exploitation. From the bribes required to secure and complete construction projects, which press construction companies to skimp on wages and work conditions, to the blatantly exploitative system of *jamadar*-based labor recruitment and management, the construction sector across South Asia seems frozen in a time when construction projects from the Qutab Minar to the Taj Mahal were erected through the mass use of servile labor. One would expect that, centuries later, some measure of fairness and basic human rights would have entered the sector responsible for building South Asia into a modern center of global commerce—from every flat people live in, to the roads they drive on, to the offices they work in. The persistence of an unabashed system of forced, bonded, and child labor that is promoted by a pathetic immunity claimed by companies and government agencies who "did not know" what the *jamadars* were up to should be an outrage to every right-minded individual in South Asia and the world.

The Business of Construction

The construction industry in South Asia is highly fragmented. In India, the top ten construction companies capture only 10 percent of the market, with hundreds of other underregulated companies accounting for the remainder. There are a few trade associations and government agencies that loosely oversee the industry,[5] but overall there is a paucity of systematic regulation and enforcement of standards. The general sectors in which construction takes place in South Asia are (1) real estate: residential (housing and development); industrial (industrial parks, factories, plants, etc.); corporate (office, research centers); and commercial (retail: malls, shops, hotels, stadiums); and (2) infrastructure: roads, railway, water and sanitation, universities, health, utilities, ports, and airports. Most of my research focused on the real estate sector, with a small amount in infrastructure. Forced, bonded, and child labor were more prevalent in real estate, but I did document these modes of exploitation in portions of the infrastructure sector as well.

It is difficult to quantify the total size and scale of South Asia's construction sector. There are easily forty million laborers across South Asia involved in some form of construction, excluding downstream inputs such as bricks and stones. Sampling for labor exploitation across the spectrum of the industry proved more challenging than other industries such as agriculture or bidi rolling, whose economic models are far less layered. Having said this, I can safely say that somewhere between 20 to 30 percent of individuals working in the construction sector in South Asia are caught in some form of bonded, forced, or child labor. This is second only to agriculture in terms of the total number of exploited workers (again excluding downstream inputs such as bricks and stones). What this number represents in terms of overall net profits that can be attributed to these forms of labor exploitation is another challenging question.

My best estimate is that the total value of the construction projects underway across South Asia during 2011 exceeded $130 billion ($100 billion in India alone). However, the labor exploitation is only occurring at the bottom end of the value chain, which accounts for a portion of this $130 billion number. In other words, the market value of a finished building may be $20 million, but only a fraction of this value can be attributed to the labor and raw materials that went into making the building. With regard to this bottom end of the value chain, it is difficult to ascertain exactly how much of the overall labor budget is retained by the tens of thousands of *jamadars* across South Asia and how much is kicked back to the construction companies as commissions or bribes for being granted the labor contracts in the first place. No matter the ratio, there is a net sum of economic benefit that accrues to these parties. This sum is the value of the labor exploitation in the construction sector.

For the sake of simplicity, I have outlined in table B.6 in the appendix the debt bondage economics of the typical construction project, where all the benefit is retained by the *jamadar*. After expenses for transport of the labor, as well as reduced wage payments, facilities and living expenses, and general monitoring costs, the *jamadar* enjoys an annual net economic benefit of almost $1,000 per bonded laborer (or roughly $83 per month for shorter projects or for laborers who are not exploited across multiple projects spanning a year or longer), which represents the difference between the legitimate funds allocated to him relating to labor and what he disburses. In all cases, some of this benefit is kicked back to his employer. The split between the *jamadar* and his employer fluctuates from one case to the next, but overall it is a tremendous sum that clearly fuels the intransigence of a system that is already quite immense and growing at breakneck speed.

As robust as the economic value of construction labor exploitation is now, it will only increase in the years to come, especially given the rapid economic growth of India. The construction sector alone is responsible for 11 percent of India's GDP (third behind agriculture and services), and over $350 billion will be invested by the government across the next ten years in infrastructure projects. On the residential side, at least $40 billion will be invested between 2010 and 2015 to meet the need for approximately thirty to forty million new residential units to keep up with demand. In the corporate sector, an estimated 220 to 250 million square feet of additional office space will be required by 2015.[6] To meet this tremendous demand in the residential and commercial sectors, the government of India has recently liberalized foreign investment rules in the construction sector, bringing in tens of billions of dollars in foreign monies for construction projects from some of the largest construction conglomerates in the United States, European Union, and Middle East.

With this vast and growing demand for new construction, one can only assume that the demand for labor will increase. As long as the underregulated system of *jamadar*-based labor recruitment and management remains intact, there will only be more men, women, and children caught in coerced and bonded labor for construction projects ranging from small apartment buildings to behemoth international sporting events. It may be too much to ask for a near-term redesign of the entire business model of construction in South Asia, but one would have hoped that in the thirty years since the PUDR, 1982, case there would have been ample time to reform, regulate, and enforce decent working conditions in the sector. Without question, the scope of vicarious liability laws must be expanded to include the employer-*jamadar* relationship (or the *jamadar* system should be abolished all together), so that construction companies and even government agencies contracting for projects can be held liable for any and all labor violations by *jamadars* with whom they subcontract. This reform alone (and the enforcement of it) would go a long way toward negating the impunity-by-deniability practice that is built into the system. It would also go a long way toward redressing the callous and archaic mode of low-caste labor exploitation that has persisted in the region for far too long. As a

Photo 5.2. Bonded laborers at Connaught Place in New Delhi.

delicate woman named Rashmi, whose family was working on an immense residential construction project in sector 4 of Navi Mumbai, told me:

> We are treated like cockroaches. It is not just the *jamadars*—the government has betrayed the people. We are like dogs in the street scrounging for food and shelter. They promise us wages, but we have been here five months with no wages and barely enough food to eat. I feel no human dignity. Every week I go to Taloje Creek and pray for the day my life will end.

There are no excuses for allowing a system that is inherently designed to promote slavelike exploitation to persist, no matter how profitable or expedient that system may be. The level of misery I witnessed in the construction sector in South Asia was deeply troubling. The workers simply had no way out of the urban slums and subhuman work conditions to which they were forced to submit. Trafficked into cities; worked day and night; kept destitute and hungry; forced to sleep, eat, and use the toilet on the side of roads; and left to fend for themselves with no way home at the end of projects, with wages largely unpaid by unscrupulous *jamadars*—entry into construction work was almost always a bleak sentence.[7] The interests of governments and international corporations remain far too powerful to accommodate the radical systemic change required to ensure that those who are building South Asia's tomorrow remain alive long enough to see it. That change will have to come by the force and persistence of sweeping social revolution. I hope that revolution comes soon, for the sake of millions of construction laborers in South Asia, whose lives are reduced to little more than birth, bondage, suffering, and death.

BROKEN STONES, BROKEN LIVES

The Quarries of Faridabad

Stop me if this sounds familiar.

Thirty years ago, there was a landmark Supreme Court case in India relating to bonded labor. This case was called *Bandhua Mukti Morcha vs. Union of India and Others*, 1983. The plaintiff in the case was the bonded labor abolition organization founded by Swami Agnivesh, India's foremost expert and activist against bonded labor. Along with the PUDR, 1982, case, these two cases provide the foundation for bonded labor jurisprudence in India and, by extension, South Asia. I will discuss both cases in more detail in chapter 7, but the basic facts of the BMM, 1983, case involved twenty-two stone quarry workers in the city of Faridabad near New Delhi who had been trafficked from numerous other states in India with offers of advances. Upon arrival at the stone quarries, the individuals were exploited as bonded laborers, tasked with breaking stones for construction in the blazing heat and under atrocious working conditions. As with the PUDR, 1982, case, the plaintiff was victorious on all counts, and a blistering indictment of the bonded labor exploiters was pronounced by the Supreme Court (see the quotation from this case that opens chapter 1). Detailed instructions came down from the court on steps that should be taken to prevent the exploitation of bonded laborers in any context, and the state of Haryana (in which Faridabad is located) was mandated to establish specific monitoring mechanisms to ensure that this kind of exploitation never occurred again.

Let me describe what I saw at some of the exact same stone quarries, in Faridabad, in the summer of 2010, almost thirty years after the BMM, 1983, case. The stone quarries I visited were large pits in the ground filled with giant granite boulders the workers called "blue stone." The quarries were originally dug around the presence of large granite deposits, but as the local supply dwindled, fresh boulders were transported from nearby mines into the existing quarries. The job of the stonebreakers is to lift a sixteen-kilogram metal sledgehammer over their heads and whack it down with as much force as possible to break the granite boulders into smaller and smaller stones, until they are pebbles. It takes the better part of a day to bash just one boulder down to the desired size. Once broken, the stones are used for construction in commercial and residential buildings, bridges, roads, dams, and canals. For their efforts under temperatures exceeding forty degrees centigrade, the stonebreakers are compensated Rs. 1 ($0.02) per square foot of crushed stones. The average stonebreaker can crush about seventy square feet of stone in a day, for a maximum daily income of $1.40. Excluding deductions, their maximum annual salary is approximately $436 (working twenty-six days per month), but, of course, most bonded laborers see about half this amount. The pathetic sum of roughly $218 in actual annual wages compares to an average annual net profit per bonded laborer in the stonebreaking sector that exceeds $1,300 (see table B.7 in the appendix), on a net profit margin of over 55 percent.

I documented twenty-eight bonded laborers at three different stone quarries in Faridabad. They were all provided small advances, which they had to work off at varying rates, all exploitative. Wages were routinely underpaid, or the square footage of the stones they crushed was undercounted. The workers (82 percent of them adult males) were not allowed to leave the quarries, and there was little in the way of clean drinking water, toilet facilities, or shelter available to them. I tried my hand at wielding the hammer and breaking the boulders, but I could barely lift the hammer over my head. When I swung it into the granite, I felt like my shoulders were about to pop out of their sockets from the powerful jarring that reverberated up my arms. Within ten minutes of this activity under the baking sun, I was drenched in sweat and utterly exhausted. I desperately wanted a sip of water, but none of the workers around me had any, so I first shared sips of water from my water bottle with the workers, then finished the last few sips myself.

The bonded laborers I documented ranged from ages twenty-four to fifty-five. They were all illiterate, as were 94 percent of the quarry workers I documented across South Asia. They were frail, malnourished, and suffered numerous injuries. "Here I bashed two of my toes," an elderly stonebreaker named Anil told me. "And you can see here where I broke my finger." Two of Anil's flat, crushed toes poked out of his sandals, and one of his fingers was missing the top half. Anil was the oldest stonebreaker I interviewed; he had been breaking stones for thirty-eight years. He was not in Faridabad during the 1983 case, but he was at other stone quarries in the state of Haryana. He was barely able to stand straight, and he seemed to be little more than a curtain of skin draped over crumbling bones.

As with Anil, fatigue overwhelms most of the workers in stone quarries, and they regularly crush their hands and feet with the hammer. Twisted ankles and gashed feet from slipping on sharp granite boulders are also common injuries. Respiratory ailments, sunstroke, eye injuries, fever, joint and muscle pain, and diarrhea round out the maladies the stonebreakers suffer. As with other industries in which bonded laborers are exploited, whenever they fall ill or are injured and cannot work, they are not paid, and they must take loans to pay for medicines.

In addition to the bonded laborers I documented, there were just as many laborers who claimed they were paid full wages (which are still pathetic at roughly $1.20 per day), were free to leave at any time, and were provided adequate food and water but were not compensated for time off because of an injury or given funds for medicines. In 87 percent of cases, the stonebreakers were migrants from other states, and their families required the meager incomes in order to survive.

"I know I am not paid fairly," a laborer named Ustav told me. "But what little I get keeps my family from starving." When I asked Ustav how he gets the money to his family, he told me the *jamadar* who recruited him from his village provides the wages to his wife. "Do you know how much your wife is given? Do you know if he gives the amount he is supposed to?" "Like I said," Ustav replied, "I know I am not paid fairly, and who knows, maybe the *jamadar* does not give my wife what he says, but I know it is enough for her and my two sons to eat. As long as they eat, I will keep working here."

When I asked the workers in the Faridabad quarries if they knew about the 1983 Supreme Court case, much to my surprise most said "yes." Aware-

Photo 5.3. Bonded laborer breaking stones at a granite quarry in Faridabad.

ness campaigns conducted by Bandhua Mukti Morcha had been successful at informing these and other stonebreakers of their rights. When I asked
if they felt they were being treated in accordance with the law, the answers
were mixed. Some said no, some said yes, but most were not sure. As I
pressed further to understand the reasons for the confusion, some interesting answers came to light.

Many of the *jamadars* or moneylenders had adapted their techniques to
evade the definitions of bonded labor found in the law, especially after the
1983 Supreme Court case. One technique was to provide minor advances
of no more than Rs. 500 to Rs. 1,000 ($11 to $22), then only apply deductions
for repayment after a few months of paid work. Once the debts were repaid, the pattern was repeated again and again. Another technique was to
pay full wages but charge high prices for food, medicine, clothes, and shelter and restrict the workers from securing supplies from anywhere else. Another technique was to charge fees for delivering wages to family members.
Another technique was to undercount the weight of the stones broken. Yet

another technique was to extract periods of unpaid labor at various points during the year or at the beginning of the season—such as unloading truckloads of boulders for several days, repairing damaged equipment, or loading broken stones into trucks for hours on end. In short, numerous techniques were used to achieve the desired result—unpaid work or the repayment of loans without formally deducting wages.

Overall, I estimate that approximately 41 to 49 percent of the workers at stone quarries across South Asia are being exploited in some form of bonded, forced, or child labor. It is difficult to estimate the total number of quarries and workers in South Asia, but I conservatively calculate that there are 37,000 to 41,000 total mine and river quarries across South Asia, with approximately 3.9 to 4.5 million workers. The areas in which I was able to document quarries most extensively include the Indian states of Haryana, Rajasthan, Uttar Pradesh, and Madhya Pradesh, as well as stone quarries throughout Nepal and a small number in Bangladesh. In aggregate, South Asia's stone quarries produce between $7.6 and $8.0 billion in crushed stones per year. Granite quarries such as those near Faridabad will be among the most profitable, and basic stone river quarries in Nepal (see the *Janajati* section, below) will be among the least profitable.

Beyond the Faridabad quarries, I explored various nearby work colonies, such as Mehethru Dera and Shradhanand Dera, where I met several workers who were breaking stones in this area prior to the BMM, 1983, case. Most were still involved in stonebreaking, though some had moved to construction. They all lived in abject misery. The eldest among them, a woman named Nirmala, complained vehemently about the wretched state of affairs despite all the laws, court cases, and NGOs that tried to help:

> My husband died in a stone quarry not one kilometer from here. All our men die in these quarries. Do you think the government cares? They do not even give us our widow's pension.[8] So, we are left trying to break these stones. Even our children must break these stones. Let me tell you, even now the *jamadars* deduct our wages. No one is stopping them. When we borrow for ill health or a wedding, they will only give us a maximum of Rs. 1,000 ($22). So, four or five of us must take loans, and it takes each of us one year to pay back this amount. We are always in debt. We live like insects here. There is no water, no electricity, no sewage. I can see the lights from Delhi just over that hill, but here we have nothing. Our children are suffering. Please, help us.

After detailing her predicament, Nirmala took hold of my hands and continued to cry out, "Please help us! Please help us!" I felt absolutely miserable as I gazed at her tortured face. It was the same feeling I had with Sumaiya near Munshiganj, and also with Ranaji near Alwar. It was the aspect of my research I most dreaded—encountering incalculable human suffering without being able to do anything about it. Waves of guilt washed over me. What was the purpose of anything I was doing? Merciless people continued to devour the weak despite every supposed advancement in human rights. Even worse, so many of the people who were supposed to be helping these individuals were taking advantage of them as well. Money was raised by NGOs and careers were built by those who claimed to be doing something to help, but so often they were really only helping themselves. I could not help but wonder whether I too was one of these people. Sitting there with Nirmala's trembling hands in mine—was I really helping anyone other than myself? I tried to believe so, but to this day, I do not know.

The *Janajati*

As bleak as my experiences were researching stonebreaking in the quarries in and around Faridabad and other states in India, they only grew darker when I researched riverbed stonebreaking among the *janajati* people of Nepal. *Janajati* is an umbrella term for several minority ethnic groups who are originally from Mongolia. Like other minority ethnicities who break stones in Nepal, such as *dalits, sherpa, gurung*, and *tamang*, the *janajati* live on the fringes of society, often exploited, eking out the barest of human existences. The *janajati* stonebreakers I visited in central Nepal were no exception.

Most stone quarries in Nepal are in the hill and lowland districts of the country. I took a three-hour jeep ride west of Kathmandu through winding mountain roads clogged with boulders and major auto accidents, then stopped at a small roadside town to hike along a riverbed to find the *janajati* stonebreakers. The path was narrow and muddy, involving several crossings of the river at shallow points. The riverbed was filled with boulders, and steep green hills rose hundreds of meters on either side. After a two-hour hike, a series of riverside villages emerged. There were twenty-four villages in total, each separated by a twenty-minute walk further up the river, for a total of 496 *janajati* households. Every one of them was home to

Photo 5.4. Janajati stonebreaker at a remote riverbed in Nepal.

a family that broke stones for a living. I visited six of the villages and documented several families per village. Aside from thatched huts with plastic
tarp roofing, the villages consisted of piles of broken pebbles, no electricity, and clothes drying on stones by the riverside. Only one of the villages I
visited had a goat. Each of the families I interviewed shared the exact same
story. A *janajati* elder named Karma Lama summarized it best:

> During the monsoons, the water comes down from the mountains and
> brings stones and boulders to the riverbed. Each day, two of my family
> members walk into the river and bring up to three hundred kilograms of
> stones to the riverbank. My eldest son and I use a big hammer to break
> these large stones into smaller stones. Then we take the smaller stones to
> the village, where my wife uses a smaller hammer to break them further.
> To do this she places the stones inside a rubber ring so that as she ham-
> mers the stones they do not fly away. We put these broken stones into
> empty kerosene canisters. The contractor comes every two weeks on a

tractor high up on the hillside to collect the canisters. We must carry each canister up to him. Just this process takes one entire day. He pays us NR 11 ($0.15) per canister that we fill. We can fill at most six canisters per day.

Karma Lama had a family of five (relatively) healthy people working on the various steps of the stonebreaking process, and at best they managed to earn around $0.90 per day—as a family. Other families were not as large, healthy, or capable. Children were either too young to help (the youngest I documented was five years old), or parents were too old or sick to work (the eldest I documented was sixty-nine years old). In these cases, the healthy family members might spend one day gathering stones and the second day breaking them. In all cases, none of the families earned anywhere near enough income to survive. They were able to get drinking and cleaning water from the river, but ensuring adequate food and supplies in their remote location was a major challenge. A villager named Kumar Rai explained how they managed:

> The contractor brings us rice and lentils when he picks up the stones. He also brings medicine, clothes, and other supplies. We must pay for these supplies from our wages, so we have nothing left for ourselves. I have been living here sixteen years breaking these stones, and I do not have one rupee that I can call my own. There is no way out of this system. There is no other option for our people.

I asked the *janajati* villagers how they survived during the non-monsoon season, when there were not as many stones to break, and they said they took loans from the contractor for food and supplies, which they had to pay back with unpaid labor during the next monsoon season. They even had to take loans of NR 250 ($3.44) per hammer and NR 40 ($0.55) for the rubber rings used in the stonebreaking process. Of course, any sort of illness meant disaster. One elderly villager named Ratna Rai developed throat cancer and had to borrow $410 for surgery to remove the tumor. This loan was equal to eighteen months of income for his entire family, excluding any sort of expenses. Ratna Rai had been trying to work back this loan for seven years, but his debts kept piling up because he continued to borrow for food, supplies, and medicine. "My sons will be paying off this loan long after I am gone." Ratna Rai told me. "I wish I had chosen to die instead."

Photo 5.5. Janajati woman in Nepal breaking stones in rubber ring.

Many other *janajati* villagers were also ill with various ailments, from strained backs and legs to coughs, diarrhea, and infections. Their thatched huts were highly exposed to the elements, and none of them had grazing animals for milk. The most telling feature of their bleak existences is that every one of the *janajati* I met looked ten to fifteen years older than they were, which means a lot in a country where people typically look ten years younger than they are. The *janajati* stonebreakers along the river I visited were the epitome of isolated and exploited slaves. They were almost completely cut off from society and beyond impoverished. Like many of the more than three thousand stone quarries in Nepal (especially the remote river quarries), the river along which these people labored was completely unmonitored and unregistered. There were no official records or books, nor was anyone in the government inspecting the conditions of work. Contractors and agents of the construction companies were in complete control and maintained a system of prisonlike exploitation. If the laborers had the slightest notion of trying to break free or moving some place else for a better life, the contractor made sure they paid for it. "If we try to leave," Kamala Magar told me, "the contractor's men patrol the river and beat us. If we do not work, he will not give us food. We do not own this land, so he can evict us at any time. We are trapped here."

As for the contractor who controlled the villages I visited, he was one of scores of agents of large construction companies in Kathmandu, where 90 percent of these stones are transported for construction of residences and commercial buildings. The typical sales rate for each canister of stones from the contractor to construction company is between NR 30 and NR 35 ($0.41 to $0.48), a nice markup from the NR 11 he pays. Despite my best efforts, I was not able to track down or speak to any contractors working in this area nor any other contractors operating in and around Kathmandu.

I have made special note of the *janajati* stonebreakers in this isolated pocket of Nepal because there is almost no human rights intervention to fight back against their exploitation. The more time I spent with them, the more difficult it was for me to escape the impression that each and every one of these people was doomed. I have not mentioned their specific location, because I fear reprisal against them for speaking with me. As isolated as they are, there would be no one to prevent them from being severely punished, if not evicted or even executed. Since the time of my visit, I have been coordinating with a few activists to attempt to bring some relief to their plight. The task is daunting. Every one of these people is caught in bonded and child labor not more than a half-day journey from Kathmandu, but there is very little interest by the government of Nepal to do anything about it. The *janajati* I met represent the most reprehensible example of slave labor in South Asia—an exiled class of disenfranchised, low-caste individuals who are completely discarded by society while being blatantly and callously exploited in subhuman conditions without the slightest intervention. Very few people in Nepal are even aware that these people exist. Fewer still are attempting to improve their fates. The *janajati* stonebreakers were clinging to the last thread of human life, and I pray assistance will be provided to them soon, before that final thread snaps.

{ 6 }

Carpets and Other Sectors

One is not low because of birth, nor does birth make one holy. Deeds alone make one low; deeds alone make one holy.

—BUDDHA

THE MISERABLE FINGERS WEAVING OUR CARPETS

The "carpet belt" of northern India stretches across the state of Uttar Pradesh, from the town of Allahabad east to Bhadohi, ending in the rural reaches beyond Varanasi. The states of Bihar and Madhya Pradesh are also populated with carpet weavers, but the main region is in Uttar Pradesh. Here, countless huts, shacks, and small carpet "factories" in remote rural areas are filled with individuals who work fourteen to twenty hours a day painstakingly weaving knotted carpets by hand.[1] These carpets are purchased regionally and exported abroad. All of these weavers are poor, low-caste peasants who are either paid a pittance for their efforts or are exploited through outright bonded and child labor. More than any other sector I researched, the carpet-weaving industry is especially reliant on the exploitation of child labor, a high proportion of whom are coerced or otherwise enslaved. Their tiny, nimble fingers and good eyesight are well suited for the intricate motions required to weave carpets of all sizes, one thread at a time.

At a shelter that maintains a secret location near Allahabad, I met thirty-four former child slaves who had been freed from two different carpet shacks housing up to twenty children each. One of these young boys,

Arjun, remained deeply traumatized by the violence he suffered in one of these shacks. With the help of one of the shelter volunteers who rescued him, he narrated the following bleak story:

> Some time ago, this man named Ali who was known to my father came to my village and said he could take me for work in the carpet factory. Ali promised my father Rs. 1,000 ($22) if I go with him and a wage of Rs. 50 ($1.11) per day working in the factory. He said the factory was only twenty kilometers away and my father could visit any time. I was afraid to leave home, but Ali said I could see my family whenever I want. We were very poor and hungry, so eventually I went with Ali. He took me and three other boys from my village in a car. He brought us to this shack where there were many boys making carpets. It was very dark and had a very bad smell. Ali locked us inside and beat us with a wooden cane. He said we would be taught how to do the carpets and we must do this work every day. He said our parents had abandoned us and we can never go home. He told us that there were wild dogs in the forest outside, so if we try to run we will be eaten. I was so frightened. One other boy from my village named Kamal did not stop crying for many days. Ali and one other man beat him very badly and dragged him from the shack.

Arjun stopped speaking at this point. He tightened his face and his eyes moistened. We brought Arjun a Limca soda and I showed him photos of some of the places I had visited to get his mind off his ordeal. Arjun remained very uncomfortable, so he went to his room to rest, and I continued with other interviews. That evening, Arjun returned and asked if he could finish telling me about his time in the carpet shack. This is some of what he said:

> I did not like being in that place. It was very difficult. Most days we were only given one break for eating and one break for toilet. If we tried to sleep, they would beat us. Sometimes they gave us pills so we can work all night. I felt so tired I cut myself by accident. If the blood from my fingers came on the carpet, they would take green chili and rub it on my wound for punishment. I do not know how long I was in that place, but God blessed me one day when the people from this shelter rescued me. I have been here for one month. I had contact with my father last week.

I miss my family so much, but here I am in school, and I hope one day I can be a doctor.

Arjun's story was one of the worst I documented in the carpet sector. The level of abuse perpetrated by his captors was beyond most of the stories I heard. Arjun and the other boys rescued from his shack were suffering from numerous ailments as a result of their abuse, including poor vision, spinal deformation, respiratory ailments, muscle atrophy, gashes in their fingers, and bruises and broken bones from numerous beatings.

It took three courageous men who operate a shelter for boys like Arjun near Allahabad to track down this shack through rumor and anecdote, observe it for several days, and attempt a daring raid when no guards were present. A total of fifteen boys were rescued, and reintegrating them back into normal life has been a monumental task. As the man who runs the shelter, Rajiv, explained to me:

> These children have suffered very badly. The abuse is terrible. Once we rescue them, it is very important that we have enough time to heal them through counseling and play and prayer. Their families are not always the best advocates for them, so we must also be very careful before we send them home, or else they will end up in another bad situation. These children feel no love from the world, so we try to teach them that they are special and that God loves them very much.

The courageous men who work with Rajiv and conduct these raids take their lives into their hands each time they attempt to save these children. Rajiv told me that one of his staff had been shot by guards during a previous raid; thankfully, he survived. Rajiv and his colleagues used to receive regular threats of violence from goons and contractors until three years earlier, when they moved to a secret location outside Allahabad. The anonymity has provided much needed safety for everyone at the shelter.

As for the agents who troll villages and recruit the children in the first place—I have met and interviewed two of them. In my earlier book *Sex Trafficking*, I described the first such meeting, on a crisp, sunny day in Bihar, with a child trafficker named Salim:

> He was so ordinary—just a man, wearing simple village clothes. His aspect was common, his mustache trimmed, his hair neatly combed. He

spoke without emotion of how he took male children for carpet weaving to the carpet-belt towns of Varanasi and Bhadohi and female children for sex work in New Delhi and Mumbai.

"A man with money meets me in Varanasi," he explained. "I send the children with him. When I return, I use some of this money as payment to parents for the next children."

Salim told me that parents often asked for money in exchange for their children.

"I am paid usually five thousand rupees [$110] for a male child and seven or eight thousand rupees [$178] for females. From this I give one thousand [$22] to the parents. I am also paid one hundred sixty rupees' commission for each square meter of carpet made by the children I bring. I do not receive commission for female children."[2]

When I met Salim in 2004, he had been involved in child trafficking for ten years and estimated he had "found work" for more than three hundred children.

In 2010 near the town of Bhadohi, I met my second trafficker of children for carpet work—Rahul. With a nonchalant attitude, he described a process that was remarkably similar to Salim's narrative six years earlier:

Parents come to me often and ask for a job for their children. I take the children to Varanasi, and there an agent takes the boys to carpet looms and the girls to brothels. I am paid usually Rs. 4,000 or Rs. 5,000 for boys ($90 to $110) and usually Rs. 7,000 to Rs. 8,000 for girls ($155 to $178). From this amount, I return 20 percent to the parents. They also receive income from the child's work of maybe Rs. 100 ($2.20) per month. This is a good opportunity for them.

Rahul explained to me that he also receives orders from loom operators and brothel owners for the child labor they need—in his case usually two boys for every one girl. I pushed Rahul harder than I pushed Salim, particularly on the issue of the violent exploitation of children. He shrugged his shoulders and replied, "I don't know about this. You must talk to the people who put the children to work." When I asked Rahul to put me in touch with those people, he replied, "This is not possible."

I asked Rahul if he knew that child labor was illegal in India and that many of these carpet factories keep the children confined against their wills and violently abuse them to make them work day and night. Here is how Rahul responded:

> If this work is illegal, why does it happen everyday? The families wish their children to work. The children are given food and money. They cannot have this otherwise. Maybe sometimes they are punished if they misbehave, but even I was punished by my mother if I misbehaved. You cannot come here and tell us what is right and what is wrong. We decide this for ourselves.

It was clear to me there was no point in trying to reason with Rahul; he strongly believed every word of the cultural relativist argument he made. It was no surprise that he suggested the food and shelter he arranged for the children (as he saw it) were preferable to the alternative—everywhere I went in South Asia, I was presented with the reality that in most cases bondage, exploitation, and even violent enslavement of men, women, and children was at least temporarily advantageous from a material standpoint to the alternative of utter destitution and starvation. Laws and morals meant very little in the face of the need to survive, so as long as these nations allowed hundreds of millions to subsist at the brink of extinction, of course these impoverished individuals would desperately opt for the only alternative presented to them. There was little point in confronting greedy and opportunistic loom owners and child traffickers without also confronting the most culpable criminal of all—the nations that allowed such extreme levels of poverty to persist, such that millions are forced to take the desperate measures of selling one of their children in order to save the others.

Villages in Bondage

Though hidden shacks that exploit child slaves for the carpet-weaving industry are not uncommon, the vast majority of bonded labor exploitation in the carpet sector of South Asia takes place in thousands of village huts across the region. This is primarily the case in India and Pakistan. In Nepal, most of the carpet weaving is done in nondescript carpet factories (often little more than one floor in an abandoned or half-completed building) in the Kathmandu Valley. Bangladesh does not have much in the way of a hand-woven carpet sector. In the rural areas I visited in northern India across Uttar Pradesh and Bihar, entire villages were caught in bondage for carpet weaving. One village not far west of Varanasi typified what I saw.

The village possessed thirty-six huts of varying sizes (none larger than 150 square feet), each with around five to six inhabitants, all *dalits*. Twenty-eight of the huts had carpet looms inside them, usually taking up to half of the available living space. The dignified village elder, named Prakash, who bore a striking resemblance to the poet Rabindranath Tagore, explained to me that everyone in the village had borrowed money from two brothers who owned all of the land in the area. Three other villages were also on their land, and the inhabitants in these villages were also in debt to the land-owners. The reasons for the debts were myriad, from basic consumption to life ceremonies (weddings and funerals), medicine, hut repairs, and the inheritance of debt from a previous generation. Prakash himself was a third-generation bonded laborer, and he had no idea how much his debt was.

Photo 6.1 Carpet loom inside hut in Prakash's village.

Once indebted, each of the villagers was put to work in three sectors—
carpet weaving, agriculture (potato, wheat, and maize), and seasonal brickmaking at several kilns not far from the villages. They were paid state-
stipulated wages—less the deductions by agents of the landowners who
visited the villages regularly to ensure that the work was being completed
to schedule. Prakash told me that these agents were merciless and often
beat the villagers if they did not work quickly enough or if they broke any
rules, such as leaving the village area without permission. Prakash also told
me that on a few occasions these men forcibly took women and children
when a family's debts became too great or when there was a major injury
that meant that the head of the household could no longer work. As for
their wage payments, the agents deducted up to half the wage for debt repayment and penalties. Some villagers I met had entered in and out of
bondage as they took loans, paid them off after a few years, then took loans
again; others, like Prakash, had been in debt for most of their lives.

Prakash showed me the carpet looms inside several of the village huts.
Two or three teenage boys were typically at work behind the looms. The
huts were cramped and dark, with no electricity, much like the shacks in
which boys like Arjun were exploited. There was poor ventilation and a
high level of particulate matter from thread dust in the air. Many of the
villagers were suffering from respiratory ailments and severe joint pain. I
spent several hours documenting the conditions at Prakash's village and
interviewing several of the villagers. It was one of the most open and can-
did villages I visited, despite the risk of harsh punishment faced by the villagers for speaking with me. Just when I was ready to return to my vehicle
after several hours of research, Prakash asked me, "Would you like to visit
one of the other villages?"

The second village was slightly more than a thirty-minute walk away,
across several large fields of wheat and maize. Prakash sent one of his fellow villagers with me and my guide to show us the way. As we approached
the second village, I saw one large Tata commercial truck, with two men
loading carpets into the back. I was sure these were men who worked for
the landowners and were picking up completed carpets for transport to a
wholesaler or distributor. They had not spotted me yet, so I had to make a
quick decision as to whether I should turn back or continue forward and
see what I might be able to accomplish. There was no way to know in advance whether the agents might take exception to an outsider poking
around in their employer's business. I asked the man from Prakash's village

what he thought we should do, and he said it would be okay to continue. I did not know if he was saying this just to be helpful or whether he really believed it, but I took his advice and prayed that nothing negative would occur to the villagers as a result of my visit.

Once I was about fifteen meters from the village, the carpet agents spotted me. I waved and approached their truck. They were younger than I had imagined, maybe twenty years old, and were dressed in blue jeans and short-sleeve shirts. I peeked in the back of their truck and saw at least fifty or sixty stacked carpets of various sizes. Before they became suspicious, I explained that I was an economics researcher from America trying to understand how the carpet industry in India works. I told them I was touring villages throughout Uttar Pradesh, where I was gathering data on how the carpets were made, how long it took, and what happened after the villagers finished making them.

"Oh, you are from America?" one of the agents replied in fairly good English. "Which city are you from?" I told the agent where I was from and where I lived. We made small talk about America, then about the agents and where they were from, and eventually we spoke about their work. "We come every month to the villages in this area and pick up the carpets," one of the agents explained. "Then we drive to Delhi to sell them."

The agents were both nephews of one of the landowners and had been doing this transportation work for a few years. In addition to the carpets, they also transported agricultural products during the harvest season. There were four other people who did the transportation work for the landowners, along with a total of four or five men that Prakash had described who regularly trolled the villages to ensure that the work was being completed on time. These men also disbursed wages and meted out punishments when required. I felt comfortable with the transportation agents and thought about asking them about wage deductions and physical punishment, but I knew that once I left they would report back to the landowner that the villagers had been speaking to me about these issues. Knowing that the villagers would likely be punished for doing so, I chose not bring up the issue of wages or labor treatment with the agents. I did, however, ask if I could meet the landowners, but I was told they were both away in London on business. "The landowners travel very often," one of the agents explained. "That is why we are here to keep the business going."

As I rounded up my conversation with the agents, I asked if they would mind if I walked around the village for a short while to document the conditions. They carried on with their work, and I took a short stroll through the village. A crowd had gathered during my discussion, and that crowd followed me nervously as I broke away from the agents and headed toward some of the huts. My guide and the young man from Prakash's village explained who I was. While some of the nervousness was alleviated, as long as the agents were nearby, it was clear that the villagers were not going to be very comfortable with my presence, no matter how innocuous my conversation with them had been. There was simply too much risk that something could go wrong while the agents were there. I did not want to force any conversations or maintain my presence any longer than necessary, so after handing out some candy to the children, I took my leave and made my way back to Prakash's village. Though I was not able to document the conditions in this second village in great detail, I felt confident they were similar to those at Prakash's village. Of course, there was little point in going to the local police to discuss my findings, as they were likely allies of the powerful landowners. Police in a nearby city, such as Varanasi, would simply defer to their local counterparts.

I walked back to Prakash's village as the sun was setting. He and his son, Baldev, were scooping buffalo manure when I returned, which they would dry and use to reinforce their huts. I told Prakash about my conversations with the transportation agents, and I assured him that I did not ask anything that would land the villagers in trouble. Prakash wiped the sweat from his brow and asked me, "When will you come back here?"

"I do not know," I replied, "There are many places I still need to go."

"I hope you got the information you needed. I hope you will not forget people like us."

"I will not forget you, Prakash. I promise I will try to come back."

I took my leave of Prakash, feeling guilty that I probably would never be able to return. He had been one of the most friendly and decent individuals I met during my research, even though he was fully aware that there was little advantage to him for doing so. Prakash's dignified and kind countenance remained with me, and six years after I met him, I was in that same region of Uttar Pradesh again, and I made a special trip to his village so I could keep my promise. I approached by foot with much anticipation at the long-overdue reunion. I saw his hut, same as before. A young lady was inside. When I asked after Prakash, she told me he had passed away three years earlier. Baldev, his son, was away at a brick kiln. He had inherited his father's debt.

The Carpet Factories of Kathmandu

Ninety percent of the hand-woven carpets exported from Nepal are produced in carpet factories in the Kathmandu Valley. These factories range from large, licensed factories that employ more than two hundred workers to hidden looms on the third floors of half-built, abandoned buildings, where foremen extract forced labor from ten or fifteen children at a time. With the help of colleagues from a few NGOs in Nepal, particularly those at the Nepal GoodWeave Foundation (NRF), I managed to inspect several of these clandestine factories inside which trafficked children were forced to weave carpets, in conditions similar to those endured by children like Arjun in northern India. The primary difference between the carpet shacks and huts I investigated in northern India and the quasi-clandestine carpet factories in Kathmandu was that there was almost three times the number of girls working in the latter than the former.

My guides at NRF were very effective at helping me research the carpet sector in Kathmandu, and they took me to inspect several nondescript carpet factories that were filled with children. NRF was working in these and other factories to extricate the children safely and get them into shelters and schools supported by the organization. Each factory had a male guard who was overseeing children working at two or three looms. Most of the children looked nine to twelve years old, though when I asked them their ages they either remained silent or said they were fifteen, which is the legal age for work in the carpet sector in Nepal. Inside the factories, I viewed order slips from distributors who exported almost entirely to the United States and the European Union. The conditions were similar to other child labor carpet factories I had seen—dark and cramped quarters, high levels of particulate matter in the air, rusty scissors and metal claws strewn across the work area, and rows of children quietly working their tiny fingers as swiftly as possible to thread the carpets into place.

At one of the shelters operated by NRF, I interviewed several children who had been rescued from carpet factories such as the ones I saw. A thirteen-year-old *tamang* boy named Tenzin shared the following story:

When I was ten years old, my father left for work on a stone quarry. He died at the quarry one year later. My mother tried to find work in farming, but we did not have enough money. An agent came to our village in Sindhupalchok district and offered my mother NR 1,000 ($13.80) to take

Photo 6.2. Forced child carpet weavers in Kathmandu.

me for work at a carpet factory. He said after I do training for two months, I can send half my wage to my mother. I came to Kathmandu with this agent and worked in four different factories for two years. It was very difficult work, and I never received any wage. We worked on the carpets from three in the morning until nine at night. We worked seven days a week. We slept on mats on the floor. We were locked inside, and they only gave us two meals each day. I wanted to leave, but they threatened us. I felt so tired and the work was difficult. They would beat us whenever we displeased them. I was so afraid when they rescued me, but I have been in this school for five months now, and I feel good. I want to keep studying so I can be a teacher.

Several other children at two different shelters narrated similar stories. Agents came to their villages with payments of $10 to $20 for boys and girls around ten years of age with promises of work in carpet factories and the eventual payment of monthly wages back to the parents. For some of the children, a small amount of money was sent every few months, but for others, no wages were ever paid. The children all worked from three or four in the morning until nine or ten at night. They slept on mats, and many were force-fed stimulants to keep them working sixteen or more hours a day, seven days a week. All the children were from rural areas spanning the western Terai or from the nearby Sindhupalchok and Makwanpur districts. All the children belonged to disenfranchised minority ethnic groups and castes. Poverty or a recent calamity were the major forces that pressured parents into selling their children, though in some cases outright greed was a factor. A few children told me that their fathers wasted money on alcohol and sent them with agents as a way to make extra income. I also met two children who altruistically heard about carpet factory work and wanted to go themselves to help their destitute families survive. For some of the children, sexual exploitation was a terrible addition to their abuse in the carpet factories. Especially for girls, work in the carpet factory was often a first step toward being trafficked into commercial sex work in the dance clubs and massage parlors of Kathmandu, which in turn often led to transnational trafficking to brothels in India.

I did not uncover entire villages that were bonded into carpet weaving in Nepal as I had in northern India, but this is likely a function of the fact that most of the carpet factories in Nepal are in and around Kathmandu, where labor is easily trafficked in from rural areas. The model in Pakistan is closer to India's, in which a cottage industry of thousands of workers throughout rural Sindh, Punjab, and Balochistan provinces ensnares countless bonded and child laborers in carpet weaving in their huts or in small factories near urban centers such as Karachi, Lahore, and Quetta.

A special note should be made regarding the efforts of the Nepal Good-Weave Foundation to certify carpets produced without child labor for export to Western markets. Through their GoodWeave certification program, NRF has established a reliable certification process in Nepal involving spot inspections and rigorous criteria to ensure that no child labor or forced labor is involved in the production of the carpets that receive their approval. At the end of 2010, NRF had established certification programs with factories capturing roughly 37 percent of carpets exported to the United States from Nepal. More than 380,000 NRF-certified carpets from Nepal have been sold in the United States and European Union since the beginning of their certification program in 1996, and NRF has rescued more than 3,600 children from carpet factories in Nepal during the same period. The certification provided by the GoodWeave label allows consumers to make informed decisions about the carpets they purchase. While this kind of spot certification works more effectively when focused in a small geographic area (such as the Kathmandu Valley), it is much more difficult and cost prohibitive in the fragmented production model of northern India and Pakistan, where the carpets are woven inside thousands of huts spanning hundreds of remote villages. Having said this, there are ways of adapting a reliable certification model to other geographic areas and production environments and, more importantly, to other commodities, such as rice, sugar, bricks, bidis, shrimp, tea, gems, apparel, and minerals. Barriers relating to cost, reliability, and corruption are not insignificant, but bright minds can overcome these hurdles. The first step is accurate supply chain tracing and quantification of the contribution of tainted goods to the overall market. From there, each commodity's unique supply chain will present opportunities for an effective certification model. This is a burgeoning field of interest for many scholars involved in the antislavery field and one that is thankfully capturing more attention from NGOs, producers, retailers, and governments. It is also the best way to catalyze consumer awareness about products whose supply chains may be tainted with some form of labor exploitation, which can in turn motivate corporations to initiate the kinds of certifications required to mitigate the exploitation at various points in their supply chains. I will discuss this important issue further in chapter 8, as part of my suggested overall campaign to combat bonded, forced, and child labor in South Asia.

The Business of Carpets

In keeping with the nature of today's globalized carpet industry, the roots of South Asia's tradition of hand-woven carpets were actually imported from abroad. Most historians place the advent of carpet weaving in South Asia with the Mughal emperor Akbar,[3] who brought Persian carpet weavers to the subcontinent during the sixteenth century. Royal patronage helped the industry establish a firm footing throughout northern India and present-day Pakistan, ultimately spreading to Nepal as well. Today, India, Pakistan, and Nepal are responsible for roughly 55 percent of the global market of hand-woven carpets. The other major exporters include Iran, China, Turkey, and Afghanistan. As noted, the contemporary carpet weaving sector in India and Pakistan is largely a cottage industry, similar to the bidi-rolling sector. Well over a million carpets worth between $850 million and $900 million on the export market are woven each year in tens of thousands of village huts, rural shacks, and makeshift carpet factories across South Asia. Loom owners sell the carpets to a plethora of distributors, who arrange for export to foreign markets. Once imported into the United States or European Union, carpets from some of the villages and factories I documented that were exploiting bonded and child labor have made their way into the showrooms of major retailers. Be it a small hut with a single family of bonded carpet weavers or a larger shack with twenty child slaves weaving carpets, the steps in the process are similar.

Hand weaving of knotted carpets is an exceedingly labor-intensive process, especially for more thickly knotted carpets, which can contain up to two hundred knots per square meter. It can take four people working twelve hours a day at a single loom three months or more to complete a large five-meter-by-five-meter carpet with two hundred knots per square meter. The looms themselves are simple in design, consisting of two wooden or steel horizontal rods attached to vertical poles on either side. Depending on the size of the loom, they can cost from $80 to $200 and last ten or fifteen years. Hundreds of vertical cords (depending on the density of knots per square meter) are attached to the horizontal rods, and the weavers follow a pattern usually printed on plastic to work their way from the bottom of the loom up by pulling yarn of various colors down the vertical cords. As they pull the colors of yarn down the vertical cords, the pattern of the carpet emerges. The weavers use a dangerously sharp claw tool to pull the yarn down the cords, then pack the yarn down tightly against the previous layer with a more blunt metal tool. Scissors are used to trim away excess yarn. No matter how many times I watched the process, I could not understand how the workers were able to work in unison and follow the printed pattern to near perfection one tiny thread at a time.

Once the carpets are completed, the contractor or loom owner transports them to the wholesaler/exporter who originally placed the order. If preexisting orders have not been taken, the loom owners simply take the carpets to distributor markets and sell them to the highest bidder. After sale, the exporter (sometimes the loom owner) will perform a chemical washing of the carpet before shipment abroad. This process involves cleaning the carpets and setting the colors through a rinse that usually includes solutions of diluted sulfuric acid, followed by water. The carpets then dry and may

Photo 6.3. Girl pulling yarn down a carpet loom.

be further clipped into a final shape before shipment. This step typically involves more experienced workers who are fairly compensated, but on occasion debt bondage can be found at this step in the supply chain as well.

Most of the debt bondage and child labor exploitation in the carpet sector takes place at the weaving stage. Some workers may be provided advances that they must work off through carpet weaving; others may be promised piece-rate wages that work out to a little more than one dollar per day, with violent coercion and underpayment of wages among the numerous tactics used to extract servile labor. Table B.8 in the appendix shows the basic bonded labor economics for a landowner with thirty carpet-weaving bonded laborers in a single village working at various sizes of carpets, such as Prakash's village. The exploiter in this scenario enjoys net profits per bonded laborer of approximately $700 per year. Other modes of carpet-weaving exploitation, such as a makeshift factory involving child slaves with token monthly payments sent to parents, would typically prove more profitable. My best estimate is that approximately 33 to 39 percent of the 1.4 to 1.8 million hand carpet weavers in South Asia are caught in some form of bonded, forced, or child labor.

Of all the products whose supply chains I managed to trace from production in South Asia to markets in the European Union and United States, I have had the most success in effecting tangible progress to disrupt the supply chains of the tainted goods within the carpet sector. My efforts to do so with shrimp, tea, rice, and other products have proved challenging, but with carpets, data from my research is being used by U.S. government officials to investigate carpets produced with child labor in Nepal that are ultimately being sold by major U.S. retailers. At the time of this book's writing, those investigations are ongoing, and I am optimistic tangible action will be taken in the future.

OTHER SECTORS WITH BONDED LABOR

There are several other industries beyond those discussed in the preceding chapters in which I documented bonded labor in South Asia. Most of these industries follow models similar to the sectors already described. They each primarily exploit migrants and low-caste groups, most of them involve advances paid by agents and contractors that the laborers must work off in severely exploitative conditions, many sectors are seasonal, and, often times, one worker may be involved in labor in several sectors during the course of his or her bondage. While the sectors previously outlined contain the majority of bonded laborers in South Asia, several million bonded laborers are caught in other sectors, such as domestic servitude, mining, glasswork, tanneries, precious stones and gem cutting, fireworks, silk work, sari embroidery, and others. In aggregate, these sectors generate billions of dollars in profits from bonded labor exploitation. A brief outline of some of these sectors will round out our investigation of bonded labor in South Asia.

Domestic Servitude

We already met child domestic slaves with the *kamaliri* practice in Nepal. While this practice may fit more within the definition of outright forced labor, one could also see it as a traditional debt bondage agreement in which room and board serve as the credit against which the laborer works for minimal to no wages. Along the same lines, many domestic servants throughout South Asia are caught in traditional debt bondage. Low-caste groups in every South Asian nation are often recruited into domestic bondage through advances or offers of lump-sum payments that the servant must work off. Wages are often promised and then typically rescinded, underpaid, or deducted for debt repayment and living expenses. Every single domestic slave that I documented belonged to a low caste or minority ethnicity. Most were minors.

A former domestic slave named Pratima from the Kantakhal area of West Bengal told me that when she was fourteen, her parents were offered an advance of Rs. 3,000 ($67) in exchange for sending her to work as a servant for a wealthy family in Kolkata. Pratima was told she would be paid Rs. 300 ($6.67) per month (10 percent of the advance; roughly $0.22 per day) and that half the wage would be deducted for debt repayment for twenty months, after which point she would receive the full wage. "I worked for this family for three years," Pratima told me. "I was never paid any wage. I did all the cleaning, dusting, washing, and cooking seven days a week. I slept on a mat on the floor, and I was given only two meals a day of the leftover food that I cooked for them. They did not abuse me physically, but they would often shout at me and insult me."

While Pratima was fortunate not to be physically abused, numerous other girls I met nervously described considerable physical and sexual exploitation at the hands of their owners. As low-caste, poor, and illiterate women and children, they often felt obliged to endure the abuse quietly. Speaking about sexual violence to family members upon returning home almost always resulted in being shamed and ostracized. Such women were deemed unworthy to be married and often ended up being trafficked to brothels across India. One such girl, Kamala, explained her situation through torrents of tears:

> The homeowner in Noida would rape me. It was so painful. I was only twelve years old, and he would leave me bleeding and crying. I prayed the nightmare would end. After eight months, they sent me back home without any payment. When I told my family what happened, my father was angry. He said, "How can you come home with no money?" My mother showed compassion to me, but what could she do? My father arranged for a *dalal* (trafficker) to take me to Delhi. I worked there in a *kotha* for three years. I felt so sad in that place. The *kothawali* made us

work no matter how much pain we felt. It was only when my father died that I could return home.

Kamala had just turned seventeen when I met her, and I could not fathom the intensity of suffering and abuse she had already endured during her precious few years of life. She felt helpless about finding a better future and lacked any sort of education or reasonable opportunity to build a life for herself. Offers from *dalals* and agents for domestic work continued to arrive, and though she had resisted them for many months, her widow mother and two younger brothers needed income. Kamala was their only option, and I could see in her eyes that it would not be long before she accepted one of these offers, hoping and praying that she might find a better situation than before.

Several other former domestic slaves I met across India, Nepal, and Bangladesh described similar experiences to Pratima and Kamala—advances that led to unpaid work, which ultimately ended in the girls' being sent back to their villages penniless. Abuse and exploitation led to shame, stigma, and in many cases, prostitution and sex slavery. For many of these girls, this pattern repeated itself several times.

Perhaps even more prevalent than direct bondage into domestic servitude is the ancillary domestic servitude performed by countless women and children as part of the repayment of loans taken by the male head of households for work in other sectors. With just about every migrant male I met who took a loan and brought his family to the work site and almost every landless agricultural family that took loans as part of their arrangement each season, women and children were often coerced into performing various kinds of free labor as part of the debt repayment. Domestic servitude at the landowner's home each day was one of the primary ways in which unpaid labor was extracted by the exploiter pursuant to overall debt repayment. Not surprisingly, the sexual exploitation of women and children by the landowner or his men occurred often, compounding the abuse inflicted on the bonded slaves. It is difficult to quantify the level of debt bondage in the domestic sector of South Asia, especially when one includes the servitude that is extracted as part of the loan repayment of a male agricultural or migrant laborer. Of course, there is no profit generation associated with this kind of labor; rather, it facilitates the avoidance of expenses that easily add up to tens of millions of dollars in lost income each year for South Asia's domestic slaves.

Mining

Mining is another sector in South Asia that captures millions of bonded laborers. Labor exploitation in this sector dates back to the predations of the British East India Company, which first mined for coal in Bengal in the 1770s. All South Asian countries have well-developed mining industries, with minerals and stones mined by migrant laborers under extremely dangerous conditions. In India, the state of Rajasthan is one of the industry's leaders, with up to three million men, women, and children involved in mining for dimensional stones such as limestone, slate, granite, marble, sandstone, and quartzite, along with numerous minerals consumed domestically and abroad. I visited a few mines in Rajasthan, and to say the conditions were brutish would be a gross understatement. The heat in the mines was unbearable, and the air was stagnant and impossible to breathe. I felt like the insides of my lungs were drenched in sweat within minutes. Aside from the intense heat and stagnant air, explosives were used recklessly, and in one of the limestone mines the workers were actually chained together at the ankles. Perhaps the most disconcerting condition I observed at one of the mines was that the carbon released from the flame lamps used to illuminate the mines was inhaled by the workers to such an extent that their saliva literally turned black. Diseases suffered by the miners included heat stroke, lung cancer, skin infections, carbon dioxide poisoning, tuberculosis, hearing loss, vision ailments, and cuts, bruises, and broken bones. As for safety equipment, goggles, face masks, gloves, back braces, and even shoes were rarely provided. This was even the case for the workers involved in cutting the mined stones with huge electric saws or crushing other stones to pebbles with hammers, like the stonebreakers in Faridabad. When the work day (and night) inside the mines was completed, life outside the mines was not much better. Most of the miners and their families had to build their own homes out of stacked flat stones, often times with a corrugated steel roof. The homes functioned like a stone oven during the summer months, when temperatures in Rajasthan regularly pass forty-five degrees centigrade. And of course, there is little in the way of fresh water, electricity, or toilet facilities.

Approximately 81 percent of the miners I documented in India were recruited through advances provided by *jamadars* ranging from Rs. 2,000 ($44) to Rs. 15,000 ($333). Similar to other industries, wages were deducted for debt repayment as well as for food and water, mistakes during work, and damage to equipment. Injuries always resulted in more debt. Unlike other industries I researched, bonded laborers at the mines were also solicited by *jamadars* and foremen to buy luxury items like jewelry and alcohol at inflated prices, exacerbating their debt. Like the stonebreaking industry, the wages for the workers were based on how many square feet of minerals and stones they mined, and, depending on the type of mine and geographic location, the typical daily wage across the various categories of workers at the average mine worked out to roughly $1.67 per day, prior to deductions. Table B.9 in the appendix shows the economics of the average limestone mining operation in Rajasthan, in which the exploiter enjoys annual net profits per bonded laborer of approximately $1,500. This is second only to brickmaking in terms of net cash generated.

Mines are supposed to be operated on twenty-year leases issued by the relevant state government, but colleagues told me that many mines were being operated illegally without a lease or on expired leases. Numerous laws in each South Asian country are meant to govern working conditions, wages, and safety standards at mines,[4] but as far as I could see these laws were being flouted with impunity. At the mines I visited in Rajasthan, there was virtually no regulation, inspection, or enforcement of the law, even though there is an official Indian Bureau of Mines that is supposed to do just that for the country's more than 2,700 official mines.[5] Mines in and around the Kathmandu Valley were not much better than their Indian counterparts and in fact had a higher rate of child labor (31 percent) than the mines I documented in India (22 percent). In Pakistan, colleagues provided data from copper, sulfur, and coal mines in Punjab and Sindh provinces, where conditions were largely similar to the mines in India and Nepal. Child labor was prevalent (24 percent), and the absence of safety equipment and the use of *peshgis* to extract bonded labor from the miners was common practice. As with India and Nepal, the miners were primarily migrants and minority ethnic groups such as Afghan migrants, Christians, and Hindus.

Most of the mining in South Asia is done seasonally during the non-monsoon months. It is among the most corrosive, dangerous, and exploitative work that I have documented anywhere in the world. All of the workers knew exactly how dangerous the work could be, yet there was no shortage of workers in the sector. Some of the miners I met had returned to the same region to work for ten or more years in a row. Others had simply moved to the area and made a life in casual labor during the off-season.

When I asked some of these workers why they took advances to work in a job that they knew was so dangerous that it could cost them their lives at any time, they almost all responded the same way: "This is the work we take when we cannot find anything else."

Glass Bangles and Glasswork

The winter months in South Asia bring two cherished gifts—cooler air and weddings. The wedding season in turn stimulates a massive increase in the demand for glass bangles and other wedding-related glass items. About forty kilometers east of the Taj Mahal and the city of Agra, along National Highway 2, one arrives in the glass capital of India—Firozabad. The glass industry began here during the sixteenth century under Mughal rule and has gone strong ever since. Anything one can imagine being made with glass is produced in Firozabad's high-intensity furnaces, by the city's more than four hundred glass producers—glass bangles, beads, chandeliers, crockery, dinnerware, wine and beer glasses, light bulbs, test tubes, Christmas ornaments, statuettes of deities, vehicle decorations, cut glass items, and much more. Wedding-related glass items are among the most popular in Firozabad, so much so that the nickname for Firozabad is Suhag Nagari, or "City of Married Women."[6] Because of the considerable increase in the need for wedding-related glass items leading up to and during the wedding season, there is a corresponding increase in need for workers during this time, which is often filled through debt bondage and child labor.

The first thing one notices when entering a glass factory in Firozabad is the intense heat. The high-intensity coal and gas furnaces reach hellish temperatures of 1,300 degrees centigrade. That is about 30 percent hotter than the average brick kiln oven, and like the kilns, these furnaces run twenty-four hours a day. Everyone in the vicinity of the oven is drenched in sweat. Heat is not the only hazard—there is poor ventilation, toxic fumes, broken glass everywhere, stray electrical wires, and limited light. I spoke to workers at four different glass-producing facilities, and 80 percent of them were migrants who had accepted advances for the season. Here is how one man named Jai Prakash described his situation:

I take an advance of Rs. 5,000 ($111) from the *jamadar*, then I come to Firozabad from my village with my family. We do the first stage in the process, which is to make the open bangles. I receive a daily wage of Rs. 65 ($1.44). More than half of this wage is taken to repay my advance and expenses. At the end of the season, there is always debt remaining, which is added to my advance the next season. During the other part of the year, we work in agriculture for the landowner. I must also take advances from him.

While Jai Prakash was paid a daily wage in exchange for a minimum quota, other laborers who made the open bangles worked on a piece-rate basis that worked out to around the same as his day wage. The open bangle production process requires a higher degree of skill than just molding bricks or rolling bidis, though there seemed to be little in the way of elevated wage rates to account for the higher skills required.

The full production process of manufacturing the tens of millions of brilliantly colored glass bangles in South Asia involves three stages. Jai Prakash and bonded laborers like him are often found in the first stage, which contains three steps. First, the workers take silica sand (primarily consisting of silicon dioxide, which is the main ingredient in glass) and mix it with soda ash, potash, borax, lime, feldspar, and other minerals. Next, they melt the batch in a pot furnace overnight. Pot furnaces can be open or closed, the former being the most common for glass bangle production. The workers colloquially refer to these as "Japanese furnaces." After the glass melts, a long metal pipe is inserted into the furnace by workers called *gulliwallas*. The molten glass adheres to the pipe in a globular shape. After the pipe is removed, the workers pound the glob into shape to make its dimensions as equal as possible. The rounded molten glass is then taken to a second furnace for the second step, where another set of workers (*sekaiwallas*) give the glob a cylindrical shape by rotating the pipe. Sometimes an automated roller is used. A third furnace is used for step three, in which another set of workers (*belanwallas*) stretch the molten glass into a spiral. The spiral lengths are then cut with a diamond cutter to form the thin bangles, usually in bunches of 320, called a *tora*. The thin bangles still have two open ends at this stage, which is why they are called "open bangles."

These open bangles are given to a contractor, who takes them to the homes of a separate group of workers, for the *sadhai* ("straighten") process. During this stage, the raw bangle is straightened into a cylinder, to align the two open ends. This process is accomplished by heating the raw bangle over a kerosene flame, then pressing it against an iron plate. This step is mostly performed by women and children in their homes and is done on a piece-rate basis of Rs 5 ($0.11) per thousand finished bangles.

The same contractor then picks up the straightened bangles and takes them to another set of workers, who join the two straightened ends of the bangles in a process called *judai* ("joining"). This too is typically done by women and children in their homes with the use of a gas flame. The women warm the ends of the bangles so that they are malleable enough to seal with the help of a metal grip. This is strictly piece-rate work that pays around Rs. 5 ($0.11) per thousand closed bangles. From this stage, the bangles are taken to artisans who decorate and paint them. Any bangles that are broken during the process are ground down and remelted to be used in the next batch.

The workers in the *sadhai* and *judai* stages are very similar to the bidi rollers I met. Women and children do this work in thousands of village huts across India, and contractors transport materials to and from them. Approximately 35 percent had taken advances, or their husbands had taken advances and were at the factory involved in the open bangle stage. For another 22 percent, their tenancy was contingent on meeting a certain quota of work each week. Sitting in a hunched position six or seven days a week, exposed to open flames and kerosene fumes, was exceedingly taxing on the workers, especially the children. Most workers suffered from lung ailments, back and joint pain, eye strain, and sometimes severe burns.

At the end of this complex, three-stage, multistep production process, the bangles are taken to retailers, where they are proudly displayed by the thousands. While the peak season sees an influx of laborers in the sector, there are workers who toil in glass bangle production all year round. The exploiters of these individuals in turn enjoy annual net profits per bonded laborer across all three stages of approximately $900 (see table B.10 in the appendix). Like the brickmaking business, fuel (coal and gas) used to heat the high-intensity furnaces in the first stage of the process is by far the highest expense in the business. Ultimately, blushing brides purchase the bangles to adorn their arms on their wedding days. Even Jai Prakash's wife, Gita, enjoyed bangle-adorned arms and ankles on her wedding day: "Gita wore one hundred bangles that day," Jai Prakash proudly told me. "I did not know back then how difficult it was to make these bangles. Now I have been working so many years to make these bangles for such low wages; I wish more people knew how difficult this work is."

Precious Stones and Gem Cutting

In the districts of Tiruchirapalli ("Trichy"), Karur, and Pudukkottai in the tropical southern Indian state of Tamil Nadu, almost two hundred thousand villagers work in their huts cutting and polishing precious and synthetic stones and gems. Cubic zirconium is a top product in this area, with almost all exports going to the United States. The model works like bidi rolling in West Bengal. Landless or poor villagers take advances from contractors who provide stones to the villagers for polishing and cutting every two to three weeks. The contractors also pick up the stones that have been polished and cut since their last visit. The fundamental difference between the bidi model and the gem cutting and polishing model is that, unlike bidis, the gems are individually quite valuable, so guards employed by the gem exporter live in and patrol the villages, collecting each day's stones for safekeeping until the contractor returns. Meticulous records are kept of the stones dropped off at each hut, and if there is any variance at the time of pickup, "We are whipped or tortured," a villager named K. P. told me.

The process of cutting and polishing stones and gems requires considerable skill. Fire is used to heat the stone or gem to make it more malleable. A chisel is used to break it down to shape and remove external impurities. Then a stone wheel laced with diamond dust[7] that may be manually or electrically operated is spun against the gem to grind it to shape. In some cases, I saw the use of steel saws laced with diamond dust instead of the grinding wheels, but the latter was by far more prevalent. After grinding, the stones might be sanded with less harsh abrasives for more delicate shaping, after which point the stones receive a final polish. Polishing usually involves the use of strong chemical solutions, such as aluminum oxide or ferric oxide, to give the gems a lustrous appearance. Most of the villagers in Tamil Nadu were involved in cutting and grinding only; the polishing was performed by other workers at the exporter's facilities. Beyond the state of Tamil Nadu, the states of Gujarat and Rajasthan also have large gem and diamond polishing sectors, especially in the cities of Surat and Jaipur, respectively. Both cities are replete with bonded and child laborers in the gem polishing sector.

Like the bidi rollers of West Bengal, the gem cutters of Tamil Nadu have a quota to meet. The usual quota is around one hundred to 120 cut stones per day, for which they receive a wage of Rs. 50 to Rs. 60 ($1.11 to $1.33). Up to half of this wage is deducted for debt repayment, mistakes, and supplies sold to the villagers by the contractors at inflated prices. To meet the quota, usually two or three members of the family must be involved with the work, including children. The conditions are harsh and can cause injuries from the use of the saws and grinding devices, not to mention back and joint pain from being hunched over all day. Eye strain is also a major ailment, following from the intense focus required to ensure all cutting is performed to specifications. As with other bonded laborers, the gem cutters explained to me that they had no other option and that there was no escape. "We are trapped here," a gem cutter named Chittranjan told me. "The contractor's men keep us working day and night, and they give us barely any wage. It is impossible to live like this."

I tried to speak to some of the gem exporters in Chennai about the labor situation in the villages, but none were willing to meet with me no matter how persistent I was. Though I did not manage to speak with any of the owners of these export companies, a security guard at one of the establishments had a friendly conversation with me. He was well aware of the problems of bonded and child labor and very low wages, but in response he had something quite interesting to say: "The wages must be like this or else our companies cannot compete with the Chinese. They pay their people nothing, so their gems are very cheap. If we do not do the same here, all these companies will go out of business. Then what will we do?"

At first blush, it was difficult for me to accept that Chinese labor practices were responsible for the prevalence of bonded and child labor in the gem-cutting villages of Tamil Nadu. On the other hand, this dynamic was perhaps the essence of globalization—promoting the exploitation of labor in all ways that a jurisdiction will allow so as to provide the most cost-competitive (and profit-enhancing) products and services on the global market. Even if bondage and labor exploitation had existed for decades in gem polishing and other sectors in South Asia, it was more than plausible that the forces of economic globalization that hunt for and reward underregulated and cost-minimizing labor environments would only reinforce, if not expand, this type of exploitation. In this context, India's gems and countless other products across South Asia may be able to maximize their price competitiveness by virtue of myriad forms of labor exploitation, but what can one say about the "moral competitiveness" of a country whose poorest and most vulnerable men, women, and children are reduced to little more than an expendable class of perpetually exploited workers? What of the dignity of a nation that allows its most downtrodden citizens to become the slave-labor class of the global economy? These are the questions that must be tackled by all of the nations of South Asia if bonded and child labor are ever to be eliminated. Beyond South Asia, those jurisdictions that allow the most extreme systems of labor exploitation to persist—from debt bondage to human trafficking and everything in between—harbor a legacy of slavelike exploitation that should not be tolerated anywhere in the world.

Even More Sectors with Bonded Labor

There are several other sectors in which bonded laborers are exploited in South Asia that I investigated during my five research trips for this book but have not discussed in the preceding chapters. Those sectors include tanneries, silk production, sari embroidery, knifemaking, and commercial sex. There are also sectors that I did not manage to research comprehensively, such as pottery, sporting goods, coffee harvesting/processing, rubber production, fireworks, rice mills, and match manufacture. The models of each of these sectors are similar to the models of the sectors covered in this book. In all cases, minority castes and ethnic groups are the primary individuals exploited; advances are offered by landowners or contractors in exchange for pledged labor; migrants are typically more severely exploited than local populations; women and children often work for free to meet production quotas; deductions for debt repayment, food, shelter, and medicine exacerbate debt levels; and an absolute lack of reasonable sources of alternate income or credit leaves the laborers with no choice but to accept the deeply exploitative arrangements.

Now that we have completed our multisector journey through the myriad modes and industries in which bonded labor exploitation occurs across South Asia, it is time to turn our attention to how to design more effective efforts to eliminate this unconscionable system of servitude once and for all. Among other forces that promote the system of bonded labor, perhaps the most foundational is the absence of rule of law, which allows the system to persist with impunity. A solid foundation of law is the first crucial step toward catalyzing more effective attempts to eliminate bonded labor. India is by far the leader in terms of establishing a solid legal foundation and history of jurisprudence against bonded labor. Pakistan would be next, followed by Nepal. In Bangladesh (also Afghanistan and Sri Lanka), there is still no specific law outlawing bonded labor. In none of these countries do

I feel that the legal foundation against bonded labor is adequate, even were it to be enforced flawlessly. This means that eliminating bonded labor is not simply a matter of rigorous enforcement of existing laws—the laws and policies currently in place are simply inadequate to the task. To design the most effective attack on the system of bonded labor, a more comprehensive and effectively designed legal foundation must be established. To do so requires an understanding of the existing scope of laws and jurisprudence against bonded labor, focusing particularly on the fundamental gaps that allow ruthless individuals to continue ensnaring, enslaving, and exploiting their fellow citizens without shame or consequence.

{ 7 }

Bonded Labor and the Law

Man, when perfected, is the best of animals, but when separated from law and justice, he is the worst of all.

—ARISTOTLE

Efforts to regulate and abolish bonded labor and other forms of slavery in South Asia date back centuries. In the modern context, truly comprehensive efforts to do so largely commence with India's Bonded Labour System (Abolition) Act, 1976. Pakistan passed its Bonded Labour System (Abolition) Act in 1992, and Nepal passed the Kamaiya Labour (Prohibition) Act in 2002. As of January 2012, Bangladesh still lacks a law that recognizes the existence of bonded labor, though it did pass a general unifying labor law in 2006, the Bangladesh Labour Act. Each country does have constitutional prohibitions against forced labor.[1]

To offer a comprehensive plan on how to tackle bonded labor, one must first understand the wide-ranging legislative and jurisprudential history on the issue. India has by far the most extensive accumulation of laws and jurisprudence on bonded labor of any nation in South Asia, and much of what one finds in Pakistan's and Nepal's acts to abolish bonded labor are modifications of India's 1976 act. This chapter will provide a brief overview of historic laws on slavery in South Asia dating back to ancient times up through the colonial period, followed by a detailed overview of current efforts in India to tackle bonded labor after independence and the passage of the 1976 act. Covering the recent history of bonded labor law and jurisprudence in India will largely subsume developments in the rest of South Asia; hence the focus in this chapter will primarily be on India. Appendix E provides additional details on some of the key laws and efforts to eliminate bonded and child labor in Pakistan, Nepal, and Bangladesh, as well as a brief summary of several Supreme Court cases on bonded labor in India beyond the two seminal cases (PUDR, 1982; and BMM, 1983) that are discussed in this chapter.

It should be noted from the outset that the case law in India on bonded labor is nothing short of fascinating. Contemporary efforts to eradicate this abuse by civil society, the National Human Rights Commission of India, and the Supreme Court of India are passionate and intelligent. Nevertheless, there are still millions of bonded laborers in India today. With all the country's resources and its well-developed system of justice and human rights, it is difficult to comprehend why the most essential of those rights—freedom—remains a faint rumor for the most oppressed and disenfranchised members of society. The truth is that laws—even if perfectly designed—only go so far as the will to enforce them. The renowned American judicial scholar and judge Billings Learned Hand once said: "I often wonder if we do not rest our hopes too much on constitutions, upon laws and upon courts. These are false hopes; believe me, these are false hopes. Liberty lies in the hearts of men and women; when it dies there, no constitution, no law, no court can do much to help it."[2]

Assuming that liberty for all does reside in the hearts of the majority of men and women of South Asia, the need for an effective foundation of law that can be enforced pursuant to the eradication of bonded labor is imperative. Much of the plan I will outline in chapter 8 is predicated on filling the gaps in the contemporary legislative and tactical framework relating to bonded labor. In brief: while India has offered the world a near-comprehensive system through which to outlaw bonded labor, child labor, and forced labor of all kinds, as well as to provide for the care of the victims of these abuses and ensure that no individuals are caught in these forms of exploitation in the future—dizzying levels of apathy, corruption, and bureaucratic callousness; key deficiencies in the law that include criminal law penalties that do not reflect the nature and benefit of slave-related crimes; and a general social acceptance that it is reasonable to exploit the labor of a certain outcast segment of society render all best laws, systems, mandates, and efforts to eradicate bonded labor highly ineffective.

With this thesis established, the first step in a review of the contemporary legal situation in India as it relates to bonded labor is a general summary of the history of the slavery laws in ancient India (which includes present-day Pakistan and Bangladesh), up through colonial times.

HINDU AND MUSLIM LAW ON SLAVERY IN ANCIENT INDIA

As discussed in chapter 1, five ancient Hindu lawgivers set forth the legal rules on slavery in ancient India: Kautilya, Manu, Narada, Katayayana, and Yajnavalkhya. Narada provided the most comprehensive classification of slavery, involving fifteen different categories (listed in chapter 1). Categories 5, 6, 7, and 13 contain those that would later be encapsulated by bonded labor. Those categories include *ankulabritta*, one whose life was saved during famine in exchange for enslavement; *ahita*, one pledged to be a slave upon acceptance of money by a master; *rinadasa*, one who becomes a slave upon release from a heavy debt; and *bhuktadasa*, one who becomes a slave in order to receive basic maintenance. From the outset, caste was an integral component of slavery, and the caste that happened to set down these laws (the Brahmins) determined that all other castes except themselves could become slaves. From a legal standpoint, slaves did not have a right to acquire or possess property, and in general, they were not allowed to provide testimony in a trial or to enter into contracts, because of the presumption of incompetency.[3] By law, slaves could only be freed by their masters. This rarely happened. However, in the event that a slave saved his master's life from immanent danger, it was encouraged that the master should free him.[4] For those categories of slavery as outlined by Narada that involved a tangible economic exchange (*ahita*, *rinadasa*), freedom was legally possible by settling the accounts, with interest. For slaves in certain other categories (*ankulabritta*, and also *lubdha* or *joodhprapta*), freedom may be possible by providing a suitable substitute.[5] Though these and other modes of potential freedom were outlined in the law, in general, once a person became a slave in ancient India, they were enslaved for life. By the time the British colonists arrived, these laws were well entrenched in Hindu society. In 1772, the British established a firm principle of noninterference in these laws, and they allowed any legal cases solely involving Hindus to be administered by Hindu law as expounded by *pundits* (Hindu scholars).[6]

Similar to Hindu lawgivers, Muslim lawgivers also set down rules relating to the regulation of slavery in ancient times. Hedaya and Futwa Alamgiri were the two primary sources of religious rules relating to slavery in the Islamic tradition that developed in ancient India.[7] Muslim law established that all men were by nature free and independent, except those who were not Muslims and not living in lands controlled by Muslims. If such people were conquered, they could rightfully be enslaved. Even if they later converted to Islam, because they were born outside of the faith, they would remain slaves, though they could no longer be put to death. No Muslim could sell himself into slavery unless it was to save himself from starvation,[8] similar to the *ankulabritta* category of slavery in the Hindu tradition. Both traditions were clear to specify laws relating to this category of slavery, because it was one of the most common ways in which slaves were acquired during ancient times, when famines were a regular occurrence. Unfortunately, salvation from famine or starvation remains a prominent mode of entry into debt bondage even today, which serves as a sharp reminder that no one who chooses subservience in exchange for survival should be deemed to have entered the condition voluntarily. As with the laws in ancient times, those who accept this devil's bargain today must be considered slaves.

Overall, the Muslim tradition in South Asia stipulated fewer categories of slaves than the Hindu tradition. There were generally five types of slaves, falling into two categories—absolute (*kinn* or *rukeek*) and qualified (*mukatab, muddabar,* or *um-ul-vald*). *Kinn* and *rukeek* were slaves who could be sold by their masters at will, killed without punishment, and otherwise treated at the master's whim, which could theoretically include freeing them. All children born by slaves in these categories were automatically slaves. In the qualified category, *mukatabs* were slaves by contract who could secure their freedom by paying an agreed-upon sum. This was the primary form of bonded labor in the ancient Muslim tradition. *Mudabbars* were slaves to whom freedom was promised after the death of the master. *Um-ul-valds* were female slaves who had borne a child fathered by her master, who were in turn promised freedom after the master perished.[9] Similar to the Hindu tradition, Muslim slaves could not provide legal testimony and could not own or inherit property.[10] As with the Hindu tradition, British colonists initially deferred to *muftis* (Muslim scholars) for interpretation of the Koran in legal cases involving Muslims.

While there are some interesting differences between the Hindu and Muslim religious laws relating to slavery (namely that in the Muslim tradition slavery was largely regarded as relating solely to conquered non-Muslims, whereas any Hindu outside of the Brahmin caste could theoretically become a slave), the traditions were similar in that a slave was largely held to be the absolute property of his or her master, and a master could do almost entirely what he pleased with the slave. Both traditions included specific categories of debt bondage, and both specified a form of slavery that resulted from being saved from starvation. Opportunities for freedom were rare. The descendants of slaves were almost always slaves as well. These religious tenets carried through to feudal and modern times, and they very much framed the evolution of legal thought on slavery and bondage in South Asia across the centuries.

BRITISH COLONIAL LAWS ON SLAVERY: 1770 TO 1920

Slavery in the Indian subcontinent drew more interest from British colonists beginning in the 1770s, when antislavery sentiment first began to develop in England. In 1807, the British Parliament passed the Slave Trade Abolition Act, and in 1833 the Slavery Abolition Act was passed. As noted in chapter 1, the territories of the East India Trading Company were specifically excluded from the 1833 act. This exclusion allowed slavery to exist legally in India after it was abolished throughout the remainder of the British Empire. In that way, Indians became a replacement slave labor force for lost African slaves. The exclusion of India from the 1833 act was not without debate. Just before the passage of the 1833 act, the Charter Act of 1832 included recommendations that slavery be abolished as soon as possible in India; however, the recommendation was not included in the 1833 act. In 1835, an Indian Law Commission was formed and tasked with, among other things, studying the issue of slavery in India.[11] This commission issued an *Indian Law Commission Report* in 1841.[12] The report included thirty-three recommendations relating to various types of labor. The first ten related to contract labor, the next seventeen related to slave labor, and the last six were regulatory in nature. None of the recommendations sought to abolish slavery in India. In fact, the majority view in the report firmly stated that slaves in India did not desire freedom and would not choose to trade security under their masters for a life of destitution, providing yet another justification of slavery based on the avoidance of deprivation. The 1841 report also recommended that slave masters should retain their power to punish their slaves physically, but it also recommended considering the possibility that slaves could purchase their freedom. The report did state that by attempting to regulate some of the evils associated with slavery in India, it was hopeful that one day the system might eliminate itself. It is worth noting that in the minority, Lord Auckland and W. W. Bird both decried the system of slavery and recommended that the report declare that slavery is an evil that should not be legally recognized or tolerated in any form. The 1841 report was followed by the Anti-Slavery Act of 1843 and Act V of 1843, both of which continued to attempt to regulate slavery and improve the basic treatment of slaves in India—but not to abolish slavery.

As detailed in chapter 1, the net result of these and other policies of the British colonial authorities beginning with the 1807 act through the mid 1800s was to transform India into a primary source of trafficked and bonded labor for the British Empire. For several decades, the traffic in slaves from India throughout the British colonies increased substantially, resulting in a global slave-trading network of Indians that surpassed in complexity and expanse the peak of the North Atlantic slave trade. This slave-trading expansion, along with the specific exclusion of the territories of the East India Trading Company from the subsequent 1833 act, provide ample space to argue that the British approach to slavery in India was to maintain a ready supply of indentured laborers for its empire. The passage of the Workman's Breach of Contract Act of 1859 further supports this view. This act was specifically designed to enforce performance of labor pledged in exchange for an economic advance. In other words, this law gave British slave masters the legal ability to enforce bonded labor.[13] The self-serving legal maneuvering of substituting deeds for sales of human beings with contracts of pledged labor to repay debts as a means of avoiding the narrow definitions of chattel slavery found in the 1833 act was an odious attempt to perpetuate slavery in the form of debt bondage throughout colonial India. The result was a vast expansion in bonded labor in India and throughout the British Empire. From the 1830s until the 1920s, much of the British Empire filled with millions of indentured Indian slaves as a direct result of these colonial laws on slavery. From nearby Bengal to the distant Caribbean isles, Indian bonded laborers provided servile labor for British colonial exploiters for several decades after slavery was supposedly abolished. The suffering that resulted from this series of colonial laws culminating in the 1859 act is incalculable. As Mahatma Gandhi once said, "An unjust law is itself a species of violence. Arrest for its breach is more so."

Though the colonial approach to slavery in India during the late 1700s began by largely deferring to local authorities on the issue, the laws passed throughout the 1800s directly facilitated the mass bondage of countless Indian slaves within India and across the British Empire. The British did not bring slavery to India, but their legal (and economic) systems directly expanded slave trading and debt bondage in India for the better part of a century. By that time, abolitionists back in England finally gathered sufficient strength to fight back more effectively against the persistence of slavery in India, particularly in the form of bonded labor.

ATTEMPTS TO ABOLISH BONDED LABOR IN INDIA: 1920–1975

The period from 1920 to 1975 saw the enactment of several laws attempting to abolish bonded labor in India, first beginning under colonial rule and later after India gained independence in 1947. The Bihar Orissa Kamaiuti Agreement Act, 1920; the Madras Agency Debt Bondage Abolition Regulations, 1940; and the Hyderabad Bhagela Agreement, 1943, were all laws passed during the colonial period that attempted to abolish pockets of bonded labor as it existed in certain states in India. At independence, the Constitution of India, 1949, included specific prohibitions against forced labor and child labor (Articles 23 and 24 respectively). After independence, the abolitionist trend continued with the Orissa Agency Debt Bondage Abolition Act, 1948; the Rajasthan Sagri System Abolition Act, 1961; and the Bonded Labour System Abolition Act (Kerala), 1975. The jurisdictions of these and other laws were restricted to the particular states in which the laws were passed. By and large they were limited in efficacy and punitive severity. Combined with a lack of adequate enforcement, the absence of severe penalties meant that the laws had a negligible effect on the bonded labor systems that they were attempting to abolish. However, in 1976 the first national law abolishing bonded labor was passed in India: The Bonded Labour System (Abolition) Act. This groundbreaking and remarkable piece of legislation has served as a model for similar legislation in other South Asian countries, and it has been the subject of several fascinating judgments by the Supreme Court of India.

THE BONDED LABOUR SYSTEM (ABOLITION) ACT, 1976

The celebrated jurist P. N. Bhagwati described the Bonded Labour System (Abolition) Act (Act 19 of 1976) in the landmark Supreme Court case *Bandhua Mukti Morcha vs. Union of India and Others*, 1983, as follows: "the [act] is intended to strike against the system of bonded labour which has been a shameful scar on the Indian social scene for decades and which has continued to disfigure the life of the nation even after independence."[14] In seeking to abolish the system of bonded labor, the act was designed to give effect to Article 23 of the Constitution of India, which prohibits the traffic in human beings and forced labor. There are several other articles in the Indian Constitution that have bearing on bonded labor, including Article 21: protection of life and personal liberty; Article 24: prohibition of employment of children in factories, etc.; Article 32: remedies for enforcement of rights; and Article 43: living wage, etc. for workers.

The preamble of the 1976 act states that it is intended to "provide for the abolition of bonded labour system with a view to preventing the economic and physical exploitation of the weaker sections of the people." Section 4 states that as of October, 25, 1975, "the bonded labour system shall stand abolished and every bonded labourer shall . . . stand freed and discharged from any obligation to render, any bonded labour." The offering of an advance in pursuit of bonded labor is outlawed, and no person can be compelled "to render any bonded labour or other form of forced labour." All bonded debts are extinguished (§6); all property of bonded laborers is freed from mortgage (§7); freed bonded laborers cannot be evicted from their homes (§8); payments against a bonded debt can no longer be accepted (§9); district magistrates are charged with implementing the act (§10); further duties of the district magistrates are outlined in detail, including ensuring that offenders of the act are prosecuted (§11–12); vigilance committees are to be created by each state and mandated to help identify, free, and rehabilitate all bonded laborers (§13–14); the burden of proof resides with the accused to establish that a debt is not a bonded debt (§15); and punishments for violations of the act are outlined, including up to three years in prison and a fine of Rs. 2,000 ($44 today; $223 in 1976, equivalent to $876 in 2011 U.S. dollars,[15]—out of which Rs. 5 per day is to be paid to the bonded laborer for each day of his servitude) (§16–19). This penalty was amended in 1996 and increased to Rs. 20,000 ($445 today; $632 in 1996, equivalent to

$900 in 2011 U.S. dollars).[16] The next few sections of the act relate to legal procedural matters, but §23 is of interest, as it includes a provision whereby if the act is violated by a company, "every person who, at the time the offence was committed, was in charge of, and was responsible to, the company for the conduct of the business of the company, as well as the company, shall be deemed to be guilty of the offence." The scope and importance of this section cannot be overstated, in that it renders companies as well as individual directors and managers of the company liable and punishable for a violation of the act. There has been virtually no enforcement of this section, and I will discuss it further as part of my overall plan to eradicate bonded labor in chapter 8.

The primary section of the act not yet discussed is section 2, which includes the definition of bonded labor. I have included the full text of the definition in appendix D, as it is quite illuminating and provides, among other things, a list of not less than thirty-one different forms of forced labor found in India at the time the act was drafted. Bonded labor itself is defined as a system of forced or partly forced[17] labor under which a debtor accepts an advance of cash or payment in kind in exchange for a pledge of his or any family member's or other dependant's labor or service to, or for the benefit of, the creditor. The agreement can be oral or in writing or some mix therein; of a fixed duration of time, or not; and with or without wages paid. An individual born into such an agreement made by an ascendant is included, and any forfeiture of the freedom of movement, employment, or the right to sell any product of the labor during the agreement at market value constitutes bonded labor. In other words, if someone takes an advance in exchange for his or any dependant's pledged labor or service and is confined to a specific geographic area, *or* cannot work for someone else, *or* is not allowed to sell his labor or goods at market value—this person is a bonded laborer under the 1976 act. The definition I provided in chapter 1 is similar but attempts to simplify the language and widen to the fullest the scope of terms such as coercion, restricted liberty, and advance. I also include the crucial category of those tied credit-labor agreements where the laborer entered the agreement because he or she lacked any reasonable alternative.

The government of India set forth "Guidelines for Release of Funds Under the Centrally Sponsored Scheme for Rehabilitation of Bonded Labour" in 1978 (amended in 1986, 1995, and 1999), which stipulated in 1978 that up to Rs. 4,000, and eventually by 1999 that up to Rs. 20,000 ($445 today; $463 in 1999, equivalent to $621 in 2011 U.S. dollars)[18] is to be expended on a 50/50 basis between the state and national governments for each identified and released bonded laborer, to provide the laborer with necessary assets (such as land and pigs, goats, sheep), training, raw materials, and working capital for a craft, funds for migration back to their home area if required, and a maximum of Rs. 1,000 ($22) in cash for subsistence.

If the act were implemented as designed, vigilance committees would be constituted by district magistrates or subdistrict magistrates in every state and would be charged with identifying bonded laborers, registering them, providing them with release certificates, and administering their rehabilitation. District magistrates would also be charged with ensuring that all offenders are prosecuted. They would also work with the vigilance committees to ensure that anyone newly caught in the system of bonded labor would be able to make a complaint and receive justice. In short, bonded labor would be a nightmare of the past. However, in the decades since the act was passed, its prescriptions and aspirations have remained largely unfulfilled. The reasons for these shortcomings are many, and the failures are even greater when one considers the extraordinary role the Supreme Court of India has taken in interpreting the act and further mandating its implementation.

THE SUPREME COURT OF INDIA

The Supreme Court of India has heard several cases since the early 1980s on the issue of bonded labor. Much of the focus of their judgments has been to interpret the meaning and scope of the 1976 act, to stress the importance of eradicating bonded labor in India, and to empower the National Human Rights Commission of India to monitor implementation of the 1976 act. Though there have been several cases that made important contributions to the fight against bonded labor (see appendix E for details), the two primary cases that set the foundation for how to construe and tackle bonded labor in India are those that I have already mentioned several times in this book: *People's Union for Democratic Rights vs. Union of India and Others*, 1982; and *Bandhua Mukti Morcha vs. Union of India and Others*, 1983. In both cases, the celebrated Supreme Court jurist P. N. Bhagwati outlined in poetic and potent language the ugliness of bonded labor and how to abolish it.

People's Union for Democratic Rights
vs. Union of India and Others, 1982

The PUDR, 1982, case established three essential legal principles in the fight against bonded labor: (1) the role of public interest litigation (PIL) as a tool to enforce the fundamental rights of India's poorest masses, (2) that bonded labor is a form of forced labor captured by Article 23 of the Constitution of India, and (3) anyone paid less than the government-stipulated minimum wage for a job is to be considered a forced laborer. By this definition, it is not unreasonable to estimate that there are easily several hundred million forced laborers in the world today.

The PUDR, 1982, case was initiated when the organization People's Union for Democratic Rights sent a letter to Justice P. N. Bhagwati of the Supreme Court of India outlining a list of complaints from specific workers involved in construction for the 1980 Asian Games held in New Delhi. For this reason, the case is sometimes referred to as the "Asiad Workers" case. The letter was based on the findings of three social scientists hired by PUDR to document the working conditions at certain construction sites relating to the Asian Games. In the letter, the Asiad workers complained of wage deductions (Rs. 1 per day on their daily wage of Rs. 9.25) for commissions to *jamadars* who had hired them, the exploitation of child labor, severely subhuman living conditions in the work areas (lack of clean water, toilets, adequate shelter), unpaid wages, restrictions on movement, and other issues that the plaintiffs in the case argued were violations of Article 23 of the Constitution of India as well as the Bonded Labour System (Abolition) Act, 1976.

The first of the three legal principles established in the Asiad Workers case has to do with a legal matter relating to the concept of *locus standi*. This legal principle stipulates that only an individual who has been harmed by an alleged legal wrong has "standing" to bring a legal claim of action. The defense attorneys in the PUDR, 1982, case argued that since the organization PUDR was not harmed by the alleged violations, they had no standing to bring the case; the laborers themselves were the only ones who could do so. Justice Bhagwati made short work of this argument, stating that where a fundamental right is concerned and the offended individuals do not have the ability (because of poverty, illiteracy, etc.) to bring a claim of action on their own behalf, the concept of PIL allows for others to bring the claim for them:

Public interest litigation, is essentially a cooperative or collabourative effort on the part of the petitioner, the State or public authority and the Court to secure observance of the constitutional or legal rights, benefits and privileges conferred upon the vulnerable sections of the community and to reach social justice to them. . . .[19]

The traditional rule of standing which confines access to the judicial process only to those to whom legal injury is caused or legal wrong is done has now been jettisoned by the Supreme Court and the narrow confines within which the rule of standing was imprisoned for long years as a result of inheritance of the Anglo-Saxon system of jurisprudence have been broken and a new dimension has been given to the doctrine of *locus standi* which has revolutionised the whole concept of access to justice in a way not known before to the Western System of jurisprudence.[20]

The second legal principle established in this case set the foundation for all future legal thinking on the issue of bonded labor as a constitutional violation in India. The defense attorneys in the case argued that bonded labor as defined by the 1976 act is not captured by Article 23 of the Constitution of India, which prohibits "Traffic in human beings and *begar*[21] and other similar forms of forced labour." The argument made was that *begar* is a form of forced labor that does not involve monetary compensation and that "similar" forms of forced labor means only those forms that similarly do not provide compensation. Since the laborers in the case were paid some compensation (though not what was promised to them and with unlawful deductions), the defense attorneys argued that this cannot be construed as forced labor and is not captured by Article 23 of the Constitution. This argument drew the ire of the Supreme Court justices, who stated unequivocally:

Article 23 strikes at forced labour in whatever form it may manifest itself, because it is violative of human dignity and is contrary to basic human values. To contend that exacting labour by passing some remuneration, though it be inadequate will not attract the provisions of Article 23 is to unduly restrict the amplitude of the prohibition against forced labour enacted in the Article.[22]

In other words, bonded labor is a form of forced labor as far as the Constitution of India is concerned.

BONDED LABOR AND THE LAW {197}

The third legal principle established in the PUDR, 1982, case is perhaps the most interesting from the standpoint of contemporary antislavery scholarship. The court held that where a person performs labor or services for remuneration that is less than the government-stipulated minimum wage, this constitutes forced labor. The reasoning behind this precedent is that "Ordinarily no one would willingly supply labour or service to another for less than the minimum wage . . . [unless] he is acting under the force of some compulsion which drives him to work though he is paid less than what he is entitled under law to receive."[23] To this end, "force" is to be construed not simply as physical force but also forces of "compulsion arising from hunger and poverty, want and destitution. Any factor which deprives a person of a choice of alternative . . . may properly be regarded as 'force,' and if labour or service is compelled as a result of such 'force,'" it would be 'forced labour.'"[24]

One can understand the wisdom of this proclamation, particularly in a country such as India or anywhere in the developing world, where so many millions of poor and vulnerable individuals who accept any offer of employment at all may do so simply to avoid starvation and destitution. As we have seen, this devil's bargain is centuries old, going back to ancient times when Hindu and Muslim scholars specifically classified a form of slavery based on this arrangement. Well into the modern era, unscrupulous individuals and human traffickers continue to exploit slave labor by capitalizing on the acute desperation of those who are on the brink of absolute deprivation. Declaring such a practice to be a form of forced labor is clearly an attempt to thwart this expansive means of entry into slavelike exploitation.

The obvious question that follows is whether the reasoning from the PUDR, 1982, case provides a reasonable way to construe forced labor not just in South Asia but anywhere in the world. Is it reasonable to assume that some form of compulsion (physical, legal, economic, or otherwise) is the only reason a person would accept payment less than the minimum wage, and if so, does this suggest that there are literally hundreds of millions of forced laborers in the world today? Such a position may stretch the reasonable meaning of the term. However, we can at least agree that people in this category are involved in some form of extreme labor exploitation that may posses some but not all of the elements of outright forced labor. Nevertheless, perpetually underpaid minimum wages represents a form of oppression that must not be tolerated anywhere in the world. The primary result of this type of exploitation is the perpetuation of a global class of destitute laborers who will never have an opportunity to elevate their overall human development, freedom, and potential. Such people are confined to eking out the barest of human existences by using the only productive asset the system allows them to possess—their meager and expendable bodies. Such people will never be free in any real sense nor able to enhance their lives or the lives of their children. They will never be in a position to bargain for decent treatment or turn away from servile labor so long as it provides the only means to survive. Any disaster will send them straight into the hands of exploiters and human traffickers. From this standpoint, there may be considerable merit in the way the Supreme Court of India defined forced labor back in 1982, as no one would willingly accept to work for less than a minimum wage unless there was some form of coercion involved, and whatever that coercion is should be sufficient to meet the burden of "forced labor." Understanding modern forms of slavery in this way may prove the most effective way to marshal sufficient attention, resources, enforcement, and overall energy to eradicate slavery once and for all. Perhaps this is what the learned justices had in mind, by defining a position that is extremely protective of the essential rights of the most vulnerable and exploited workers in India and the world.

Bandhua Mukti Morcha vs. Union of India and Others, 1983

The second of the two seminal cases relating to bonded labor heard by the Supreme Court of India is *Bandhua Mukti Morcha vs. Union of India and Others*, 1983. The plaintiff in this case was the bonded labor abolition organization founded by Swami Agnivesh. Similar to the approach in the PUDR, 1982, case, Swami Agnivesh wrote a letter to the Supreme Court (dated February 25, 1982) outlining a breach of fundamental rights against twenty-two named bonded laborers at stone quarries in the city of Faridabad outside New Delhi, in the state of Haryana. In one of my meetings at Swami Agnivesh's office in New Delhi, he explained to me that he was working as the minister of education for the state of Haryana when he first came across the bonded laborers in these stone quarries in 1980. Initially, he thought it was an isolated case, but the more he investigated, the more he realized how pervasive the problem was, and he resolved to do something about it. Leaving his post in the government, he founded Bandhua Mukti

Morcha and dedicated his life to combating bonded labor across the nation. In particular, Swami Agnivesh has focused his efforts on combating the injustices caused by the caste system in India, which he sees as one of the primary causes of exploitation and bondage. "I subscribed to the caste system when I was young," Swami Agnivesh explained, "but once I grew up I realized how this system caused so much suffering. I realized how bonded labor was used to treat these people like subhumans. It is a ruthless system. We will not stop until we have changed this system completely."

As a lawyer by training, Swami Agnivesh wrote his letter to Justice P. N. Bhagwati of the Supreme Court in the hopes that it would move the court to investigate and take action. As discussed in chapter 5, the BMM, 1983, case involved stone quarry workers who had been trafficked to Faridabad from numerous other states in India with offers of advances and then exploited as bonded laborers tasked with breaking stones for construction in blazing heat and atrocious working conditions. The complaint described the difficulties the workers faced breathing the high levels of dust in the quarries, that some of the workers suffered from several chronic diseases, and that all the workers were restricted to the quarries and could not leave. There was no clean drinking water provided, and the workers slept in the open on straw mats with no protection from the sun or rain. Women were sexually exploited at the quarries, no compensation was provided to workers who fell ill or were injured, and there were no medical treatment facilities. Justice Bhagwati described the workers' condition best:

> They are non-beings, exiles of civilization, living a life worse than animals, for the animals are at least free to roam about as they like and they can plunder or grab food whenever they are hungry but these out castes of society are held in bondage, robbed of their freedom and they are consigned to an existence where they have to live either in hovels or under the open sky and be satisfied with whatever little unwholesome food they can manage to get inadequate though it be to fill their hungry stomachs. Not having any choice, they are driven by poverty and hunger into a life of bondage a dark bottomless pit from which, in a cruel exploitative society, they cannot hope to be rescued.[25]

There were numerous points raised in this case relating to legal procedures and definitions,[26] but the precedent of primary interest is that the court held that forced labor is the same as bonded labor from the standpoint of activating the provisions of the 1976 act, following on the PUDR, 1982, case, which established that bonded labor is a form of forced labor from the standpoint of activating Article 23 of the Constitution of India. It may seem trifling, but this point had to be legally established because the defense attorneys in the BMM, 1983, case attempted to argue that the laborers in Faridabad were forced laborers, not bonded laborers who had taken loans that could be documented, and hence the 1976 act did not apply. Rejecting this argument entirely, the court held, "Whenever it is shown that a labourer is made to provide forced labour, the Court would raise a presumption that he is required to do so in consideration of an advance or other economic consideration received by him and he is therefore a bonded labourer."[27] The presumption may be rebutted by evidence offered in court, but otherwise the court considers that bonded labor is a form of forced labor. This point is crucial in that it negates any attempt by the exploiter to argue that an individual is not a bonded laborer because of the absence of reliable documentation that a loan was provided in exchange for labor. Such documentation is almost always impossible for the bonded laborer to provide; hence the presumption of bondage where any forced labor is established is vital with regard to activating the provisions of the 1976 act. The precedent also speaks to the blurry line between bonded and forced labor. Even though that line does exist, it can be very difficult to disaggregate one mode of servitude from another, and having to do so should not in any way cripple attempts by the law to inflict penalties on the offender or compensate and care for the victim.

In his further remarks, Justice Bhagwati expressed significant disapproval that eight years after the passage of the 1976 act, the system of bonded labor had not already been eliminated throughout India:

> It is absolutely essential we would unhesitatingly declare that it is a constitutional imperative that the bonded labourers must be identified and released from the shackles of bondage so that they can assimilate themselves in the main stream of civilised human society and realise the dignity, beauty and worth of human existence.[28]

The Supreme Court sided with the plaintiff in the BMM, 1983, case on all counts, and it enumerated twenty-one specific directions intended to see that the bonded laborers in Faridabad received full care and rehabilitation under the law and that the State of Haryana undertook rigorous and monitored efforts to identify, free, and rehabilitate all bonded laborers in its jurisdiction. Eight years after this case, Bandhua Mukti Morcha brought another claim (*Bandhua Mukti Morcha vs. Union of India and Others*, 1991) in which it argued that the directives from the 1983 case had still not been implemented by the state of Haryana. The Supreme Court sided again with the plaintiff. As of my research at the quarries in Faridabad in 2010, these directives still have not been met in full by the state of Haryana, let alone any of the other eight states in India in which I have conducted my research.

FAILURE TO IMPLEMENT THE LAW

With reasonably good (but not sufficient) laws in place and the highest court in India aggressively demanding the immediate elimination of bonded labor, it is difficult to understand why there are still millions of bonded laborers in India and millions more across South Asia. There are myriad reasons for this failure, but the primary forces relating to the Indian government's inability to eliminate bonded labor include corruption; an apathetic bureaucracy that refuses to implement and uphold the law; a befuddling inability of district magistrates and vigilance committees to identify, free, and rehabilitate bonded laborers; and an insufficient level of prosecutions of the crime. These same factors hold true in other South Asian nations. Beyond the governments of South Asia, there remains a general social acceptance across South Asian society that it is acceptable to exploit certain "lower" classes or castes of individuals or that the exploitation is acceptable because the alternative is worse (starvation, destitution, etc.). Finally, there remains a grave failure of the public and private sectors to alleviate many of the forces that render people vulnerable to being exploited, such as poverty, bias against female gender, exploitation of children, landlessness, internal population displacement, and an inability to access sufficient credit.

Perhaps the most comprehensive and helpful overview of these deficiencies was provided to me by the National Human Rights Commission of India, both in oral interviews and in a printed response to a series of questions I submitted in the summer of 2010. In a writ petition (no. 3922/1985)—*Public Union for Civil Liberties vs. State of Tamil Nadu and Others*, 1985—the

Supreme Court of India requested that the NHRC get involved in monitoring the implementation of the 1976 act. The NHRC has since focused its efforts on thirteen states[29] in India deemed particularly prone to bonded labor. They have worked to ensure that vigilance committees are constituted and properly functioning in each of these states, they have sent special rapporteurs to conduct investigations into the status of implementation of the 1976 act in many of these states, they have convened an expert working group to study the probiem, and they have made numerous recommendations[30] on how to improve policy and law against bonded labor.

The secretary general of the NHRC, Shri K. S. Money, and one of his leading experts on bonded labor, Dr. Sanjay Dubey, explained to me in great detail how and why many of these governmental and bureaucratic efforts to eliminate bonded labor (as well as forced labor and child labor) remain lacking. Starting with the vigilance committees, Shri Money explained that it was only recently, more than three decades after the passage of the 1976 act, that VCs had finally been constituted in most districts. However, "the vigilance committees are not working well," he stated. "Maybe they are constituted on paper, but they are apathetic, and they do not meet regularly."

During the first decade after the act, tens of thousands of bonded laborers were identified, registered, and rehabilitated. However, after an initial flurry of activity, the identification activity largely stagnated. The government of India had by then officially recorded a little over 280,000 identified and released bonded laborers, but there have been barely ten thousand more recorded since the mid-1990s.[31] What's more, there is no accounting as to how many of these individuals ended up back in debt bondage because of a lack of government assistance and support, just as we saw in chapter 2 with the *kamaiya* in Nepal. A bonded laborer named Satish in Uttar Pradesh told me that he did not even bother with the "rehabilitation" programs under the 1976 act: "If we register and apply for the rehabilitation, the landowner bribes the official and takes the money for himself." Some landowners even conjure laborers out of thin air, register them, and take the grant money for themselves. In other cases, corrupt bureaucrats deduct "processing fees" and other charges, so that the money that ends up in the laborer's hands is next to nothing. The roughly 290,000 bonded laborers officially freed thus far by the efforts of the government of India under the 1976 act represent approximately 2.3 to 2.7 percent of the 10.7 to 12.7 million bonded laborers I calculate live in India today, or almost no percentage of the tens of millions of bonded laborers who have lived and died in India from 1976 through 2011.

As for the district magistrates who are charged with, among other things, ensuring that offenders are prosecuted, Shri Money explained, "They are not really focused on rooting out the problem. Everything depends on the sincerity of the individuals to uphold the law, but most district magistrates do not take this problem seriously." Dr. Dubey added that the NHRC is supposed to receive comprehensive reports from the thirteen target states every six months with updates on progress in eliminating bonded labor and prosecuting offenders, but "these reports are still not coming in. Many states are still in denial mode about bonded labor, or they think identifying bonded laborers was a one-time event, instead of an ongoing process." Both Shri Money and Dr. Dubey stressed that even when bonded laborers are identified and freed, the rehabilitation process is exceedingly insufficient: "The laborers are just freed and given a small amount of money. This means they are back in bondage. The rehabilitation must be sustained." This deficiency in the rehabilitation of identified bonded laborers is particularly appalling, when one considers that in the Bandhua Mukti Morcha case of 1983, Justice Bhagwati made it absolutely clear how important this step was:

> If the bonded labourers who are identified and freed, are not rehabilitated, their condition would be much worse than what it was before during the period of their serfdom and they would become more exposed to exploitation and slide back once again into serfdom even in the absence of any coercion. The bonded labourer who is released would prefer slavery to hunger, a world of "bondage and (illusory) security" as against a world of freedom and starvation.[32]

These and other bureaucratic failings notwithstanding, one might reasonably ask: Even if the system is not doing its job at proactively identifying bonded laborers, surely bonded laborers can identify themselves, and would this not lead to their being freed and (hopefully) rehabilitated—as well as their exploiters being prosecuted for breaking the law? Unfortunately, the system of receiving such complaints within the exceedingly thick Indian bureaucratic system has been designed in a way that renders it almost impossible for a bonded laborer to identify himself safely. In villages and rural areas, *patwaris* serve as local land record clerks, and they are also the ones who theoretically receive complaints from individuals being exploited as bonded laborers. This complaint would then be passed to the *tehsildars*, who serve as tax collectors based on the *patwaris'* records and who would then report the complaint to the subdistrict magistrates, who would then report the complaint to the district magistrates, who would theoretically investigate the complaint and potentially order a prosecution. In almost every case I encountered, the complaints never went passed the *patwari*. When investigating such complaints deep in rural areas away from hotels and other amenities, the *patwaris* were typically invited to be the guest of the local landowner/slaveowner, who then provided the *patwari* with excellent hospitality and perhaps even bribes to quash the complaint. Even if a bribe was not paid, the bonded laborer was almost always brought into the landowner/slaveowner's home, in front of all his men, guards, and the *patwari*, and asked if he had any complaints. Knowing the harsh punishment that awaited him once the *patwari* left, the answer was always, "no Saheb, no complaints at all."

In an effort to dig deeper into these major systemic deficiencies, I endeavored to meet with district magistrates and vigilance committees in six different states in India. I was ignored or turned down in all cases except for one. The subdivisional magistrate of New Delhi, Rahul Shukla, was willing to meet with me. We met on August 13, 2010, just after he had received reports of a suicide that had occurred in his district. He had been on the job for thirteen months when we spoke, and during that time he had dealt with one case of bonded labor. "I take bonded labor cases very seriously," Mr. Shukla told me, "but there will not be many complaints in Delhi; you will have more in rural areas."

I asked him about the one case he had dealt with. "We have freed sixteen bonded laborers near Dwarka," Mr. Shukla explained, "and I have overseen their rehabilitation. If we prosecute, I will be a witness in the trial." Mr. Shukla seemed to care genuinely about the plight of bonded laborers, and he told me that he worked with local NGOs to try to identify them, as opposed to simply waiting for complaints. When I asked him what he thought could be done better to tackle the problem, he said, "I feel there should be just one person in each district focused on this issue and only this issue. I am pulled in so many directions, it is difficult for me to do as much as I would like."

The final and perhaps most important component in failures to eliminate bonded labor has to do with prosecutions. Even with a relatively paltry

290,000 or so bonded laborers identified and freed by the Indian government since 1976, one would expect there to be thousands of prosecutions (and hopefully convictions) of those who had exploited these individuals. There is no reliable data on prosecutions and convictions since the passage of the 1976 act, but the NHRC has been attempting to compile data in its thirteen target states since 1996. According to the NHRC data, there have been roughly one hundred to 250 prosecutions per state in aggregate during the last fifteen years (or seven to seventeen prosecutions per state per year), of which 80 to 90 percent of the cases are still pending. Ninety to 100 percent of those cases that have been decided have been acquittals. As an example, here is what the NHRC outlines for the state of Uttar Pradesh in a report from Special Rapporteur Shri Chaman Lal in 2005: "A total of 231 prosecutions have been launched under the Bonded Labour System (Abolition) Act 1976 since 1996–1997 (up to 30th June, 2005) . . . only 6 cases have been decided so far—all in acquittal."[33] In aggregate since 1996, the NHRC estimates that only "1.35% of the reported cases [of bonded labor] were registered . . . and only 0.08% of culprits were prosecuted."[34] In short, the judicial response to bonded labor is broken. For what it is worth, the picture on child labor is a little better. Again citing NHRC data from Uttar Pradesh: "A total of 10,916 prosecutions have been launched under the Child Labour Act, 1989 till 30th June 2005. A total of 2,213 of these have been decided so far—369 in conviction and 1,844 in acquittal."[35]

Two key problems emerge from this data. First, cases are taking years and years to be adjudicated. Second, once the cases are adjudicated, most or all the accused are acquitted. As I looked deeper into this issue, a third problem emerged: most cases are dismissed very early in the judicial process. I reviewed as many case transcripts across several years as I could find from the high courts of Allahabad, Patna, New Delhi, and Mumbai (thirty-six cases in total), and a curious trend emerged. Most bonded labor cases were PIL cases filed on behalf of bonded laborers by an NGO. Judges then ordered investigations by district magistrates into the allegations. The district magistrates then submitted reports that there were either no bonded laborers present where they were alleged to be or that they had all been freed. Upon receipt of these reports, the high courts dismissed the charges in thirty-one of the thirty-six cases I reviewed, without ordering any further investigation or even asking an independent party to verify the findings of the district magistrate.

Two examples from the High Court of Judicature in Allahabad are illustrative. In the case of *Yameen vs. State of Uttar Pradesh and Others*,
2010, the court received a writ petition on January 13, 2010, alleging the
exploitation of bonded laborers at a brick kiln. The high court ordered the
district magistrate to investigate and report by January 19, 2010. The report
was filed on time, and on January 19, 2010, the high court declared, "A report has been submitted that all bonded labourers have been got free and
at present there is no bonded labour in brick-kiln. In this view of the matter, this writ petition has become infructuous and is accordingly dismissed
as infructuous."[36] No further inquiry, investigation, or prosecution beyond
the magistrate's report was conducted. In another case, *Ravindra vs. State
of Uttar Pradesh and Others*, 2009, one bonded laborer managed to escape
and with the help of an attorney filed a claim that he and twenty-four others still held captive had been exploited as bonded laborers. The claim also
stated that on November 10, 2009, the escaped bonded laborer asked the
district magistrate to intervene and free his fellow bonded laborers but
that no action was taken. As with the previous case, the high court ordered
the magistrate to investigate and submit a report. The report was submitted on time, and the court declared, "A report has been submitted that all
bonded labourers have been got free and at present there is no bonded labour in brick-kiln. In this view of the matter, this writ petition has become
infructuous and is accordingly dismissed as infructuous."[37] This befuddling and perfunctory process was repeated in numerous cases in several
high courts that I reviewed, including verbatim language in several bonded
labor cases dismissed by the High Court of Allahabad. These results dem-
onstrate a shocking apathy toward any sincere investigation into the claims
of bonded labor exploitation by vulnerable individuals who are no doubt
desperate for some measure of justice in a system that appears to have forsaken them.

If there have been approximately 290,000 bonded laborers officially
identified by the government of India since 1976, then there have been by
necessity thousands of individuals officially exploiting these people as
bonded laborers. The inability to prosecute and convict even a handful of
these offenders means that there is utter contempt and disregard for justice for bonded laborers across the nation, along with outright apathy, corruption, and bias in the system of government, law enforcement, and the
judiciary. The situation is even worse in Pakistan, Nepal, Bangladesh, and
the rest of South Asia. Considering that there have been tens of millions of

bonded laborers who have lived and died in South Asia in the last few decades, there should have been at least tens of thousands of offenders prosecuted and convicted by now. Sadly, there has been barely a handful. Even if each and every bonded laborer in South Asia is suddenly identified, freed, and fully rehabilitated today, if virtually no one is convicted of the crime, what is to stop these scoundrels from exploiting new bonded laborers tomorrow? One final point must be made. Even if all bonded labor exploiters are prosecuted and convicted tomorrow, the maximum penalties (for example, Rs. 20,000 [$445] in India) are deeply insufficient as compared to the net profits that can be generated through the exploitation of bonded laborers. Even with a 100 percent conviction rate, the exploitation of bonded labor remains a very good business decision. This reason, above all, is why the system of bonded labor continues to thrive across South Asia.

Recognizing the immense challenges—from social apathy to systemic corruption to inadequately designed laws—that are built into the entire system of any and all efforts to eliminate bonded labor in South Asia, I provide in the next chapter my best argument as to how we can do a better job. As poor a job as India has done at eliminating bonded labor (as well as forced and child labor), the rest of South Asia has done even worse. It is my sincere hope that perhaps a few of the ideas in the following chapter will prove useful to the longstanding efforts of so many activists to tackle and eradicate bonded labor.

{ 8 }

Tackling Bonded Labor

Human dignity is the quintessence of human rights.

—CHIEF JUSTICE J. S. VERMA

I had the honor of meeting the former chief justice of India, J. S. Verma, a few years ago in New Delhi. He gave me a copy of his book, *The New Universe of Human Rights,* and I had not read more than a few pages before I came across the sentence quoted above. It seemed so simple, yet this fundamental truth is so often overlooked in the complex pursuit of ensuring that all men, women, and children are assured their basic human rights. Defining "human dignity" may seem to be a challenge, but to me it signifies that a person can wake up each day and feel secure in his rights, freedoms, opportunities, and means to pursue a decent life. Not everyone is equally endowed of opportunities and means, but a basic level of what Amartya Sen calls "primary goods,"[1] coupled with the protection of essential legal rights and freedoms, are vital components in ensuring that all citizens of the world can live with human dignity. This, in my mind, is what it means to provide human rights.

The millions of bonded laborers in South Asia do not live with human dignity. Their lives are characterized by incalculable suffering, affliction, and exploitation. Not one of them enjoys a modicum of human rights. The elimination of the system of bonded labor is a social, economic, and moral imperative if the promise of freedom and dignity for all citizens of South Asia is to be achieved. This promise is not a theoretical aspiration or an ephemeral concept. It is the birthright of every person everywhere, and it was a specific promise made by India's first prime minister, Jawaharlal Ne-hru, in the nascent moments of freedom from the British Empire:

> The future beckons to us . . . to bring freedom and opportunity to the common man, to the peasants and workers of India; to fight and end poverty and ignorance and disease . . . and to create social, economic, and political institutions which will ensure justice and fullness of life to every man and woman.

This is the future that beckoned to all of South Asia decades ago, on those first days of independence from tyranny and exploitation. Yet this promise remains deeply elusive for hundreds of millions of poor and oppressed people across South Asia—and even more so for the millions of slaves in the region, who remain subjugated by cruelty and bondage.

Bonded labor is a relic of history. It is a fundamental violation of essential human dignity that is predicated on the exploitation of the vulnerable and desperate. Bonded labor should have faded long ago into oblivion, but it persists through the pitiless reinforcement of the conditions of poverty, bias, and oppression, which ensures the existence of an ever-vulnerable and ever-desperate subclass of subcitizens across South Asia. Bonded labor is a crime. Bonded labor is a disgrace. Bonded labor is a humiliation to all of humanity. Bonded laborers may exist primarily in South Asia, but the forces that promote that deplorable system—and those who benefit from it—span the globe. Every single inhabitant of the developed world is a shareholder in the system of bonded labor. From New York to Singapore, London to Sydney, all citizens consume the products produced by bonded laborers. The list of these products is extensive, including frozen shrimp and fish, tea, coffee, rice, wheat, diamonds, gems, cubic zirconia, glassware, brassware, carpets, limestone, marble, slate, salt, matches, bidis, cigarettes, apparel, fireworks, knives, sporting goods, and much more. Even if one does not consume these or other products directly, we are all beneficiaries of the global economic regime that advances the exploitation of the lowest-cost labor environments and applies extreme market-economy pressures on producers to maximize profits while retaining optimal price competitiveness. These forces promote labor exploitation, and, in the extreme, they promote bonded labor, human trafficking, and other forms of contemporary slavery. Having said this, South Asia must take particular responsibility for the persistence of this revolting remnant of Old World barbarism.

The global capitalist world may feed upon the system, but South Asia remains home to bonded labor. South Asia allows the system to exist, and South Asia must initiate more effective efforts to eradicate the system once and for all. Many dedicated thinkers and activists have devoted their lives to this task, and I hope the ideas outlined in this chapter may assist them.

RECAPITULATION OF THE TWENTY FORCES THAT PROMOTE BONDED LABOR

In chapter 1, I enumerated twenty forces that promote bonded labor across South Asia. These forces centered around an essential thesis:

> *The persistence of bonded labor in South Asia is driven by the ability to generate substantial profits at almost no real risk, through the exploitation of an immense underclass of systemically impoverished and vulnerable people.*

The first half of this equation is driven by demand-side forces of substantial profit at no real risk; the second half of this equation is driven by supply-side forces that promote the availability of a vast pool of potential bonded laborers.

To dismantle the system of bonded labor, both the demand- and supply-side forces of the business must be inverted. The industry must become much less profitable and far more risky (demand side), and the available pool of potential bonded laborers must be substantially reduced (supply side). While tackling both sides of the system are necessary, resources are limited. If one set of tactics must be prioritized over the other, I believe that focusing on demand-side forces provides the best opportunity to create a significant dent in the industry in the near term, while addressing the supply-side forces will help eliminate bonded labor and other forms of labor exploitation in South Asia over the long term. The twenty forces listed in chapter 1 are divided into the demand and supply sides of the industry as follows:

I. Demand-Side Forces (substantial profit at no real risk)

A. Legal Deficiencies
1. Insufficient minimum wages
2. Insufficient scope of vicarious liability laws

3. Land laws that promote the ongoing landlessness of peasants and agricultural laborers
4. Deeply insufficient penalties in the law for the crime of bonded labor

B. Systemic Barriers
5. Severely lacking enforcement of labor laws, such as they exist, including flaunting of minimum-wage laws and virtually no prosecutions for offences against bonded labor
6. Corruption in government, law enforcement, and the judiciary
7. Difficulties with identification and freeing of bonded laborers
8. Reporting mechanisms that make it impossible for bonded laborers to identify themselves safely
9. The *jamadar* system of labor subcontracting

II. Supply-Side Forces (promote vulnerability to bondage)

10. Poverty
11. A lack of sufficient credit resources for the poor, especially for non-income-generating purposes
12. A lack of reasonable and sustained income opportunities for the poor, especially former bonded laborers
13. Inadequate infrastructure or means of transportation for rural laborers to access markets
14. A lack of comprehensive literacy and basic education for the poor
15. Virtually nonexistent rehabilitation of identified and freed bonded laborers, or unreasonable lag time between identification and rehabilitation
16. Poorly designed rehabilitation packages that do not provide sufficient cash income and relevant vocational training to former bonded laborers
17. Isolation and paucity of unionization of rural laborers
18. Environmental disaster or transformation
19. Insufficient access to health care and basic medicines
20. Social and systemic biases against subordinated castes and ethnic groups

If these twenty forces are adequately tackled by a fully resourced and sustained campaign across all levels of government, civil society, and citizenry, I am confident that bonded labor will become an offense of the past.

Prioritizing the demand-side forces will help significantly to dismantle the system in the near term. The remainder of this chapter will focus on the logic of the ten initiatives I described in chapter 1. I believe that these ten initiatives will provide a comprehensive strategy with which to address these twenty forces.

TEN INITIATIVES TO ELIMINATE BONDED LABOR

The ten initiatives I outlined in chapter 1 must be undertaken for several years to have a significant impact on bonded labor in South Asia. The first four initiatives address the demand-side forces, and the remaining six address the supply side of the bonded labor system. The only real consideration in terms of sequencing is that the first initiative relates to legal reform, which must precede the direct intervention strategies of the remaining demand-side initiatives. The supply-side initiatives should be undertaken at the earliest time and for as long as possible. Some of the efforts I describe are already being pursued in various forms, but they are typically resource constrained or not designed or executed effectively. I will discuss the demand-side initiatives first, and most of the details in this chapter will relate to this category, as I believe that this is where the most aggressive work can be done to have a near-term effect on dismantling the system of bonded labor in South Asia.

I. Demand-Side Initiatives

The first initiative on the demand side involves enacting a set of legal reforms that will establish the optimal environment in which to deploy the remaining demand-side interventions, which are intended to reduce the profit and elevate the risk associated with bonded labor exploitation to a severely detrimental level.

1. Legal Reform

The first legal reform is to increase minimum wages across South Asia. Each country in South Asia should create a national minimum wage of at least $5.00 per eight-hour day ($0.63 per hour) for unskilled labor, rising from there for higher-skilled positions. At present, minimum wages are

either unstipulated or hover around $1.10 to $2.60 per day for most positions to which peasants have access. Even if fully paid, these wages are insufficient to meet basic subsistence needs, let alone allow for savings to cover
emergencies. Based on the income and expense sampling I have conducted
across South Asia, $5.00 is the minimum number that can allow for a se-
cure existence. Any argument that businesses such as brickmaking, carpet
weaving, or agricultural production cannot afford these wages are soundly
rejected by the conservatively estimated profit-and-loss tables found in appendix B. Every single business described in this book can afford to pay
these minimum wages and still generate ample net profits. They may not
show 50 percent or higher net profits, but they will still be viable, healthy
businesses. Finally, the minimum wages should be increased by a consumer
price index (CPI) or similar rate every five years, particularly given the
high inflation rates in most South Asian countries.

The second legal reform is to expand the scope of vicarious liability laws
across South Asia to include in the strictest sense the relationship between
employers and labor subcontractors (*jamadars*).[2] This can be done through
case law precedent or, more efficaciously, by passing a law. If a labor sub-
contractor violates labor laws in any way, the commercial entity that hired
him must be jointly and severally liable to the violation. So long as commercial entities are able to claim ignorance of and immunity from a *jamadar*'s violations, the entire system is set up to promote corruption and exploitation. This is not to say that the principle of vicarious liability should
include all categories of independent contractors, but as far as South Asia
and bonded labor are concerned, it should include the employer-*jamadar*
relationship. Any expansion of the principle of vicarious liability to include
the employer-*jamadar* relationship must be rigorously enforced through
severe economic penalties.

The third legal reform is to provide reasonable and equitable opportunity for land ownership for the poor. Landlessness is a key driver of vulnerability to debt bondage, and fear of eviction for landless tenants ensnares
countless millions in years of slavelike exploitation. Across decades, there
has been a dizzying array of attempts to redistribute land ownership to the
poor and marginalized of South Asia, as well as to protect landless tenants
from eviction, fix tenancy rates, formalize land records to protect peasants,
and extend land ownership to females. Despite this and other activity, security of land ownership remains a myth for most peasants, rendering
them highly vulnerable to exploitation. Land policies tend to favor large

landholders and corporate interests rather than poor agricultural laborers and peasants. The issues are complex, but intransigence and corruption are the primary barriers to fair opportunities for the poor to have secure land ownership. The Government of India itself concedes:

> In an economy where over 60 per cent of the population is dependent on agriculture, the structure of land ownership is central to the well-being of the people. The government has strived to change the ownership pattern of cultivable land, but has had limited success . . . the lack of progress of the land reforms programme, viz., implementation of land ceiling laws, security of tenure to tenants and consolidation of land holdings, remains a matter of serious concern.[3]

Until these issues are tackled through aggressive and enforced legal reform, landless peasants will continue to be exploited by landowners, as they have been for centuries.

The fourth legal reform is perhaps the most crucial in the near term: to increase significantly the economic penalties associated with the crime of bonded labor. This reform and the demand-side interventions described in the next initiative are the cornerstones of the optimal near-term attack on bonded labor and all other forms of slavery in South Asia. Together, these tactics are intended to eradicate the profits and increase the risks associated with the system of bonded labor. I believe these tactics can also be used as models for an optimal attack on any other form of slavery, anywhere in the world. Determining the precise level to which the crime of bonded labor should be penalized can be done in three steps.

The first step is to understand the *real* economic penalty currently associated with bonded labor. The second is to assess the total economic profits currently associated with bonded labor. The third is to determine the level at which the real economic penalty should be set in order to diminish severely if not eliminate the economic profits associated with bonded labor.

STEP 1

A simple formula for calculating the real economic penalty would be:

Real economic penalty = probability of being prosecuted × probability of being convicted × maximum financial penalty in the law.

Simple formulas for the probabilities of being prosecuted and convicted would be:

Probability of being prosecuted = number of prosecuted criminal acts in a year/number of criminal acts in a year.

Probability of being convicted = number of convictions in a year / number of prosecutions in a year.[4]

Taking India as an example, we know that the current penalty under the 1976 act for the offense of bonded labor is Rs. 20,000 ($445). The real penalty would entail multiplying this number by the probabilities of prosecution and conviction. I calculated the average probability of being prosecuted for the offence of bonded labor in India from the years 2000 through 2010 as being less than 0.01 percent and the probability of being convicted once prosecuted as being 4.96 percent. Multiplying these numbers results in a real economic penalty that is essentially $0. The same value is likely to be achieved when calculations are performed for other countries in South Asia. This $0 real economic penalty is what is indicated by the phrase "no real risk" in our essential thesis. In essence, the current real economic penalty for the crime of bonded labor is meaningless, and thus it produces absolutely no incentive for offenders to obey the law. As Chief Justice Bhagwati so aptly explained:

> Magistrates and Judges in the country must view violations of labour laws with strictness and whenever any violations of labour laws are established before them, they should punish the errant employers by imposing adequate punishment. . . . If violations of labour laws are to be punished with meagre fines, it would be impossible to ensure observance of the labour laws and the labour laws would be reduced to nullity. They would remain merely paper tigers without any teeth or claws.[5]

STEP 2

The tables in appendix B provide an initial sense of the profits associated with the exploitation of bonded laborers across South Asia. These values range from approximately $300 per bonded laborer per year in certain parts of the agricultural sector to $1,990 per bonded laborer per year in the brickmaking industry. However, bonded laborers are not exploited for just one year. As table 1.2 (in chapter 1) shows, the weighted average duration of exploitation of a bonded laborer in South Asia is 6.3 years. Some individuals may be exploited for a few months each season and others may be held in bondage for decades, but 6.3 years is the calculated weighted average of all the cases I documented. To calculate the total economic profits associated with the crime of bonded labor, we can use a concept that I introduced in my first book, *Sex Trafficking*, and further detailed in a subsequent law article in the *Northwestern Journal of International Human Rights*, "Designing More Effective Laws Against Human Trafficking."[6] This concept is called the "exploitation value" (EV) of a slave. This blunt economic term is not intended to lose sight of the severe human suffering bonded labor entails but rather simply to capture the total economic value of a bonded laborer to his exploiter across the weighted average duration of enslavement.

I have included the full explanation of EV calculations in table A.6 in the appendix, but table 8.1 contains a summary of certain key sectors in 2011 U.S. dollars. The numbers in table 8.1 are derived from highly conservative calculations of the total economic value of a bonded laborer to an exploiter in select industries, across the aggregate duration of bondage. In

TABLE 8.1
Exploitation Value of a Bonded Laborer in Key
Industries

Industry	Exploitation Value ($)
Brickmaking	4,911
Mining	3,425
Stonebreaking	3,310
Glass bangles	2,079
Carpet weaving	1,779
Bidi rolling	1,432
Kamaiya	848
South Asia weighted average	**2,585**
Global weighted average	**2,778**

other words, for each industry, this is the total economic value of a bonded laborer to the exploiter. Bonded laborers often work in several industries over the course of their bondage, so a blended average of these numbers would capture their total exploitation value to the exploiter in these cases. To decrease the exploitation value of a bonded laborer, an upward shock to the economic costs of operating the business must be created, and this can only be done by elevating the real economic penalty of committing the crime to a profit-compromising level. The level to which this penalty should be increased is discussed in step 3.

STEP 3

To elevate the economic costs of exploiting bonded laborers to a profit-compromising level is a matter of maximizing the formula discussed in step 1: real economic penalty = probability of being prosecuted × probability of being convicted × maximum financial penalty in the law. At present, that value is close to $0 across South Asia, whereas the weighted average EV of a bonded laborer across all industries in South Asia is $2,585 ($2,778 globally). Some industries have greater profits than others, but as many slaveowners exploit bonded laborers in numerous sectors, it is reasonable to attempt to elevate the real penalty of the crime to at least the weighted average across all industries. While the precise level of economic penalty stipulated in the law is open to debate, the concept is clear: the greater the real economic penalty of bonded labor, the lower the profitability, desirability, and viability of the crime.

One benchmark for more economically meaningful penalties could be drug laws. In India, the Narcotic Drugs and Psychotropic Substances Act, 1985, stipulates a penalty for trafficking in controlled substances of ten to twenty years in prison and a fine of up to Rs. 200,000 ($4,445). This financial penalty is ten times more severe than the current fine for bonded labor. Given the moral repugnance of the crime of bonded labor, as well as its substantial economic benefits, one could argue that the economic penalty for enslaving another human being should be several times greater than that of trafficking in hashish. Having said this, simply substituting Rs. 400,000 or Rs. 600,000 for Rs. 20,000 as the penalty for bonded labor would still result in a real penalty that is virtually nil, because of the minimal levels of prosecution and conviction of the crime. Hence, in addition to elevating the economic penalty, the probabilities of prosecution and conviction must be increased. The optimal means of accomplishing this goal will be discussed in initiative 2, below.

Assume for the sake of argument that the penalty in the law for each offense of bonded labor was Rs. 500,000 ($11,111), that the prosecution probability of the crime of bonded labor was 33 percent (one in three criminal acts are prosecuted in a given year), and that the probability of conviction was 67 percent (two in three prosecutions result in a conviction or settlement). Then the real economic penalty would be $11,111 × 33% × 67% = $2,457. This not far from the weighted average EV of a bonded laborer in South Asia, and it is a far more profit-compromising number than a real penalty of $0. Most important, a value like this would make bonded labor a nearly profitless crime, if not unprofitable, particularly if the offender is brought to justice and convicted well in advance of the expected average duration of exploitation of 6.3 years. Also, ensuring that a company's executives and directors are equally liable for bonded labor offenses—as is already mandated under §23 of India's Bonded Labour System (Abolition) Act, 1976—and can be penalized at a level even more substantial than the hypothetical $11,111 per infraction would further deter any commercial entities from allowing labor exploitation to occur. Add to this expanded vicarious liability laws that include *jamadars*, and the economic logic of the entire system of bonded labor will begin to crumble. With the above legal and regulatory reforms in place, the environment would be optimal to ensure that the system of bonded labor would no longer be a risk worth taking for any slave exploiter or commercial entity in South Asia.

Setting aside theoretical arguments, the point of this exercise is to show the importance of creating a legal and law enforcement regime that massively elevates the deterrent and retributive value of the real economic penalty of bonded labor. Criminals, like all people, are rational economic agents, and where a high-profit, low-risk business opportunity presents itself, they will pursue it and fight to maintain it until that reality is forcibly and irrevocably altered. Whatever the paper penalty stipulated in the law may be, and whatever the prosecution and conviction probabilities that are ultimately achieved, the outcome must transform the reality of bonded labor into a highly toxic, costly, and risky business venture. Amending laws is one thing, but achieving enormously elevated prosecution and conviction levels is quite another. The second initiative in the demand-side attack on the system on bonded labor is intended to achieve these increased probabilities.

2. *Transnational Slavery Intervention Force*

The second initiative is designed to increase substantially the probabilities that the criminals who exploit bonded laborers will be prosecuted and convicted of their crimes. It is also intended to reduce the average duration of enslavement of bonded laborers, which, when coupled with elevated economic penalties and higher probabilities of being prosecuted and convicted, will greatly reduce the overall profitability and increase the risk and cost of the business of bonded labor. In doing so, these initiatives will hopefully invert the demand-side forces of the crime, rendering it untenable.

The second initiative involves the creation of an elite, fully trained, and fully resourced transnational slavery intervention force in South Asia. The intervention force would comprise personnel from all willing and able South Asian nations, with (preferably) international jurisdiction. It would serve under the direction of an executive committee consisting of bonded labor experts from the Human Rights Commissions of all contributing nations and select NGOs. Among other initiatives, the force would be tasked with the following:

- To investigate any and all areas where there is a suspicion of bonded, child, or forced labor
- To identify, free, and register all victims and liaise with rapid-response rehabilitation teams to assist them
- To track down and detain exploiters and gather evidence required to prosecute and convict them in fast-track courts
- To trace ill-gotten funds and freeze them for potential economic penalties
- To conduct random minimum wage and labor-condition inspections throughout the informal and low-wage sectors of the economy, as well as inspect large-scale projects (such as the Commonwealth Games or other major infrastructure and construction projects)
- To monitor and inspect the activities of *jamadars* to ensure compliance with all labor laws
- To replace the current self-identification system of bonded laborer reporting to local *patwaris* with mobile teams that can receive and investigate bonded labor complaints anonymously and rapidly
- To provide, or arrange to provide, protection for freed bonded laborers during a trial against their exploiters

These are some of the activities that a transnational intervention force can undertake to mitigate the powerful demand-side forces that promote bonded labor. The intervention force will help ensure that minimum wages are paid without deductions, that bonded laborers are freed at far greater levels than they are today, and that bonded laborers will be able to identify themselves safely rather than submit to endless exploitation. The force will also help ensure that offenders are detained, that investigations are thorough, that all available evidence is gathered so as to maximize the potential for successful prosecutions, and that the key witness-victim is protected for the duration of the trial. A dedicated mission of unrelenting, broad-scale, and aggressive intervention can help bring the system of bonded labor to its knees, leaving little space for apathy or corruption. With large numbers of bonded laborers freed each year, with evidence gathered and criminals prosecuted and convicted in a timely fashion, and with those convictions resulting in severe economic penalties that negate any potential benefit of the crime, the entire system of impunity-based, slavelike exploitation of the poor and vulnerable masses of South Asia will begin to crumble. Of course, any initiative such as this is vulnerable to inefficiency or corruption, but blending international forces under the watchful eyes of a transnational executive committee, as well as the world, will leave much less space for corruption or failure. Those who doubt the efficacy of any sort of intervention force at reliably investigating, documenting, and freeing bonded and child laborers across the rural reaches of South Asia need only be reminded of the following: if someone like me is able to track down thousands of bonded laborers and actually document more than five hundred cases in comprehensive detail, then surely an elite and fully resourced intervention force can bring an end to these abhorrent crimes. To aid their efficacy, the intervention force can sequence its efforts at strategic points of intervention in the supply chains of industries tainted by bonded labor.

Appendix C includes diagrams of four industry supply chains in which bonded labor occurs in South Asia. Though there are numerous sectors in which bonded laborers are exploited, the supply chains for these sectors primarily fall into two categories:

1. Fixed point of production
2. Fragmented point of production/cottage industry

Industries that are typified by category 1 include bricks, agriculture, construction (for the duration of the project), stonebreaking, mining, and aquaculture. Industries that are typified by category 2 include bidi rolling, glass bangles, gem cutting and polishing, domestic servitude, and carpet weaving.[7]

I have provided two examples of each category in appendix C. Understanding the structure and functioning of these supply chains is vital in order to identify strategic points of intervention for the transnational slavery intervention force to prioritize. To optimize this force's efficacy in the near term, I recommend that it commence by targeting the points of production in the first category of supply chains. Within this category, brick kilns should be targeted first (see figure C.1, in the appendix), as this is the most cash-profitable sector in which bonded laborers are exploited. More important, two of the three steps in the supply chain are actually found in a single, fixed place and time on a regular basis: the brick kilns. Bonded and child laborers toil at highly visible and easily accessible brick kilns day and night to mold and bake bricks, and distributors also use bonded and child laborers to transport the bricks from the kilns into trucks for transport to construction areas. Targeting the kilns when bricks are being transported to trucks by wholesalers/distributors can maximize the immediate effect on bonded and child labor exploitation by the thousands.

Construction sites and stone quarries are also highly fixed, visible, and easily inspected by an intervention force, and they also tend to generate substantial profits. Targeting these sectors can be a priority, after bricks. Agriculture and aquaculture round out the primary sectors that tend to involve highly fixed and immovable points of production, but agriculture in particular tends to be the least cash-profitable sector in which bonded laborers are exploited, whereas brickmaking is the most cash profitable. Further, many brickmaking bonded laborers are involved in other sectors during the off-season, such as agriculture or carpet weaving, so intervening at brick kilns will have a cascading effect on other sectors. Nevertheless, sectors like agriculture and aquaculture must also be targeted, and when they are, each point in the supply chain will demand intervention. For example, with shrimp aquaculture (see figure C.2, in the appendix) the fixed locations in which baby shrimp are caught can easily be investigated, along with the shrimp farms and processing facilities. All of the steps in the supply chain are fixed and easily identifiable. Ensuring that child, bonded, or forced labor are not present in any of these steps in the supply chain is the only way to cleanse all of the products that are purchased by consumers. Bearing in mind that a majority of the individuals who may be involved in child or bonded labor at these sites may be doing so under a devil's bargain of servitude or starvation, any demand-side intervention must run concurrent with robust and sustained efforts to transition these individuals to self-sustaining freedom, as provided for in several of the initiatives described below.

Other activities the intervention force can engage in include working with certification agencies to provide certification that the products exiting the supply chains are not tainted by any form of labor exploitation, from outright slavery to deficient wages to child labor. The contribution of an independent and/or transnational intervention force in any mass certification venture is vital in order to obviate the issues of corruption that would otherwise develop, such as bribes to local inspectors or even black-market "certifications" (such as a stamp or label) being used to defeat the system.

After first targeting those industries with fixed points of production, the intervention force can expand its efforts to the second category, those industries with more fragmented points of production. With sectors like carpets (see figure C.3 in the appendix) and bidis (see figure C.4 in the appendix), tens of thousands of village huts across South Asia serve as the venues in which the exploitation occurs. Working with local NGOs will allow the intervention force to focus its efforts on villages where the exploitation is taking place. This will be a more labor-intensive campaign, but with sufficient resources and commitment, labor exploitation of all kinds can be eliminated from even the most remote villages in South Asia.

There are numerous other advantages to analyzing the supply chains of bonded labor industries in detail, but the most crucial one is to provide guidance and prioritization for the intervention of law enforcement and even everyday activism in the sphere of bonded and child labor. Documenting and quantifying the contribution of the tainted goods to the overall market for each product also allows for more effective arguments to corporations, governments, and consumers with regard to the level of resources and aggressiveness required to stamp out the exploitation.

By focusing on direct and aggressive intervention in supply chains, liberation of slaves and investigation of criminals, ensuring adherence to labor laws, providing safe space for self-identification of bonded laborers, and other activities that directly dismantle the economic functioning of the system of bonded labor, this kind of targeted and sustained intervention will help invert the perception that bonded labor is a robust system of impunity and profitability. The final two demand-side initiatives will round out the efforts to help achieve this goal.

3. Fast-Track Courts

In chapter 7, I discussed how the judicial process is deeply insufficient at adjudicating cases involving claims for bonded labor violations in a fair and timely fashion. Court cases across South Asia drag on for years with endless backlogs and severe inefficiencies. The majority of bonded labor cases are dismissed after a superficial investigation, and apathy and corruption appear to taint much of the system. Caught in the mire are the bonded and child laborers of South Asia. There will never be a fair and timely adjudication of cases nor any semblance of real penalty for the crime of bonded labor until this broken judicial process is repaired.

Comprehensive reform of the judiciary in South Asia in the near future is unlikely. In the near term, fast-track courts should be established across South Asia that focus solely on bonded, forced, and child labor cases. Rigorous standards for investigation should be established. It is not good enough for the local district magistrate—often times the ally of the local landowner/exploiter—to say that he conducted an investigation and could not find any bonded laborers. Independent observers should be a part of every proceeding, and judicial review should be conducted to minimize corruption. These courts should be designed to perform with the seriousness, thoroughness, and swiftness with which the Supreme Court of India handled the PUDR, 1982; and BMM, 1983, cases. Finally, alternate dispute resolution (ADR) committees can be formed to work in rural areas to adjudicate swiftly any other minor labor complaints.

4. Redesign or Abolition of the Jamadar System

As we have seen throughout this book, *jamadars* are at the heart of the recruitment, bondage, and exploitation of innumerable men, women, and children across South Asia. There are two options to address this problem. The first is to redesign the system to achieve maximum oversight and regulation. For example, all *jamadars* could be registered and their activities regulated by an independent law enforcement or judicial entity. *Jamadars* would then be trained in best practices and receive a renewable license upon signing a code of conduct that upholds all standards of the law. Aggressive and comprehensive oversight and random auditing of their activities would help minimize exploitation, including the monitoring and tracing of all monies allocated to *jamadars* pursuant to any commercial project in any sector. Going one step further, *jamadars* could also be reclassified as employees (there is sound legal reasoning for doing so), which would help tighten the noose on vicarious liability.

To the extent these and other regulations prove too challenging, the second option is to discard the system all together. The Supreme Court of Pakistan did just that in the Darshan, 1990, case, though virtually nothing has been done since then to enforce this pronouncement. Assuming the *jamadar* system is completely and forever abolished, commercial projects would be staffed by employees of the producers, and all labor that is recruited would similarly be managed by employees of the producers. Executives would agree to taking full fiduciary responsibility for the contracted workers, including the invocation of those clauses in the relevant bonded labor abolition acts (§23 in India's 1976 act) that render corporate executives, directors, and managers who are responsible for the actions of a company criminally liable for breach of the legislation. Elevated penalties will help deter apathy and ensure compliance. This same clause could also be invoked in the first option for a redesign of the *jamadar* system, so long as the scope of vicarious liability laws are expanded to include *jamadars*. There may be other ways of eliminating the abuses inherent to the *jamadar* system as it is currently practiced in South Asia, but I believe one of these two options will prove most effective.

II. Supply-Side Initiatives

The demand-side initiatives discussed above represent the optimal opportunity to make a significant near-term dent in, if not to virtually eliminate, the system of bonded labor in South Asia. By inverting the essential logic of the industry—substantial profits at no real risk—the system will hopefully become too risky, costly, and unviable for any slave exploiter. However, the second half of the essential thesis for bonded labor is also important: the immense and ever-present supply of systemically impoverished and vulnerable people. While I do not think these forces are as amenable to disruption in the near term as the demand-side forces, they must also be addressed if the system is to be truly and completely eradicated, if not to ensure the overall decency, sustainability, and security of all societies in South Asia.

The supply-side initiatives that follow are focused on mitigating those forces that promote the supply of potential bonded laborers. These forces are among the most complex and pervasive in South Asia, spanning poverty to infrastructure to environmental disaster. They are also responsible for a host of other crimes and human rights violations. These initiatives will be discussed in general terms, in the hopes that doing so will catalyze further discussion and creativity around accomplishing these goals.

5. Elevated Scaling and Effectiveness of Select Government Antipoverty Programs

This is the most complex, resource intensive, and ultimately important of the supply-side initiatives I am proposing. Extreme poverty, a lack of sufficient credit resources and alternative income opportunities, and inadequate infrastructure and means to access markets are among the most powerful forces that render individuals in South Asia vulnerable to bonded labor and other forms of exploitation. A comprehensive and fully resourced antipoverty initiative that targets these forces will go a long way toward attenuating in the long term some of the most fundamental vulnerabilities faced by the poor across South Asia. Many of these issues are already a focus of government initiatives, but corruption, a lack of funding, inadequate execution, overcentralization, mismanagement, and numerous other barriers render these programs largely ineffective.

The government of India, for example, has comprehensive antipoverty initiatives, which have been a part of almost every one of the country's five-year plans since independence. These schemes are divided into five categories: (1) self-employment, (2) wage employment, (3) food security, (4) social security, and (5) urban poverty alleviation.[8] Were these programs adequately resourced and effectively delivered, poverty levels in India would be significantly decreased. Unfortunately, barely half of the allocated resources actually reaches the poor; the rest is consumed by graft, inefficiency, and corruption. Some of what I discuss below is already encapsulated by current government programs in South Asia, but a focus on three specific components to poverty alleviation, with adequate funding and execution, will be most effective at mitigating the key supply-side forces that render people vulnerable to bonded labor and other forms of exploitation. A minimum rate of 90 percent of allocated resources reaching their targets must be achieved.

MICROCREDIT EXPANSION

It is no mystery that the absence of reliable and sufficient credit sources pushes many peasants in South Asia to take loans from *jamadars* or local landowners/producers, which often results in varying degrees of bondage. Microcredit was born in South Asia through the genius of the Nobel Peace Prize winner Mohammed Yunus of Bangladesh. In 1976 he founded the Grameen Bank[9] ("Village Bank"), which focuses on providing small loans to the poor (mostly women) for small business ventures. The added elements of promoting savings and self-help groups, business training, and a low cost of borrowing have assisted millions in climbing out of poverty. Microcredit has expanded to dozens of countries around the world and has become a dominant model for poverty alleviation. Having said this, microcredit is still limited by access to capital and the need to be a self-sustaining business. This means that loans have to "perform," which in turn requires that a high percentage of the loans must go toward income-generating activities (IGAs), so that they can be repaid to the microcredit lender, who can then repay its own lender and also fund operations. Unfortunately, the credit needs of the poorest of the poor are often not income generating. Those needs may be for basic consumption, medicine, or life rituals. In fact, table 1.3 from chapter 1 shows that from the data I have gathered, upward of 80 percent of the credit needs of the bonded laborers I documented were not related to income-generating opportunities. Microcredit or other alternative credit sources must be designed so that they can meet the spectrum of credit needs of the poorest of the poor, especially for non-IGAs. In addition, far more capital must be made available to microcredit lenders so that they can expand their reach to as many of the poor as possible, while also blending their lending portfolios to increase the ratio of lending that does not have to go toward IGAs.[10] Many of the bonded laborers I met did not have any idea what microcredit was nor that this kind of credit might be available to them. Others knew of microcredit and even were aware of possible credit sources in their areas but were prevented from accessing them by landowners, moneylenders, *jamadars*, or producers under threat of violence or eviction. Expanding and redesigning microcredit in the ways described will take time and trial and error, but doing so would go a long way toward addressing the inadequate credit availability for the poor in South Asia.

GLOBAL ECONOMY INTEGRATION

The poor in South Asia (and all over the world) must be integrated more completely, directly, and equitably into the global economy. Saying this is a mouthful, but the further we can go in this direction, the better for the overall income reliability and human development of rural and impoverished people everywhere. There are immense global economic forces and trade barriers that disenfranchise the poor in developing nations from participating fully and equitably in the global economy. Initiatives based on tying the products of rural labor directly to Western consumers represent a prime opportunity to integrate the poor into global markets while providing them with myriad and sustained sources of income. There are dozens of NGOs and even small enterprises that are focused on everything from Fair Trade initiatives to investing in the production and distribution of rural products straight to Western (or nearby urban) markets. These types of efforts must be expanded through elevated funding by governments and foundations. Governments should also create and expand initiatives designed to integrate the poor into markets, without exploitative intermediaries. For example, the government of India could work directly (or contract with NGOs to work directly) with bidi rollers in West Bengal at distributing their products directly to bidi distributors, while returning a fair level of profit participation back to the bidi rollers (most easily through the elevation and full payment of minimum wages). Exploitative *jamadars* could be completely disintermediated, helping to contribute to the abolition or comprehensive redesign of the *jamadar* system discussed in initiative 4. The same could be done for hand-woven carpets, cut gems, and many other products. Government initiatives could also focus on providing subsidized transit to markets for the rural poor (once infrastructure is expanded). These may not be completely free-market ways of doing things, but for a period of time this type of government involvement may help make markets more accessible and equitable for low-end workers in the long term.

EXPANSION OF RURAL INFRASTRUCTURE AND MANUFACTURING

All governments in South Asia already invest in rural infrastructure, but they do not invest enough. Roads, electricity grids, bridges, irrigation, transit, housing, and sanitation are but a few of the sectors that can enhance rural well-being and all-important access to markets. Local labor should be used for all such projects. The labor should be contracted and managed directly by a partnership between the government or contracting construction company and NGOs focused on rural development, not by *jamadars*. South Asian bureaucrats can be just as corrupt as local *jamadars*, so partnership with a local NGO can help assure corruption is at a minimum and work standards are maintained. There is also a precedent in Indian case law that could be used to hold the government vicariously liable for violations of essential laws and basic human rights committed by government officials involved in these projects.[11] The slavery intervention force described in initiative 2 can also be tasked with helping to maintain labor standards and assuring that the projects achieve maximum employment and benefit for the rural poor. In the same vein, governments can also invest in the expansion of manufacturing, which represents a disproportionately lower portion of GDP in South Asia than in comparable countries in East Asia or other regions in the world. Special economic zones can be created in rural areas and tax incentives provided to the private sector for training and factory employment for residents in the designated zones, starting with low-technology production and expanding from there. Tens of millions of sustainable jobs could eventually be created, dissipating the pool of impoverished and vulnerable South Asians substantially.

These are ambitious and complex initiatives that will take time. Even if achieved, these initiatives alone would not be adequate at eliminating poverty across South Asia. However, these are the kinds of supply-side programs that will be most effective at providing alternative sources of credit and sufficient income to the poor while also enhancing rural employment and access to markets. The more successful and expansive these efforts are, the smaller the available supply of potential bonded laborers will be. Adequate provision of resources and effective execution must be the priorities; otherwise, the pattern of corruption and ineffectiveness in government antipoverty initiatives will continue to cripple such efforts.

Finally, and perhaps most important—as discussed at the end of chapter 1, NGOs and philanthropic foundations can (and must) undertake their own efforts to accomplish these same goals on smaller scales in select areas. Such efforts can often be the starting point to tremendous change. Once successful, these modest efforts can be scaled through collaboration with government resources.

6. Expanded and Free Rural Education Programs

Illiteracy and a lack of education directly promote the exploitation of bonded laborers and limit their access to income-generating opportunities. The governments of South Asia and numerous NGOs provide varying degrees of free or subsidized education programs, especially for rural children who may be caught in bondage and unable to attend school. In India, for example, the Right to Education Bill, 2009, requires that states ensure all children ages six to fourteen attend school full time and includes the provision of education services for migrant children who travel with parents to work sites. Unfortunately, implementation has been severely lacking. During my research in 2010, I did not see one single provision by the state of Haryana for child education services at more than twenty construction sites where migrant/trafficked parents—and their children—were working day and night to complete the preparations for the Commonwealth Games. These types of education programs must be executed effectively, especially in migrant or rural areas. (There have been numerous occasions when I visited a government-funded rural school in South Asia where the teacher had not shown up for days and books and supplies were nonexistent.) A particular focus of the rural education programs should be on developing economic literacy, small business skills, and training on how to use infrastructure and transit to access markets.

7. Rapid-Response Registration and Rehabilitation Teams

The entire process of identifying, registering, and rehabilitating bonded laborers under the respective bonded labor system abolition laws of South Asia should be handed over to privately managed rapid-response teams focused on conducting this work effectively and efficiently. At present, virtually no activity is undertaken by district magistrates or vigilance committees to identify bonded laborers. Once identified, months may pass before they are registered. Once registered, months or years may pass before they are provided with rehabilitation assistance under the law. By that time, the individuals have moved on to some other exploitative condition. Fully funded teams tasked with doing nothing other than roaming rural areas and fulfilling the mandates of identification, registration, and rehabilitation of bonded laborers would provide far more effective results. These teams would also work directly with the intervention force during raids on slave establishments to ensure that all liberated individuals are immediately and effectively transitioned to freedom. The design of the rehabilitation packages and the level and duration of support must also be expanded beyond current mandates in the law. More cash support is required up front, ongoing educational and vocational training is a must, and the development of relevant skills that can lead to sustained income opportunities should be a focus of all rehabilitation efforts.

8. Rural Integration and Information Dissemination Efforts

Exploiters of bonded labor thrive by isolating the individuals they exploit, limiting their horizon of social networks and opportunities, and preventing any sort of organized unionization or bargaining. Networks of communication and integration of villages across rural areas will help dismantle these forces. The mass distribution of solar-charged mobile phones will enhance communication and information sharing between villagers, and it will also open channels of information and opportunity dissemination by NGOs, the government, and the private sector to rural peasants. These individuals can also reach out to law enforcement (or the slavery intervention force) through the establishment of SMS hotlines. With the right guidance, they can share information, form commercial networks, and mobilize unions and collective-bargaining programs. Migrants can form ties to local support in destination areas, rendering them less likely to be exploited. The mobile phones can be distributed by the government or handset manufacturers, with an initial period of free SMS usage. Data rates in South Asia are extremely low, and they can be further subsidized for low-income users. It is impossible to enumerate the plethora of ways in which enhanced mobile communication and rural integration can help stem the forces of isolation and limited opportunity that consign so many rural poor in South Asia to exploitation an bondage.

9. Rapid-Response Environmental Teams

From the monsoon floods of 2010 to Hurricane Aila the year before, we saw how environmental disaster directly led to increased levels of bonded labor, child labor, and human trafficking across South Asia. When those who have almost nothing lose what little they have and are utterly displaced and unable to survive, *jamadars*, exploiters, and traffickers swoop in with offers. The exploitation that follows ensnares millions after every major disaster. Rapid-response teams that descend on disaster zones immediately with a focus on alleviating economic and medical needs will provide crucial relief to vulnerable people. When not responding to large-scale disasters, the teams can also be tasked with the provision of basic healthcare and medicines in rural areas—something expanded mobile communication can also help with. The more resourced, comprehensive, and sustained these efforts are, the more effective they will be.

10. National Awareness and Educational Campaigns

This final initiative is vital in order to promote the long-term legitimacy and security of South Asian society. The initiative would involve national awareness campaigns for the general public, as well as educational programs for law enforcement, judiciary, and government officials, focused on promoting the equality of minority castes and ethnicities across South Asia and on raising awareness of the issues of bonded and child labor. I firmly believe that if a sufficient proportion of South Asian society felt that bonded labor and the exploitation of subordinated ethnic groups, castes, and children were repugnant anachronisms, these issues would no longer exist. All necessary initiatives, resources, and campaigns to eradicate these offenses would be catalyzed from within South Asian society. Sadly, a sizeable proportion of South Asian society and its governing structures remain generally apathetic toward issues such as bonded and child labor, and hence these offences continue to scar the face of the region.

Creative media personnel will no doubt devise the most effective ways to disseminate these messages, but a few key elements are necessary. First, the realities of the oppressive nature of bonded labor, as well as its extent across South Asia, must be conveyed accurately. Second, consumers must be made aware that they purchase products produced by bonded and child laborers every day. Third, the educational and sensitization efforts created for law enforcement, the judiciary, and government officials must be focused on disseminating accurate (not anecdotal) knowledge of how and why bonded labor works, along with the manner in which it harms the nation ethically, economically, and from a security standpoint. Fourth, the general sense among some South Asians that child labor and bonded labor are acceptable because the alternatives are worse must be dispelled. Of course it is true that given the conditions associated with most cases today, the alternatives (starvation, etc.) are indeed worse at that point in time, but that does not mean that bonded labor and child labor are acceptable. In fact, it is unacceptable that a society would allow any single citizen to be faced with a hopeless choice between starvation and slavery. This type of bleak bargain represents a catastrophic failure to produce any measure of sustainable and just society.

To be most effective, Bollywood and cricket stars can be recruited to support these initiatives. They could spearhead programs such as a "Bonded Labor Awareness Day" or "Child Labor Awareness Day." Their ability to sway public opinion will prove crucial to the overall efficacy of social awareness campaigns. Bollywood can also invest in a series of public relations messages or even short-form and long-form documentaries highlighting bonded labor and the need for caste and minority equality in South Asia. On the day that a critical mass of South Asians are catalyzed to reject the oppression of minority castes and the exploitation of bonded and child laborers, everything else that is necessary to abolish these offenses will follow.

The totality of these supply-side initiatives, undertaken to whatever degree possible, will alleviate many of the forces that promote bondage and other forms of labor exploitation across South Asia. The road to a sustainable and just society will be long, but prosperity and fairness for all people in the region will help end the centuries of pain and degradation of the most downtrodden sectors of society. Ensuring that all people are protected by law and enjoy full freedom and human dignity will result in a proud legacy for the generation that achieves these long-overdue imperatives. In the meantime, aggressively dismantling the fundamental economic logic of bonded labor through the demand-side initiatives discussed above will hopefully diminish, if not virtually eliminate, the entire system of human bondage in the near term and help bury once and for all this most ignoble of human evils.

A CHILD NAMED ANAND

I would like to end this book with the story of a remarkable child, named Anand. I met Anand at a shelter for boys in Bihar. He was a *dalit*, small for his age, and suffered from frequent throat and lung infections. He had a large scar along the left side of his head where his hair did not grow. Anand told me a story that was one of the most devastating I heard, but in the midst of all that he had suffered, his strength of spirit and innocent heart completely overwhelmed me. This is the story he shared:

My name is Anand. I am eleven years old. I was born in Nalanda district in Bihar. My elder brother died when I was young. My father and mother and my elder sister worked in brick molding. I was too young to help at that time, so I would play with the clay and make small statues of animals. My favorite was elephant. The *maliks* were very cruel. They would beat my father often. Sometimes they also beat my mother and sister. One day, they said my mother and sister must go away. My father pleaded that they must be allowed to stay. I did not understand what was happening. I ran to my mother and held her leg, but the *malik* kicked me, so I fell to the ground. My father shouted at the *malik*, but he hit my father with a cane on the head. He kept beating my father. I was crying "Papa! Papa!" but my father would not wake up.

After that day, the *malik* took me to the landowner's home, and I lived with the servants. I cried every night. I missed my mother and father so much. One servant named Vidhi was kind to me, and she comforted me. I asked her to help me find my parents. She said my father was with God. I asked her if my mother was also with God, but she did not know.

After some time, I ran from the landowner's home to find my family. It was easy to run away. I took some roti from where the servants eat, and I went to the main road. There were so many people on the road. I asked them if they had seen my mother. Her name is Anju. The servants found me that day and brought me back. They were very cross with me. The landowner was also cross, and he sent me to work at the brick kiln even though I was young. I did brick molding like my father. It was very difficult. If I did not work fast enough, the *maliks* would shout at me. One time, the same *malik* who beat my father hit me in the head here and I went unconscious. When I woke, I felt very sick. I was scared and I wanted to run away, but I was afraid I would be punished.

One night, I ran as far as I could. I did not have shoes, so my feet were bleeding. I came to a town and found some place to sleep in one alley. A man who owned one shop woke me. I told this man what happened to me. He gave me food. He bandaged my feet and gave me slippers.

This man took me to this home for boys. I have been here almost one year. I have been learning to read and write. I want to be a lawyer so I can protect the rights of children. Children must be protected from bad people.

I understand now what happened to my father. I pray my mother and sister are okay. I know I will see them again. I will be so happy to see my mother and show her how much I have learned. She will say, "I am so proud of you, my little raja."

Anand smiled as bright as the sunrise as he imagined his mother proudly commending her little king. The more time I spent with him, the more I was amazed at his inner glow and positive spirit. There was a sparkle in his eyes that was magnificent. After spending so many years encountering destitution, torment, and darkness across South Asia, when I met this precious little boy who remained innocent and untainted by the cruelty around him, I felt the first flicker of hope in years—there just might be the chance of a brighter future for the millions like him.

Later, Anand told me he still liked to make clay statues of animals. I asked him to show me his favorite. He gleefully brought me an elephant and a horse. "You take the horse; I will take the elephant," he said. I took the horse, and we played together for a time, riding to a faraway land that was filled with magic. We rode side by side—a weary traveler and a young king—to a place where his mother and father were waiting for him, where everyone was joyful and free, and where the future of an untouchable child like Anand was not crushed by prejudice and greed but was as boundless and pure as his God-given soul.

Appendix A

SLAVERY ESTIMATES

Tables A.1 and A.2 provide further details on my calculations of the number of slaves in the world and the number of bonded laborers in South Asia at the end of 2011, based on the definitions provided in chapter 1. In table A.1, I have divided slavery into three broad categories: bonded labor, trafficked slaves, and forced labor. Table A.2 provides a breakdown of the number of bonded laborers in South Asia by country. The data in the two tables are based on calculations of 95% confidence intervals (CI)[1] of the number of slaves in the world and the number of bonded laborers in South Asia at the end of the year 2011. The total number of slaves ranged from 28.4 to 32.6 million. The mean of the range suggests that there were 30.5 million slaves in the world at the end of 2011: 19.2 million bonded laborers, 3.0 million trafficked slaves, and 8.3 million forced laborers. Out of the 19.2 million bonded laborer/debt bondage slaves in the world, 16.5 million were in South Asia.

The definition of slavery I provided in chapter 1 is construed with the broader qualifications and interpretations of the terms "restricted liberty," "coerced," and "reasonable alternative"—such that the estimates above include seasonal, serial, and other forms of partial debt bondage in the bonded labor category; a slightly broader range of victims in the trafficking

TABLE A.1
Slavery Breakdown—End of Year 2011

	95% CI: Millions of Slaves	Mean: Millions of Slaves	Percentage of Total
Bonded Labor/Debt Bondage	17.9–20.5	19.2	63.0
Trafficked Slaves			
Sexual Exploitation	1.3–1.5	1.4	4.6
Other Forced Labor	1.5–1.7	1.6	5.2
Total Trafficked Slaves	2.8–3.2	3.0	9.8
Forced Labor	7.7–8.9	8.3	27.2
Total	**28.4–32.6**	**30.5**	**100.0**

TABLE A.2
Bonded Laborers in South Asia—End of Year 2011

	Total Pop. (millions)	95% CI: Millions of Bonded Laborers	Mean: Millions of Bonded Laborers	Percentage of Population	Percentage of Total Bonded Laborers in S. Asia
India	1,150	10.7–12.7	11.7	1.0	70.9
Pakistan	184	2.0–2.6	2.3	1.3	13.9
Bangladesh	156	1.6–1.8	1.7	1.1	10.3
Nepal	29	.37–.43	0.4	1.4	2.4
Sri Lanka and Afghanistan	46	.37–.43	0.4	0.9	2.4
Total	**1,565**	**15.0–18.0**	**16.5**	**1.1**	**100.0**

category; and forced military, and seasonal or other forms of partial forced labor in the forced labor category.

Construing these key terms such that the categories listed above are excluded provides the results shown on table A.3. The net number of bonded laborers in the world is reduced by 7.0 million (mean), the net number of forced laborers in the world is reduced by 0.8 million (mean), and the net number of trafficked slaves in the world is reduced by 0.3 million (mean). I believe the 30.5 million number is the more accurate estimate.

TABLE A.3
Slavery Breakdown (Restrictive)—End of Year 2011

	95% CI: Millions of Slaves	Mean: Millions of Slaves	Percentage of Total
Bonded Labor/Debt Bondage	11.3–13.1	12.2	54.5
Trafficked Slaves			
Sexual Exploitation	1.2–1.4	1.3	5.8
Other Forced Labor	1.3–1.5	1.4	6.2
Total Trafficked Slaves	2.5–2.9	2.7	12.0
Forced Labor	7.0–8.0	7.5	33.5
Total	**20.8–24.0**	**22.4**	**100.0**

In *Sex Trafficking*, I provided an estimate of 28.4 million slaves at the end of 2006 (18.1 million bonded laborers; 2.7 million trafficked slaves; 7.6 million forced labor slaves), which was the mean of my CI calculations for 2006. The data used to calculate all past and current estimates are based on three sources: (1) a broad level of direct capture-recapture $(CR)^2$ and random sampling observation and calculation that I began to conduct in 2004, (2) the aggregation of as much reliable second-hand data on regional or country-based slavery estimates as possible (weighted downwards because of its being second hand), and (3) a conservative model that utilizes various drivers and assumptions to calculate global slavery numbers by type based on an accruing data set that I have acquired. These numbers in turn provide individual samples that I feed into a CI calculation each year.

My updated calculations for the end of 2011 include revisions based on refined definitions, as well as organic, five-year compound annual growth rates (CAGR)[3] of 0.9% per year for bonded labor, 2.8% per year for trafficked sex slaves, 2.0% per year for other trafficked slaves, and 1.2% per year for forced labor. These growth rates from 2006 to 2011 were driven in large part by the exacerbation of certain supply-side drivers of vulnerability to slavery relating to the commodity bubble of 2007 and the subsequent global economic meltdown of 2008 through 2010. Several environmental disasters, from earthquakes to hurricanes to floods, also contributed to growth rates during this period. The most powerful factor, however, was related to the global economic upheavals spanning 2007 to 2010. The 2007 commodity bubble more than doubled the prices of basic food and fuel inputs for billions of the poorest people in the world (which was repeated during the summer of 2011), who could barely afford the prebubble prices. The subsequent global economic meltdown further exacerbated supply-side forces of slavery by evaporating markets for many goods and services provided by the poor, by causing cuts to social safety nets and poverty alleviation schemes, and by increasing migration levels across the developing world. It can be argued that diminishing disposable income of the consumers of slave-generated goods and services would reduce demand-side drivers of slavery, but I believe basic economic theory suggests the supply-side forces would be stronger and that even the demand-side forces could result in increased slavery levels. Where disposable incomes diminish, it does not necessarily reduce or eliminate demand for certain goods and services. It in fact may drive consumers toward the lower-priced version of the same good or service, which in many cases can only be provided by the retailer by virtue of reduced operating costs achieved through some level of labor exploitation. Retailer demand for low-wage or slave labor would also arguably increase during times of economic freefall. Where margins may be pressured because of diminishing consumption or aggressive price cutting as a means to boost consumption, the minimization of operating costs, especially labor, can be an effective way of preserving or minimizing the decrease in profits. Going forward, I would expect CAGRs for each category of slavery to be lower in the next five years than the previous five years, barring a double-dip global recession, another commodity bubble, or other significant global economic upheaval.

SLAVERY ECONOMICS

Tables A.4 and A.5 provide my updated calculations of global slavery profits for the end of year 2011 (based on the mean 30.5 million slaves estimate). Slave labor generated revenues of $164.7 billion in 2011, with total profits of $96.5 billion accruing to the exploiters of these slaves: $17.6 billion from bonded labor, $42.2 billion from trafficked slaves (of which $38.3 billion is from trafficked sex slaves), and $36.7 billion from forced labor.[4] Worldwide, the average slave generated $3,165 in net profits for his exploiter during 2011, at an average net profit margin of 59%. Bonded laborers are the least profitable, at $920 per year per slave, and trafficked sex slaves are by far the most profitable, at $28,357 per year per slave. The aggregate

TABLE A.4
Summary of Global Slavery Profits—End of Year 2011

	Weighted Average Annual Revenues per Slave ($)[1]	Implied Annual Revenues from Slave Labor ($B)[2]	Weighted Average Net Profit Margin (%)[3]	Weighted Average Annual Profits per Slave ($)	Implied Annual Profits from Slave Labor ($B)	Percentage of Total
Bonded Labor/Debt Bondage	1,840	35.2	50.0	920	17.6	18.3
Trafficked Slaves						
Sexual Exploitation	42,010	56.7	67.5	28,357	38.3	39.6
Other Forced Labor	4,820	7.5	52.5	2,530	3.9	4.1
Total Trafficked Slaves		64.2			42.2	43.7
Forced Labor[4]	7,910	65.3	56.3	4,451	36.7	38.0
Total		164.7			96.5	100.0

per slave 5,399   per slave 3,165

Global Slavery
Net Profit Margin (%): 59

Dollar values in 2011 U.S. dollars.

[1] 2011 U.S. dollar valuation based on relevant CPI adjustment from the dates of slave's exploitation(s).

[2] Based on average of starting and ending number of slaves during 2011.

[3] For bonded labor, some forms of forced labor, and where the sale of commercial sex is legal, this is a pretax profit margin, though it includes an assumption of bribes paid to avoid full tax rates; ill-gotten profits in these cases are also often kept "off the books" to minimize tax payments.

[4] Includes forced commercial sex work of individuals not trafficked.

average slavery profit numbers are weighted downward because of the large number of bonded laborers, who represent approximately six out of ten slaves in the world.

Table A.5 summarizes the key metrics I have calculated relating to global slavery economics, the most important of which are the exploitation value (EV) and the return on investment (ROI) calculations. The first column of this table is carried over from table A.1, and the second column is carried over from table A.4. The weighted average acquisition costs for each category of slavery are based on data from the greater than one thousand case studies I have gathered on slaves of all kinds around the world. The acquisition costs range from $230 for bonded laborer/debt bondage slaves to $1,910 for trafficked sex slaves. *The weighted average acquisition price of today's 30.5 million slaves is $440. This compares to a global weighted average acquisition price of approximately $4,900 to $5,500 in 2011 dollars for a slave roughly two hundred years ago in 1810.* This value was calculated through a sampling of acquisition prices of slaves around the world in 1810, which on average ranged from approximately $7,000 to $10,500 (depending on age, gender, health, time of year, geography, skill, and other factors) in 2011 dollars[5] for African slaves in or trafficked to/within the Americas, to $900 to $3,500 in 2011 dollars for slaves in or trafficked to/within South Asia, Africa, East Asia, and the Middle East (prices determined by similar factors as in the Americas). In addition to these average ranges for the prices of slaves sold in 1810, it is important to note that some slaves were sold for much less—in some cases for less than the price of a cup of tea—and others were born into slavery, which renders their acquisition costs close to nil.[6] Even though the weighted average cost of a slave has decreased substantially across time, there are slaves purchased today for several thousand dollars, and there were slaves purchased two hundred years ago for a few dollars. The ban on European slave trading from Africa to the Americas is one of many reasons for a sharp increase (up to 100%) in the market value of a slave in the Americas between 1810 and 1860. Prices in Africa, the Middle East, and Asia did not increase nearly as sharply, primarily because slave trading continued within and to/from many of these regions through the 1800s and into the early 1900s (especially in Asia). *A price sampling from 1860 results in a global weighted average acquisition price of approximately $9,000 to $9,900 in 2011 dollars.*[7] Weighted average slave prices largely decreased around the world shortly after this time through to the present day. It must be stressed again that

TABLE A.5
Slavery Economics Summary—End of Year 2011

Type	Millions of Slaves	Weighted Average Annual Profits per Slave ($)	Weighted Average Acquisition Cost per Slave ($)[1]	Weighted Average Exploitation Value ($)	Implied Total ROI (%)	Implied Annualized ROI (%)
Bonded Labor/Debt Bondage	19.2	920	230	2,778	1,208	191
Trafficked Slaves						
Sexual Exploitation	1.4	28,357	1,910	59,185	3,099	931
Other Forced Labor	1.6	2,530	540	6,142	1,137	271
Forced Labor[2]	8.3	4,451	660	10,512	1,593	398
Total/Weighted Average	**30.5**	**3,165**	**440**	**7,648**	**1,396**	**285**

Dollar values in 2011 U.S. dollars.

[1] 2011 U.S. dollar valuation based on average of relevant CPI and GDP deflator adjustments from the dates of slave's acquisition(s).

[2] Includes forced commercial sex work of individuals not trafficked.

despite this downward trend, slave prices centuries ago, as with the present day, ranged from nominal to several thousand dollars.

With regards to bonded labor acquisition costs, these were calculated as the loans or assets provided by the slave owner to the slave, including subsequent loans offered throughout the course of the weighted average duration of enslavement. For seasonal bonded laborers, each season's advance is used as a single cost of acquisition, as opposed to adding up each season's advance for all the years of the individual's bondage. For other slaves, actual sales prices are used. Many slaves have no idea what they were sold for, and the debts they may be told to repay often have little to do with their true acquisition cost. I have only used the case studies where I was able to acquire reliable acquisition cost data, and I have supplemented these studies within the trafficked slave segment with data generated by virtue of unit economic calculations by slave type and region, based on conservative assessments of the pure costs of acquisition and transport of a trafficked slave. The same also applies for certain categories of forced labor.

EXPLOITATION VALUE OF A SLAVE

Perhaps the most important metric in table A.5 is the exploitation value (EV) of each slave category. I first introduced the concept of the EV of a slave in the last chapter of my book *Sex Trafficking*. I subsequently discussed the concept in more detail in "Designing More Effective Laws Against Human Trafficking," in the summer 2011 issue of the *Northwestern Journal of International Human Rights*. Without knowing this value, it is impossible to understand just how profitable contemporary human enslavement is, and in turn it is very challenging to design effective laws against those who seek to engage in human enslavement. The weighted average EVs by category of slavery range from $2,778 for bonded laborer/debt bondage slaves to $10,512 for forced laborers to a startling $59,185 for trafficked sex slaves. This means that when a slave exploiter acquires a bonded laborer for a global weighted average of $230 ($200 for South Asia; $410 for non–South Asia), he can expect to enjoy net profits from the exploitation of that slave of $2,778 ($2,585 for South Asia; $3,960 for non–South Asia) before the individual either escapes, is freed, or perishes. These global debt bondage numbers provide a percentage total ROI of 1,208%, or

191% per year for the average duration of enslavement (~6.3 years). Trafficked sex slaves have the highest percentage ROI, of almost 3,100%, or 931% per year for the average duration of enslavement (~3.3 years). The annual ROI for forced labor is 398%, and the global weighted average annual ROI for all forms of slavery is 285% for the average duration of enslavement (~4.0 years). This aggregate data is based on a global weighted average acquisition cost of a slave of $440, after which the exploiter can expect to enjoy net profits generated through the exploitation of that slave of $7,648, before that slave either escapes, is freed, or perishes. This net cash return per slave around the world demonstrates the powerful demand-side forces to acquire and exploit slaves of all kinds.

The annualized ROI numbers, as well as the EVs, are dependent on the calculated average durations of enslavement for each category, which I determined from the same case studies used to determined the acquisition prices. It is also worth noting that the forced laborer ROIs are reduced because of two categories—forced military and domestic servitude—neither of which produce any ongoing economic profits (other than one-time fees for the latter category). Forced labor ROIs are higher than trafficked forced labor ROIs because the former category includes some forced prostitution.

Table A.6 includes the summary calculations of some of the EVs for select bonded labor industries as well as a discussion of how these values are calculated. I have included a sample of some of the bonded labor industries in South Asia that contribute to the total weighted averages per bonded laborer in the two columns on the far right: one for South Asia and one for the world. The EV is calculated by deducting operating costs from revenues, which provides a monthly recurring contribution. This figure is multiplied by the average number of months of enslavement to generate an operating EV. Deducting the weighted average acquisition cost of the bonded laborer from operating EV provides the net EV of a bonded laborer.[8]

The EVs in South Asia range from a high of $4,911 for a brick kiln bonded laborer to a low of $848 for a *kamaiya* bonded laborer. The weighted average EV for all forms of bonded labor in South Asia is $2,585. Globally, the number is $2,778. I also provide ROI calculations, which represent the net EV divided by the acquisition cost. The percentages range from a high of 1754% for the brickmaking sector to a low of 499% for *kamaiya* bonded labor. The average for all forms of bonded labor in South Asia is 1,293%.

TABLE A.6
Bonded Labor Exploitation Value (EV) Summary

	Brickmaking	Carpet Weaving	Kamaiya	Glass Bangles	Bidi Rolling	Mining	Stonebreaking	South Asia Bonded Labor Weighted Average	Global Bonded Labor Weighted Average
Revenues	**310**	**117**	**78**	**192**	**96**	**253**	**200**	**176**	**192**
Total Operating Costs	144	51	40	114	45	128	86	81	90
Recurring Contribution	**166**	**66**	**38**	**78**	**51**	**125**	**114**	**95**	**102**
Avg. Monthly Churn Rate (%)	*1.1*	*1.3*	*1.7*	*1.3*	*1.1*	*1.4*	*1.1*	*1.3*	*1.3*
Operating EV	**5,191**	**1,949**	**1,018**	**2,269**	**1,592**	**3,645**	**3,520**	**2,785**	**3,008**
Aggregate Loan Advance	280	170	170	190	160	220	210	200	230
Net EV	**4,911**	**1,779**	**848**	**2,079**	**1,432**	**3,425**	**3,310**	**2,585**	**2,778**
Implied ROI (%)	*1754*	*1046*	*499*	*1094*	*895*	*1557*	*1576*	*1293*	*1208*

Dollar values in 2011 U.S. dollars.

These numbers and metrics are indispensible for the design of more effective laws against bonded labor, and designing more effective laws is one of the most important elements to waging a more effective campaign to eliminate bonded labor. I discuss the relationship between these metrics and my recommendations relating to law and bonded labor in chapter 8.

Appendix B

SELECT BONDED LABOR ECONOMICS

TABLE B.1

Kamaiya Economics, Western Terai, Nepal, Type 2

General Assumptions

5 working members per family
50 *kattha* land worked per family
Crop cycle: 2 rice 1 wheat per season
Ratio of harvest to seed: 10.6× rice; 8.3× wheat
Yield: 90 kg rice, 85 kg wheat per *kattha*
650 kg paddy provided per family
2 meals per day provided per working family member
1 *bukura* provided
Medicine and clothes provided
2011 U.S. dollars

Unit Assumptions			Annual Profit and Loss	
Revenues	**Unit Prices ($)**		**Revenues**	
Rice (medium new)	0.22	per kg		2,011
Wheat	0.26	per kg		1,114
			Total Annual Revenues	**3,125**
Operating Costs			**Operating Expenses**	
Paddy (medium) seed	0.30	per kg		257
Wheat seed	0.33	per kg		170
Meals for *kamaiya*	0.13	per meal		468
Fertilizer, pesticide, other inputs	1.00	per *kattha*		150
Medicines	1.25	per laborer per month		75
Clothes	15.00	per laborer per season		75
Transportation	100.00	per season		100
Repairs and misc.	1.50	per laborer per month		90
Paddy for *kamaiya*	650.00	kg per household		197
			Total Operating Expenses	**1,582**
Fixed Costs			**Annual Gross Profit**	**1,543**
Equipment	400		*% Gross Margin*	*49.4*
Bukura	250			
			Depreciation	
			Equipment	40
			Bukura	25
			Total Depreciation	**65**
			Annual Net Profit[1]	**1,478**
			% Net Profit	*47.3*
			per bonded laborer	296

[1] Based on my research, there does not appear to be much in the way of taxes paid on revenues from the sale of agricultural products based on the use of *kamaiya* bonded labor. At most, some nominal amount may be worked into the exploiter's overall business. This amount would probably be offset by reductions in other expenses I have modeled, resulting in similar overall profitability.

Hari Economics, Sindh Province, Pakistan, Type 2

General Assumptions

> 5 working members per family
> 5 acres land worked per family
> Crop cycle: 2 rice 1 wheat per season
> Ratio of harvest to seed: 11.2× rice; 8.8× wheat
> Yield: 1,400 kg rice, 1,350 kg wheat per acre
> 50/50 share in input costs between owner and laborer
> 65/35 share in output revenues[1]
> *Peshgi* of $62.50 per acre
> 2011 U.S. dollars

Unit Assumptions				Annual Profit and Loss	
Revenues	**Unit Prices ($)**			**Revenues**	
Rice (medium new)	0.24	per kg			2,161
Wheat	0.26	per kg			1,152
				Total Annual Revenues	**3,313**
Operating Costs				**Operating Expenses**	
Paddy (medium) seed	0.32	per kg			200
Wheat seed	0.35	per kg			135
Fertilizer, pesticide, fuel, other inputs	90.00	per acre			225
Transportation	150.00	per season			150
Repairs and misc.	2.00	per laborer per month			120
Peshgi	62.50	per acre			313
				Total Operating Expenses	**1,143**
Fixed Costs				**Annual Gross Profit**	**2,170**
Equipment (tractor, hoes, etc.)	2,000			*% Gross Margin*	65.5
Animals	700				
				Depreciation	
				Equipment (tractor, hoes, etc.)	200
				Animals	70
				Total Depreciation	**270**
				Annual Net Profit[2]	**1,900**
				% Net Profit	57.4
				per bonded laborer	380

[1] The revenue share in type two *hari* contracts is supposed to be 50/50, but *haris* are never given access to sales figures from the market, and my best estimates are that owners take roughly two-thirds or more of the revenue share instead of 50 percent.

[2] Based on my research there does not appear to be much in the way of taxes paid on revenues from the sale of agricultural products based on the use of *kamaiya* bonded labor. At most, some nominal amount may be worked into the exploiter's overall business. This amount would probably be offset by reductions in other expenses I have modeled, resulting in similar overall profitability.

Brickmaking Economics, Bihar, India

General Assumptions

> 50 bonded laborers per brick kiln
> Loans advanced to 38 laborers out of 50
> Wages paid only to laborers receiving loans
> 550,000 bricks made each month
> 90% of bricks sold during season
> Weighted avg. brick unit sale price: Rs. 1.8
> Bricks made eight months out of the year
> Extra capacity sold during rainy season
> 20% price premium for bricks sold during rainy season
> Transportation costs paid by buyer
> 2011 U.S. dollars

Unit Assumptions				Monthly Profit and Loss	
Revenues	**Unit Prices ($)**			**Revenues**	
Bricks	0.04	per kg			19,800
Wage deduction	0.68	per kg			775
				Total Monthly Revenues	**20,575**
Operating Costs				**Operating Expenses**	
Weighted Avg. Wage[1]	1.36	per laborer per day			1,550
Foreman/manager/*kamdar* (×4)	10.00	per day			1,200
Accountant	15.00	per day			450
Government royalty[2]	750.00	per month			750
Fuel (coal, oil, diesel)	5,111.11	per month			5,111
Jamadar commission	0.44	per 1,000 bricks			244
Utilities, repairs, and misc.	0.33	per laborer per day			500
				Total Operating Expenses	**9,806**
Fixed Costs				**Gross Profit**	**10,769**
Kiln construction	25,000			*% Gross Margin*	*52.3*
Tools, molds, pump, other equipment	3,500				
Aggregate loan advance	280			**Depreciation**	
				Kiln Construction	104
				Tools, molds, and other equipment	58
				Loan advance	137
				Total Depreciation	**299**
				Taxes/Tax Bribe[3]	1,584
				Net Profit	**8,886**
				% Net Profit	*43.2*
				Annual Revenues	**185,722**
				Annual Net Profit[4]	**99,482**
				% Net Profit	*53.6*
				per bonded laborer	1,990

[1] This is a weighted average based on piece-rate wages and day wages paid to the various labor types at the kiln.

[2] The precise royalty will depend on the state in India (or state/province in other countries) in which the kiln is located. Some are fixed sums for the year; others are fixed sums plus variable amounts per 1,000 bricks made. In variable scenarios, the kiln owners can pay bribes to reduce the royalty, and they often "cook" the books to show a lower number of bricks produced and sold. A review of several kilns in Bihar revealed that the average royalty is approximately $9,000 per year.

[3] Almost all kiln owners offer bribes to local officials to avoid paying full taxes. These rates vary, but the figure tends to be around 8 percent of operating revenues (excludes laborer debt repayment) or less.

[4] Assumes remaining bricks produced but not sold during the season are sold during the off-season at a 20% price premium; only associated costs are government royalty, tax bribe, depreciation, and one foremen and accountant.

TABLE B.4
Bidi Rolling Economics, West Bengal, India

General Assumptions

100 bonded laborers per *jamadar*
Loans advanced to 70 laborers out of 100
800 bidis rolled per laborer per day
25 bidis per pack
Bidis rolled 27 days per month
2011 U.S. dollars

Unit Assumptions			Monthly Profit and Loss	
Revenues	**Unit Prices ($)**		**Revenues**	
Wholesale bidis (pack of 25)	0.10			8,640
Wage deduction	0.44			960
			Total Monthly Revenues	**9,600**
Operating Costs			**Operating Expenses**	
Wage	1.29	per 1,000 bidis		2,784
Raw materials (kendu, tobacco, thread)	0.44	per 1,000 bidis		960
Transportation	200.00	per month		200
Jamadar commission	0.22	per 1,000 bidis		480
Misc.	0.03	per laborer per day		90
			Total Operating Expenses	**4,514**
Fixed Costs			**Gross Profit**	**5,086**
Tools	300		*% Gross Margin*	*53.0*
Aggregate loan advance	160			
			Depreciation	
			Tools	12
			Loan advance	144
			Total Depreciation	**156**
			Net Profit	**4,930**
			% Net Profit	*51.4*
			Annual Revenues	**115,200**
			Annual Net Profit[1]	**59,159**
			% Net Profit	*51.4*
			per bonded laborer	592

[1] Based on my research, there does not appear to be much in the way of taxes paid on revenues from the sale of wholesale bidis produced through the use of bonded labor. At most, some nominal amount may be worked into the exploiter's overall business. This amount would probably be offset by reductions in other expenses I have modeled, resulting in similar overall profitability.

TABLE B.5

Shrimp Farming (Freshwater) Economics, Khulna Division, Bangladesh

General Assumptions

6 working members per family

10 hectare shrimp farm

Avg. 175 kg tiger shrimp harvested per hectare

Avg. wholesale trader price for shrimp:
  $4.29 per kg

Avg. $0.017 purchase price per shrimp fry

Yield is 10% of fry purchased

8-month harvest season

2011 U.S. dollars

Unit Assumptions

Revenues	Unit Prices ($)	
Shrimp	4.29	
Operating Costs		
Guard (x3)	30.00	per month
Shrimp fry	0.017	per shrimp fry
Food, fertilizer	20.00	per hectare
Transportation to distributor	0.05	per kg
Misc.	1.00	per day
Fixed Costs		
Nets	50	

Annual Profit and Loss

Revenues	
	7,500
Total Annual Revenues	**7,500**
Operating Expenses	
	720
	1,182
	200
	88
	240
Total Operating Expenses	**2,430**
Gross Profit	**5,070**
% Gross Margin	*67.6*
Depreciation	
Nets	1
Total Depreciation	**1**
Net Profit[1]	**5,069**
% Net Profit	*67.6*
per bonded laborer	845

[1] Based on my research, there does not appear to be much in the way of taxes paid on revenues from the sale of wholesale shrimp produced through the use of bonded labor. At most, some nominal amount may be worked into the exploiter's overall business. This amount would probably be offset by reductions in other expenses I have modeled, resulting in similar overall profitability.

TABLE B.6

Construction Economics, New Delhi, India

General Assumptions

30 bonded laborers per *jamadar*

Loans advanced to 25 laborers out of 30

Wages paid to all bonded laborers

One-third of workers each in unskilled,
semiskilled, and skilled work

Workers on projects 5 out of 6 months

Recruitment and transport costs paid by *jamadar*

2011 U.S. dollars

Unit Assumptions

Revenues	Unit Prices ($)	
Wages for workers (blended avg.)	4.00	
Shelter, medical, facilities	2.22	
Operating Costs		
Wages for workers (blended avg.)	1.33	per laborer per day
Shelter, medical, facilities	0.44	per laborer per day
Guard (×2)	10.00	per day
Misc.	0.33	per laborer per day
Fixed Costs		
Recruitment, transport	50	
Aggregate loan advance	200	

Monthly Profit and Loss

Revenues	
	3,600
	2,000
Total Monthly Revenues	**5,600**
Operating Expenses	
	1,200
	400
	600
	300
Total Operating Expenses	**2,500**
Gross Profit	**3,100**
% Gross Margin	*55.4*
Depreciation	
Recruitment, transport	42
Loan advance	64
Total Depreciation	**106**
Net Profit	**2,994**
% Net Profit	*53.5*
Annual Revenues	**56,000**
Annual Net Profit	**29,942**
% Net Profit	*53.5*
per bonded laborer	998

Stonebreaking (Granite Quarry) Economics, Haryana, India

General Assumptions

40 bonded laborers per quarry
Loans advanced to 40 laborers out of 40
Wages paid to all laborers
Avg. 70 sq. ft. of stones crushed per laborer per day
Laborers work 26 days per month
Wage rate of $0.02 per sq. ft. crushed
Wholesale rate of $0.10 per sq. ft.
2011 U.S. dollars

Unit Assumptions			Monthly Profit and Loss	
Revenues	**Unit Prices ($)**		**Revenues**	
Crushed stone	0.10			7,280
Wage deduction	0.01			728
			Total Monthly Revenues	**8,008**
Operating Costs			**Operating Expenses**	
Wage	0.02	per sq. ft.		1,456
Guard (×4)	10.00	per day		1,200
Transportation	400.00	per month		400
Repairs and misc	0.33	per laborer per day		400
			Total Operating Expenses	**3,456**
Fixed Costs			**Gross Profit**	**4,552**
Tools and other equipment	1,000		*% Gross Margin*	*56.8*
Aggregate loan advance	210			
			Depreciation	
			Tools and other equipment	28
			Loan advance	108
			Total Depreciation	**136**
			Net Profit	**4,416**
			% Net Profit	*55.2*
			Annual Revenues	**96,096**
			Annual Net Profit[1]	**52,998**
			% Net Profit	*55.2*
			per bonded laborer	1,325

[1] Based on my research, there does not appear to be much in the way of taxes paid on revenues from the sale of wholesale stones produced through the use of bonded labor. At most, some nominal amount may be worked into the exploiter's overall business. This amount would probably be offset by reductions in other expenses I have modeled, resulting in similar overall profitability.

Carpet Weaving Economics, Uttar Pradesh, India

General Assumptions

30 bonded laborers, 3 groups each carpet size
Loans advanced to 25 laborers out of 30
Wages paid only to laborers receiving loans
Carpets Made and Sold:
10: 2' x 5' (small)
3: 5' x 8' (medium)
0.5: 12' x 15' (large)
100 knots per square meter
Wholesale rate: $10 per sq. foot
Cost of thread: $0.56 per sq foot
5% of thread lost each month
2011 U.S. dollars

Unit Assumptions				Monthly Profit and Loss	
Revenues	**Unit Prices ($)**			**Revenues**	
Carpets—Small	100				1,000
Carpets—Medium	400				1,200
Carpets—Large	1,800				900
Wage deduction	0.55				413
				Total Monthly Revenues	**3,513**
Operating Costs				**Operating Expenses**	
Wages	1.10	per laborer per day			825
Thread	0.56	per sq. ft.			245
Gaurd	10.00	per day			300
Repairs and misc.	0.18	per laborer per day			160
				Total Operating Expenses	**1,530**
				Gross Profit	**1,984**
Fixed Costs				*% Gross Margin*	*56.5*
Looms	1,400				
Tools and other equipment	400			**Depreciation**	
Aggregate loan advance	170			Looms	12
				Tools and other equipment	11
				Loan advance	54
				Total Depreciation	**77**
				Taxes/Tax Bribe[1]	155
				Net Profit	**1,751**
				% Net Profit	*49.9*
				Annual Revenues	**42,150**
				Annual Net Profit[1]	**21,015**
				per bonded laborer	700

[1] Almost all carpet loom owners offer bribes to local officials to avoid paying full taxes. These rates vary, but the figure tends to be around 5 percent of operating revenues (excludes laborer debt repayment) or less.

TABLE B.9
Mining Economics (Limestone), Rajasthan, India

General Assumptions

20 bonded laborers per contractor
Loans advanced to 18 laborers out of 20
Wages paid only to laborers receiving loans
85 kg of limestone mined per laborer per month
90% of limestone sold during season
Weighted avg. wholesale price: $4.20 per kg[1]
Mining conducted eight months out of the year
Extra capacity sold during rainy season
Transportation costs paid by mine lessee
2011 U.S. dollars

Unit Assumptions

Revenues	Unit Prices ($)	
Limestone (wholesale)	4.20	
Wage deduction	0.84	
Operating Costs		
Weighted Average Wage	1.67	per laborer per day
Guard (×2)	10.00	per day
Accountant/foreman	15.00	per day
Government lease[2]	600.00	per month
Transportation	250.00	per month
Utilities, repairs and misc.	0.50	per laborer per day
Fixed Costs		
Tools and other equipment	4,500	
Recruitment, transport	50	
Aggregate loan advance	220	

Monthly Profit and Loss

Revenues	
	6,426
	451
Total Monthly Revenues	**6,877**
Operating Expenses	
	902
	600
	450
	600
	250
	300
Total Operating Expenses	**3,102**
Gross Profit	**3,775**
% Gross Margin	*54.9*
Depreciation	
Tools and other equipment	75
Recruitment, transport	28
Loan advance	51
Total Depreciation	**154**
Taxes/Tax Bribe[3]	321
Net Profit	**3,300**
% Net Profit	*48.0*
Annual Revenues	**60,727**
Annual Net Profit[4]	**30,099**
per bonded laborer	1,505

[1] This is a weighted average of Jaisalmer Yellow, Ita Gold, Kota Brown, and Kota Blue limestone.
[2] The precise lease rate varies by state, by stone or mineral being mined, and by mine size. Most leases researched were expired or unpaid. Legitimate lease rates for the state of Rajasthan relating to a medium-size limestone mine were approximately $7,200 per year.
[3] Almost all mine lessees offer bribes to local officials to avoid paying full taxes, especially on expired or unpaid leases. These rates vary, but the figure tends to be around 5 percent of operating revenues or less.
[4] Assumes remaining limestone mined but not sold during the season is sold during the off-season; only associated costs are government lease, tax bribe, depreciation, and one accountant.

Glass Bangle Economics, Firozabad, India

General Assumptions

25 bonded laborers per contractor (11 stage 1; 7 stage 2; 7 stage 3)
Loans advanced to 23 laborers out of 25
Wages paid only to laborers receiving loans (11 stage 1, 6 stage 2, 6 stage 3)
500,000 bangles produced each month[1]
95% of bangles sold (5% breakage)
Weighted avg. wholesale bangle sale price: $8.89 per 1,000
Transportation costs paid by contractor
2011 U.S. dollars

Unit Assumptions

Revenues	Unit Prices ($)	
Bangles (wholesale)	8.89	
Wage deductions (all stages)		

Operating Costs		
Weighted average stage 1 wage	1.44	per laborer per day
Weighted average stage 2 wage	0.11	per 1,000 straightened
Weighted average stage 3 wage	0.11	per 1,000 joined
Guard (factory only)	10.00	per day
Fuel (coal and gas)	900.00	per month
Transportation	150.00	per month
Jamadar commission	0.22	per 1,000 bangles
Repairs and misc.	0.33	per laborer per day

Fixed Costs	
Aggregate loan advance	190

Monthly Profit and Loss

Revenues	
	4,222
	572
Total Monthly Revenues	**4,794**

Operating Expenses	
	477
	333
	333
	300
	900
	150
	105
	250
Total Operating Expenses	**2,848**
Gross Profit	**1,946**
% Gross Margin	*40.6*

Depreciation	
Loan advance	56
Total Depreciation	**56**
Net Profit	**1,890**
% Net Profit	*39.4*
Annual Revenues	**57,527**
Annual Net Profit[1]	**22,680**
% Net Profit	*39.4*
per bonded laborer	907

[1] Peak production during wedding season amortized across full year.

[2] Based on my research, there does not appear to be much in the way of taxes paid on revenues from the sale of wholesale glass bangles produced through the use of bonded labor. At most, some nominal amount may be worked into the exploiter's overall business. This amount would probably be offset by reductions in other expenses I have modeled, resulting in similar overall profitability.

Appendix C

SELECT BONDED LABOR SUPPLY CHAINS

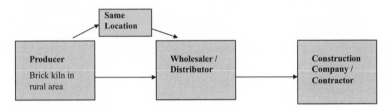

Key points:

- Impossible to relocate
- High capital expenditures
- Relatively time-consuming and high-volume production process
- Range in size from 30 to 1,000 laborers
- Typified by bonded, forced, and child labor
- Seasonal during non-monsoon months
- Total production cost approximately Rs. 0.8 per brick

Key points:

- Distributor acquires bricks at point of production
- Bonded, forced, and child labourers used for loading
- Bricks purchased all year
- Weighted avg. sales price to distributor: Rs 1.8 per brick

Key points:

- Transported to construction site by truck
- Bricks can be traced from construction site to production site because of baked-in labels
- Typified by bonded, forced, and child labor
- Retail pricing typically 1.5x to wholesale price
- Construction company may be vertically integrated and handle distribution directly; none include brickmaking stage

Figure C.1. Brickmaking supply chain.

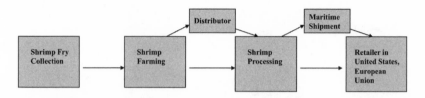

Key points:

- Saline: in rivers on northern border of Sundarban
- Fresh: primarily in hatcheries in Khulna district
- Highly fixed locations
- Very conspicuous
- Typified by child labor
- Seasonal March through July
- Sales price ~$0.01 per fry

Key points:

- Typified by debt bondage based on lease agreements
- Saline lease: $64 per 14.4k sq. ft.
- Fresh lease: $71 per 14.4k sq. ft.
- Highly fixed locations
- Highly conspicuous
- 170k hectares saline and 400k hectares freshwater farms in southwest Bangladesh
- Seasonal July through March
- 3-4 month growth cycle for shrimp
- Weighted average price point: $4.29 per kg

Key points:

- Most shrimp received from intermediary distributor
- Highly capital intensive
- Highly fixed locations
- Highly mechanized and specialized
- Highly leveraged
- Anecdotal evidence of forced labor

Key points:

- All maritime (frozen) shipments depart from two ports only: Mongla or Chittagong
- Difficult for retailer or consumer to know if supply chain is tainted
- Shrimp from numerous processors can be in one container (though remaining frozen and labeled)

Figure C.2. Frozen shrimp (tiger) supply chain.

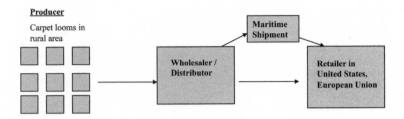

Producer

Carpet looms in
rural area

**Maritime
Shipment**

**Wholesaler /
Distributor**

**Retailer in
United States,
European Union**

Key points:

- Very fragmented
- Easy to relocate
- Low capital expenditures
- Very time consuming and low-volume production process
- Very hidden
- Range in size from hut with 3 laborers to shacks with 20 laborers
- Typified by bonded, forced, and child labor
- PK model similar; Nepal more centralized in KTM Valley
- Total production cost (100 knots) approximately $3.60 per sq. ft.

Key points:

- Transported by truck to distributor
- Low cost and easy to transport clandestinely
- Wholesaler price point typically $10 per sq. ft.

Key points:

- Maritime shipments depart from 8+ sea ports
- Carpets from numerous wholesalers mixed in shipment containers
- Very difficult for retailer or consumer to know if supply chain is tainted
- Retail pricing typically 4x to 5x wholesale price

Figure C.3. Carpet weaving supply chain (northern India).

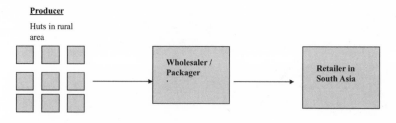

Producer

Huts in rural area

Wholesaler / Packager

Retailer in South Asia

Key points:

- Very fragmented
- Easy to relocate
- Low capital expenditures
- Very short and high-volume production process
- Very hidden
- Typified by bonded, forced, and child labor
- Total production cost approximately $0.05 per pack

Key points:

- Transported by truck to packager
- *Jamadar* usually handles transport
- Low cost and easy to transport clandestinely
- Moderate capital expenditures
- Moderate mechanization
- Wholesale price point typically $0.10 per pack

Key points:

- Transported by truck to retailer
- Difficult for retailer or consumer to know if supply chain is tainted
- Retail pricing typically 2x to 2.5x wholesale price
- Small amount of export to other countries in South Asia and Middle East

Figure C.4. Bidi rolling supply chain.

Appendix D

The following definitions relating to the system of bonded labor are provided in the Bonded Labour System (Abolition) Act, 1976. Two "Explanations" are included in the latest drafting of the act based on precedents established in the PUDR, 1982; and BMM, 1983, cases. Most definitions of bonded labor in legislation in South Asia are derived from this definition:

2.   DEFINITIONS.—In this Act, unless the context otherwise requires,—

(a) advance means an advance, whether in cash or kind, or partly in cash or partly in kind, made by one person (hereinafter referred to as the creditor) to another person (hereinafter referred to as the debtor)

(b) agreement means an agreement (whether written or oral, or partly written and partly oral) between a debtor and creditor, and includes an agreement providing for forced labour, the existence of which is presumed under any social custom prevailing in the concerned locality.

Explanation: The existence of an agreement between the debtor and creditor is ordinarily presumed, under the social customs, in relation to the following forms of forced labour, namely: Adiyamar, Baramasia, Basahya, Bethu, Bhagela, Cherumar, Garru-Galu, Hali, Hari, Harwail, Holya, Jana, Jeetha, Kamiya, Khundit-Mundit, Kuthia, Lakhari, Munjhi,

Mat, Munish system, Nit-Majoor, Paleru, Padiyal, Pannayilal, Sagri, Sanji, Sanjawat, Sewak, Sewakia, Seri, Vetti;

(c) ascendant or descendant, in relation to a person belonging to a matriarchal society, means the person who corresponds to such expression in accordance with the law of succession in force in such society;

(d) bonded debt means an advance obtained, or presumed to have been obtained, by a bonded labourer under, or in pursuance of, the bonded labour system;

(e) bonded labour means any labour or service rendered under the bonded labour system;

(f) bonded labourer means a labourer who incurs, or has, or is presumed to have, incurred, a bonded debt;

(g) bonded labour system means the system of forced, or partly forced, labour under which a debtor enters, or has, or is presumed to have, entered, into an agreement with the creditor to the effect that—

(i) in consideration of an advance obtained by him or by any of his lineal ascendants or descendants (whether or not such advance is evidenced by the document) and in consideration of the interest, if any, due on such advance, or

(ii) in pursuance of any customary or social obligation, or

(iii) in pursuance of any obligation devolving on him by succession, or

(iv) for any economic consideration received by him or by any of his lineal ascendants or descendants, or

(v) by reason of his birth in any particular caste or community, he would— (1) render, by himself or through any member of his family, or any person dependent on him, labour or service, to the creditor, or for the benefit of the creditor, for a specific period or for an unspecified period, either without wages or for nominal wages, or (2) forfeit the freedom of employment or other means of livelihood for an specified period or for an unspecified period, or (3) forfeit the right to move freely throughout the territory of India, or (4) forfeit the right to appropriate or sell at market-value any of his property or product of his labour or the labour of a member of his family or any person dependent on him and includes the system of forced, or partly forced, labour under which a surety for a debtor enters, or has, or is presumed to have, entered into an agreement with the creditor to the effect that in the event of the failure of the debtor to repay the debt, he would render the bonded labour on behalf of the debtor;

Explanation: For the removal of doubts, it is hereby declared that any system of forced, or partly forced labour under which any workman being contract labour as defined in clause (b) of sub-section (1) of Section 2 of the Contract Labour (Regulation and Abolition) Act, 1970 (37 of 1970), or an inter-State migrant workman as defined in clause (e) of sub-section (1) of Section 2 of the Inter-State Migrant Workmen (Regulation of Employment and Conditions of Service) Act, 1979 (30 of 1979), is required to render labour or service in circumstances of the nature mentioned in sub-clause (1) of this clause or is subjected to all or any of the disabilities referred to in sub-clauses (2) to (4), is "bonded labour system" within the meaning of this clause.

(h) family, in relation to a person, includes the ascendant and descendant of such person;

(i) nominal wages, in relation to any labour, means a wage which is less than,—(a) the minimum wages fixed by the Government, in relation to the same or similar labour, under any law for the time being in force; and (b) where no such minimum wage has been fixed in relation to any form of labour, the wages that are normally paid, for the same or similar labour, to the labourers working in the same locality;

(j) prescribed means prescribed by rules made under this Act.

Appendix E

BONDED LABOR LAW AND CASES: PAKISTAN, NEPAL, BANGLADESH, INDIA

PAKISTAN

The Constitution of the Islamic Republic of Pakistan, 1973, contains the following prohibitions against forced labor: Article 11(1): Slavery is nonexistent and forbidden, and no law shall permit or facilitate its introduction into Pakistan in any form; Article 11(2): All forms of forced labor and traffic in human beings is prohibited.

The primary point of interest in these constitutional provisions is that Article 11(1) declares that slavery did not exist in Pakistan at the time its constitution was written, a declaration that directly promoted the Pakistani government's general state of denial as to the existence of bonded labor and other forms of forced labor in Pakistan for decades.

After considerable internal and international pressure, Pakistan finally passed the Bonded Labour System (Abolition) Act in 1992, sixteen years after the passage of India's act. Pakistan's 1992 act is largely modeled after India's 1976 act and follows many of the same sections and stipulations. Similar definitions of bonded labor are provided, and similar enactments relating to the full and immediate abolition of the system are set forth. A similar system of vigilance committees is described, with district magistrates serving in a similar capacity to India. One interesting divergence is the stipulation of a greater penalty, of up to PNR 50,000 ($588 today; $2,128 in 1992, equivalent to $3,383 in 2011 U.S. dollars),[1] a financial penalty that the NHRC in India has been arguing for since the mid-1990s.

The mandates of Pakistan's 1992 act were given further scope in the Pakistan Bonded Labour System (Abolition) Rules, 1995. This act provides details on definitions, the powers and duties of district magistrates (such as the ability to inspect premises in their jurisdictions where there is a suspicion of bonded labor, to mobilize government and nongovernmental organizations to fulfill the mandates of the 1992 act, and to ensure the adequate rehabilitation of bonded laborers), as well as the powers and duties of the vigilance committees (such as how they should be constituted, when they should meet, and how they should handle complaints from bonded laborers). Also, a fund was created with an initial size of PNR 100 million ($1.18 million) to be used for training institutes, legal and financial assistance to bonded laborers, and other provisions related to bonded laborer rehabilitation. No one I spoke with or interviewed in Pakistan—from NGOs crusading against bonded labor to human rights barristers—was able to tell me if the fund had actually been funded and, if so, how much, if any, of the monies had been disbursed.

Other relevant legislation in Pakistan includes the Sindh Tenancy Act, 1950, which outlines tenancy rights in Sindh province among permanent and at-will sharecropping tenants. The act prohibits the eviction of permanent tenants, outlines more equitable splits of costs and revenue sharing among tenants and landlords (the *batai* system), and stipulates that disputes are to be adjudicated by a one-man tribunal with fines of up to PNR 500 ($5.88) for violations. The act prohibits landowners from extracting *begar* from tenants. A September 2002 amendment to the act prohibits the eviction of at-will tenants, and an October 2002 amendment stipulates that disputes will be heard by a tribunal instead of a by single person. These amendments also mandate that *haris* are captured by the Tenancy Act and that freedom of movement and employment for tenants cannot be restricted for any reason.

Finally, the Employment of Children Act, 1991, prohibits the employment of children under the age of fifteen from engaging in work that is deemed hazardous or dangerous, including carpet making, construction, brickmaking, manufacturing of explosives or fireworks, soap manufacturing, leather processing, fishing, power looms, precious stones, metal or wood handicrafts, and others. Children are also not allowed to work overtime or during nighttime hours. A National Committee on the Rights of the Child was established to monitor the enforcement of this law and protect children, including inspection of employment facilities. Little inspection activity actually takes place.

There have been barely a handful of convictions in Pakistan under the 1992 act, for many of the same reasons that there have been very few convictions in India under its 1976 act. The Human Rights Commission of Pakistan recently noted: "The Judiciary, on its part, was found short on its promises of expeditious disposal of cases and eradication of corruption in the judicial system. More than 1.5 million cases were pending in the courts at the end of 2009" (HRCP 2009, 2).

Two bonded labor cases of interest include *Darshan Mashih vs. State*, 1990; and Judgment of the Federal Shariat Court in the Bonded Labour System Abolition Case, 2005. The Darshan case involved bonded labor in the brickmaking industry and was the catalyst for the passage of Pakistan's 1992 act. This case was one of the first public interest litigation (PIL) cases in Pakistan and was the first to be initiated by the receipt of a telegram, which was written in 1988 by bonded laborers to the chief justice of the Supreme Court of Pakistan, following the example of the PUDR, 1982; and BMM, 1983, cases from India. The telegram pleaded for assistance in protection against exploitation as bonded laborers. Claims for violations of ten different Articles of the Constitution of Pakistan were made by lawyers for the bonded laborers, including Article 9: security of person; Article 11: prohibition against traffic in human beings and forced labor; Article 14: protecting the dignity of man; Article 15: protecting freedom of movement; and Article 25: prohibition of discrimination on basis of sex.

The court ordered several investigations that resulted in the freeing of more than twenty bonded laborers. Several directives were issued. The most important of these include the following: the abolition of the *peshgi* system except for advances of up to one week's wages; the abolition of the *jamadar* system, which is "finished and excluded for all times"; the cancellation of all past *peshgis*, which are deemed void and cannot be recovered by using the police or "coercive measures"; the prohibition of owners against asking or pressurizing women and children to work; the prohibition of deductions from wages, be it for damages or loss during the production process (which are to be borne by the owner) or due to the repayment of past *peshgis*. One glaring absence from this decision was the declaration that even though the *peshgi* system was abolished, past *peshgis* were not deemed void. The court explained: "The question, whether recoveries would be abolished altogether and whether legislation shall be made on the lines as done in India, is deferred for the time being."[2] To my knowledge, this issue was never resolved by the court.

In the 2005 case, brick kiln owners approached the Shariat Court for a declaration as to whether the provisions of the 1992 act in Pakistan are contrary to Islamic principles found in the Koran and *Sunnah*.[3] Siding against the kiln owners, the Shariat Court held that the 1992 act does not violate Islamic law. The Shariat Court cited the ILO Convention no. 29 on Forced Labour and the United Nations Declaration of Human Rights, 1948, in support of its declaration.

NEPAL

Article 20 of the Constitution of Kingdom of Nepal, 1990, prohibits the traffic in human beings and forced labor. After several years of internal and international pressure, Nepal issued a ban on the *kamaiya* system of bonded labor on July 17, 2000, then subsequently passed the *Kamaiya* Labour Prohibition Act, 2002. This act was intended to abolish the *kamaiya* system of bonded labor prevalent in the western Terai, Nepal, as well as provide for the identification, liberation, and rehabilitation of *kamaiya* bonded laborers. Although the act defines bonded labor within the context of the *kamaiya* system most often entered by people of the *tharu* ethnic group, it is generally regarded to apply to any form of bonded labor involving any ethnic group in Nepal. There have yet to be any prosecutions under the 2002 act. Further detail on the stipulations of this act and subsequent efforts to transition former *kamaiya* to freedom are discussed in chapter 2.

Other relevant legislation in Nepal includes the Labour Act, 1991, which provides for national standards relating to work hours, health, safety, and a minimum wage. The Child Labour (Prohibition and Regulation) Act, 2000, defines a child as someone under sixteen years of age and prohibits their employment in "risky" industries, including tourist-related sectors (hotels, casinos, bars, restaurants, river rafting, trekking, and mountaineering), construction, bidi manufacturing, carpet weaving, leather processing, alcohol production, mining, rickshaw pulling, and plastic production. The employment of a child under the age of fourteen is prohibited. Children over the age of fourteen must not be employed in nonrisky industries from the hours of 6 P.M. to 6 A.M., and they must also not work more than thirty-six hours per week. Inspections are meant to be undertaken by the government labor office to ensure compliance with the law, and a Child Labour Eradication Committee was formed to undertake research on how best to eliminate child labor in Nepal. Virtually no prosecutions have taken place under the 2000 act in Nepal. The absence of a well-developed tradition of public interest litigation (PIL), as one finds in India, Pakistan, and to a lesser extent Bangladesh, is one of many factors leading to the paucity of prosecutions under Nepal's bonded labor and child labor legislation.

Finally, Muluki Ain (Public Law), 1964, prohibits forced labor and bondage of any kind, as well as the transnational transport of individuals for the purposes of selling them (human trafficking).

BANGLADESH

Article 34 of the Constitution of the People's Republic of Bangladesh, 1972, prohibits forced labor; however, there is still no definition of forced labor in Bangladeshi law or any stipulation of a penalty for the offense. Bangladesh also does not yet have any specific legislation recognizing or abolishing bonded labor. Accordingly, there are no prosecutions relating to bonded labor in Bangladesh.

The most relevant labor legislation is the Bangladesh Labour Act, 2006. This act constitutes general unifying legislation of more than twenty-five scattered labor acts and ordinances in Bangladesh. Bonded labor does not appear anywhere in the act. The government has allowed the ILO's program on Prevention and Elimination of Bonded Labour in South Asia (PE-BLISA) to operate in Bangladesh, although only with the intention of preventing people from falling into debt bondage as opposed to releasing or rehabilitating any current bonded laborers. The 2006 act prohibits the employment of children under the age of fourteen and prohibits children under eighteen from working in hazardous industries, which is a higher age than other legislation in South Asia. Those industries deemed to be hazardous are similar to those outlined in other South Asian legislation relating to child labor. The act also sets a maximum thirty hours of work per week for children under the age of eighteen, and it prohibits the employment of children during nighttime hours. There has been a scattering of prosecutions under the 2006 act, but with a growing PIL tradition in Bangladesh[4] there will hopefully be more legal action in the future.

INDIA

In addition to the PUDR, 1982; and BMM, 1983, cases discussed in chapter 7, the following Supreme Court cases have all made important contributions to the fight against bonded labor in India.

Sanjit Roy vs. State of Rajasthan Supreme Court, 1983: The court held that the failure to pay minimum wages amounts to the exploitation of forced labor and that forced labor does not solely apply to physical or legal force but includes force arising from economic desperation.

Neeraja Chaudhary vs. State of Madhya Pradesh Supreme Court, 1984: The court held that a failure to rehabilitate bonded laborers is a violation of Articles 21 and 23 of the Constitution as well as of the 1976 act.

Mukesh Advani vs. State of Madhya Pradesh Supreme Court, 1985: The court held that states must implement more effective mechanisms to ensure the payment of minimum wages, and failing to do so amounts to a violation of the 1976 act.

Bandhua Mukti Morcha vs. State of Tamil Nadu, 1986: The court held that various practices, such as deductions from wages, restriction of movement, and only providing food in exchange for work, amount to bonded labor under the 1976 act.

Public Union for Civil Liberties vs. State of Tamil Nadu and Others, 1994: The court held that state governments must take all necessary action under the law to eliminate bonded labor, including a focus on initiating criminal proceedings against offenders.

People's Union for Civil Liberties vs. Union of India and Others, 1994: The court held that compensation must be paid to those whose rights have been violated under the 1976 act and that states continue to fail to meet their obligations to eliminate bonded labor.

Public Union for Civil Liberties vs. State of Tamil Nadu and Others, 2004: The court focused on the importance of clearly defined and executed rehabilitation programs for freed bonded laborers, who are vulnerable to slipping back into bondage and destitution without such programs.

Appendix F

SELECT ECONOMIC AND HUMAN DEVELOPMENT STATISTICS

TABLE F.1
Select Economic and Human Development Statistics

	Bangladesh	India	Nepal	Pakistan	Total
2010 PPP income ($)	1,650	3,350	1,180	2,480	
PPP income global rank (of 213)	181	154	192	162	
Agriculture as % of total GDP	18	16	33	22	
Agriculture as % total labor force	45	52	75	52	
Arable land %	55	49	16	24	
People living on less than $1.25 income per day (millions)	78	437	16	48	579
As percentage of total population	50	38	55	26	
People living on less than $2.00 income per day (millions)	127	892	23	121	1,163
As percentage of total population	81	78	79	66	
Life expectancy, female (yrs)	68	66	68	67	
Life expectancy, male (yrs)	67	63	66	64	
Literacy rate, female %	75	74	76	60	
Literacy rate, male %	74	88	87	80	
Female to male % completing primary enrollment	105	94	85	84	
Total population (millions)	156	1,150	29	184	1,519
Population % female	50	48	49	49	

Sources: World Bank, online statistics database, available at http://www.data.worldbank.org; United Nations Development Program, available at http://www.undp.org.

Notes

PREFACE

1. The word "labor" appears in the American English spelling throughout this book, except where an original South Asian law, legal case, or convention is cited, in which case "labour," the South Asian spelling, is used.

1. BONDED LABOR: AN OVERVIEW

1. Unless otherwise indicated, the names of all bonded or child laborers in this book are pseudonyms. In some cases where discussing precise geographic locations might risk the safety of the interviewee, I have provided a slightly alternate setting. In cases where providing the names of specific organizations or activists helping the bonded or child laborers might risk their safety, I have refrained from providing any details that would do so.

2. Throughout this book, where I quote a bonded laborer or share a narrative, that narrative may have been recorded in full as a single narrative spoken to me or as part of a conversation in which I asked questions to stimulate the conversation. In such cases, I have edited the narratives as minimally as possible to aid with readability.

3. *Pheras*, or "rounds," are a traditional aspect of weddings in India, involving the circumambulation of a sacred fire four or seven times. In the Hindu tradition, seven *pheras* are taken, the first four led by the groom and the last three led by the bride. After each *phera*, a specific wedding vow is taken relating to various pledges the bride and groom make to each other to uphold throughout their lives.

4. See Aristotle, *Poetics*, book 1, sections 3–7.

5. For a thorough discussion on medieval European feudalism, see Stephenson (1952); for feudal India under the Mughal Empire, see Habib (1963); for the economic and social structure of Tokugawa Japan, see Smith (1959); for more detail on peonage in the American South, see Pete (1990).

6. In these cases, poor women from developing countries take on debts in order to pay fees to recruiters in exchange for transport to a foreign country where they are put to work as domestic servants for a wealthy family. I have documented severe abuses in this model of debt bondage in North America, Africa, and Southeast Asia. Typically, the servants are unlawfully confined upon arrival, their documents are confiscated, and they are not paid wages because the family receiving them is told (and in some countries is allowed by policy) to withhold wages until they have recouped the fees they paid to the same recruiter who arranged the transport of the domestic servant. Abuses are rampant, from extended debt bondage to outright beatings and sexual abuse. Other sectors with similar practices of debt bondage relating to migrant workers include construction and agriculture. My estimates of the number of individuals caught in this form of debt bondage are probably conservative relative to the true size of the phenomenon, but additional data gathering is required to provide a more accurate estimate. To the extent that the estimate of this form of debt bondage increases, the proportion of slaves around the world who are caught in debt bondage would increase, and the proportion of debt bondage slaves who are in South Asia would decrease.

7. Sheth (2010, 5).

8. Other reasons for insufficient access to formal credit markets include geographic inaccessibility (individuals live far from the nearest credit office or bank branch) as well as strict repayment terms with severe penalties that deeply impoverished individuals cannot meet.

9. See Srivastava (2000) for an argument on the need for alternative income opportunities and wage labor (as well as credit smoothing) in order to attenuate forces that drive peasants into debt bondage. See Platteau (1994) for a discussion on how alternate economic opportunities helped eliminate bonded labor in Tokugawa Japan. See Acemgolu and Wolitzky (2011) for an economic model that demonstrates that enhanced alternative economic opportunities reduce the level of coercion in labor agreements.

10. Contract law is an extensive subject well beyond the scope of this book. For an excellent case-law overview of the principles of contract law, see Poole (2006).

11. See Srivastava (2003) for a discussion of why migrants are more vulnerable to bondage because they are, *inter alia*, more isolated and less able to assert their rights.

12. This is based on the 19.2 million mean estimate for total bonded laborers in the world, approximately 84 to 88 percent (86 mean) of whom are in South Asia.

13. "Paddy" refers to the prethreshed form of rice; it is derived from the Malay *padi*, which means rice.

14. See Conning (2005) for an economic model that demonstrates how total output for a society is largest under the competitive solution, whereas output suffers but profit for landowners is higher under tied labor regimes such as bonded labor. See Acemgolu

(2011) for an economic model that demonstrates how social welfare, laborer welfare, and net output are reduced in the context of coercive labor agreements.

15. See Conning (2005) for a discussion of how landlords actively minimize alternatives for peasants, forcing them to enter into worse and worse labor contracts.

16. *Darshan Mashih vs. State,* 1990 PLD 1990 SC 513.

17. Sen (1975) provides a comprehensive overview of the various forms of agricultural economic agreements, broadly divided into "Own Labor" (where the agriculture is produced by the individual land owner or renter himself) and "Hired Labor" (where the agriculture is produced by someone hired by the owner of the land). Bonded labor falls into the latter category, which Sen further divides into "Private Enterprises," such as plantations with indentured labor, and "Permanent Bonds," which amounts to long-term slavery.

18. Kosambi (1975, 96–97).

19. For more detail on various categories of *dasas* and slavery in ancient India, see Chanana (1960).

20. Mackay (1976, 40).

21. For a fascinating discussion of slavery in ancient India as depicted in Pali and Sanskrit texts, see Chanana (1960).

22. For more detail, see book 3, "Concerning Law," of the *Arthashastra.* A good English translation of the text can be found in Shamashastry (2010).

23. Macnaghten (1828, 265–266).

24. See Kumar (1965) for a thorough discussion of the links between caste and debt bondage and the role that caste has played in the broader evolution of labor relations in India.

25. The traditional caste system of Nepal is slightly different, involving three main categories: Tagadhari (twice-born), Matwali (liquor drinking), and Pani Na Chalne (untouchables). The Tagadhari consist of the highest sub-castes: Brahmin, Thakuri, and Chhetri. The Matwali consist of most of the country's Tibeto-Burmese tribal groups. The untouchables consist of three main subcategories: those living in the Terai, those living in the Pahar zone, and the Newar untouchables. This caste system was codified by the Muluki Ain of 1854 under the Rana dynasty.

26. *Laws of Manu,* VII, 410, 413.

27. Ibid., 414.

28. "Scheduled Caste" is the legal and constitutional term given to those groups that have traditionally occupied the lowest status in the Indian caste system as "untouchables." The Constitution (Scheduled Caste) Order 1950 lists 1,108 Scheduled Castes. The term *dalit* is typically used to refer to this group.

29. "Scheduled Tribe" refers to indigenous tribal groups that are spread across the central, northeastern, and southern regions of India. Also referred to as *adivasis* (original inhabitants), these groups have long been marginalized from mainstream Indian society. The Constitution (Scheduled Caste) Order 1950 lists 744 Scheduled Tribes.

30. Levi-Strauss (1955, 149).

31. Gupta (1992, 177–180).

32. For more detail on the economic developments of medieval India and the expansion of slavery during the period, see Habib (2001) and Habib (1963).

33. Beyond outright slavery and debt bondage, it can be argued that there was never really any sharp distinction between free and unfree labor for millions of Indians during the British colonial period. British authorities exerted various degrees of coercion and compulsion to extract low-wage and virtually unpaid labor in India. In its worst forms, this coercion was slavery, but "free" labor was hardly that, as millions of peasants and workers in India suffered from intense forms of economic and extraeconomic coercion that could hardly be construed as free and fair labor.

34. See Emmer (1985).

35. For a thorough account of this period of slavery in the British Empire, see Tinker (1974) and Northrup (1995).

36. Quoted from Banaji (1933), 6–7; see this publication also for an excellent summary of slavery during the British colonial period.

37. See ibid. for more detail on these and other forms of debt bondage throughout colonial India.

38. Northrup (1995, 140–142).

39. Maddison (2006, 112–115).

40. Other land revenue systems under the British that led to similar outcomes include the Ryotwari system prevalent in Bombay and Madras provinces (this system did not have an intermediary; rather, peasants paid taxes directly to the British officials) and the Mahalwari system, in which the heads of *mahals* (villages or estates) collected fixed taxes from peasants on behalf of the British.

41. For a comprehensive discussion on the impacts of British land revenue policy in Bengal, see Guha (1982).

42. Data from Maddison (2006), 92, 114–118.

43. Those definitions were: *slavery* is the process of coercing labor or other services from a captive individual, through any means, including exploitation of bodies and body parts; *slave trading* is the process of acquiring, recruiting, harboring, receiving, or transporting an individual, through any means and for any distance, into a condition of slavery or slavelike exploitation (Kara 2009, 5).

44. See Kara (2011b) for further discussion on my breakdown of these three categories of contemporary slavery and how they function in the context of the global economy, with comparisons drawn to Old World slavery.

45. In such cases, the pledged labor can be seen as securitizing the credit, as opposed to being the sole mode of repayment.

46. For examples of this argument, see Shultz (1964), Chenery and Srinivasan (1988), Stiglitz (1989), and Genicot (2002).

47. Genicot (2002), 102. Despite stating that bonded labor is ex ante voluntary, Genicot does use economic modeling and game theory to prove that it would nevertheless be more efficient to ban bonded labor than to allow it to persist.

48. See, for example, DellaVigna (2009), in which three common deviations from the traditional model of rational decision making are established: (1) nonstandard preferences, (2) incorrect beliefs, and (3) systematic biases in decision making. See

also Rabin (1998) for a general overview of behavioral economic theory and literature.

49. *People's Union for Democratic Rights vs. Union of India and Others*, 1982 1 SCR at 456, 490.

50. Vicarious liability is a principle of tort law that assigns liability for an injury to a person who did not directly cause the injury but who has a particular legal relationship to the person who did. Legal relationships that can typically lead to vicarious liability include the relationship between parent and child, husband and wife, employer and employee, and in some cases, employer and independent contractor. The Latin maxims *qui facit per alium facit per se* ("he who acts through another shall be deemed to have acted on his own") and *respondeat superior* ("let the master answer") are commonly applied in vicarious liability cases.

51. See Srivastava (2005) for a discussion on why the extremely poor are unable to access sufficient levels of microcredit or are unable to access microcredit at all.

2. AGRICULTURE: *KAMAIYA* AND *HARI*

1. Section 1(2) of the act defines *kamaiya* labor as "the labour or service to be provided by a person to his creditor without any wages or at low wages for the following reasons: 1) To repay loans obtained by him or any member of his family, or to pay interest thereon; 2) To repay loans obtained by his ancestors, or to pay interest thereon, 3) To repay the *kamaiya* loans of the *kamaiya* labourer for whom he had provided surety to the creditor." Two immediate problems with the definition are that it is too specific to one group of bonded laborers and that the term "low wages" is ambiguous.

2. One *bigha* is twenty *kattha*. One *kattha* equals approximately 3,640 square feet.

3. *Zirayat* is a system of sharecropping in western Nepal in which the laborer and the landowner share the costs of agricultural inputs such as seed, water, tools, and animal feed and then share the revenues from the output of the harvest. The terms are usually 50/50 for share of costs and revenues, but the landowner utilizes various tactics to extract more from the laborer on the expense side and shares less on the revenue side. Many laborers cannot afford the upfront costs and cannot survive on the income, so they revert back to agricultural debt bondage. This typology is very similar to the *hari* system described later in this chapter.

4. These wages are for men. Wages for women are typically 20 to 30 percent less. Women also typically do not engage in construction work, just agriculture or general labor.

5. There is also a particular variant of the *kamaiya* system that was described to me, although I did not manage to document it during my research, called the *rana* system, in which a small-scale farmer, called a *kisan*, may possess two or three *tharu* bonded laborers who work alongside him and are not deemed deeply subordinate in status to him but rather are seen as part of the overall homestead.

6. The *kamaiya* and *hari* systems are also among the most entrenched and extreme modes of agricultural bondage in South Asia, in large part because of the highly

unfavorable ratio of arable land to the percentage of the labor force involved in agriculture in Nepal and Pakistan. Whereas roughly half the land in India and Bangladesh is arable and roughly half the labor forces in these countries is involved in agricultural labor, only 16 percent and 24 percent of the land in Nepal and Pakistan respectively is arable, with 75 percent and 52 percent (see appendix F) of each country's respective labor forces involved in agriculture. These highly unfavorable proportions put considerable pressure on access to cultivable land among landless peasants and further weaken any sort of bargaining position the peasants may have, because of the high number of individuals who are desperate to take their place. These same forces hold true in India and Bangladesh, but they are more extreme in Nepal and Pakistan.

7. In each chapter, I provide estimates of the total number of bonded, forced, and child laborers in the industry investigated. I have included all three categories in order to be as inclusive as possible of all forms of servile labor exploitation found in each industry. Within these categories, there are several combinations possible. Adults and minors may be exploited in bonded labor, forced labor, or in some cases both during the course of one year. The category of child labor thus refers only to minors who work full time but are not caught in bonded or forced labor conditions. Adults and minors may also be caught in exploitation in more than one industry during the course of one year.

8. Bista (1991, 30–39).

9. "*Kamaiya* System Ends: Bonded Labourers Freed from Debts," *Kathmandu Post* (July 18, 2000).

10. The categories were: Group A—landless *kamaiya* (8,022 households); Group B—*kamaiya* with a hut but no land (5,428 households); Group C—*kamaiya* with hut and registered land less than two *kattha* (1,877 households); Group D—*kamaiyas* with hut and land exceeding two *kattha* registered land (3,073 households).

11. An additional 14,000 applications for *kamaiya* status were also submitted in 2002, of which fewer than half were accepted.

12. Khichdi is a traditional dish of rice and lentils prepared throughout South Asia.

13. The Northwest Frontier province was renamed Khyber Pakhtunkhwa province in 2010. The northwest portion of the province borders Afghanistan. The town of Peshawar is the regional capital.

14. In Balochistan province, the *buzgar* system operates similarly to the *hari* system of Sindh. The *hatup* system of Punjab province is also similar but usually involves more exploitative conditions in which the sharecropper only shares one-sixth or one-eighth of the harvest income. Finally, the *seeri* system in Pakistan involves *peshgis* given to the heavily illiterate and landless *seeri* people in exchange for seasonal bonded labor in agriculture and other sectors. These people often suffer severe beatings and abuse.

15. Data from the World Bank, http://data.worldbank.org/country/pakistan.

16. HRCP (2009, 222).

17. Data from Agricultural Census of Pakistan 2000, http://www.statpak.gov.pk/aco/?q=node/261.

18. HRCP (2009, 186).

19. Ibid., 222.

20. Sharia law is regarded as the code of religious law under Islam, derived from the Koran and the teachings of the prophet Mohammad. In more extreme interpretations, it involves a severe subordination of the rights of women.

21. HRCP (2009, 186–190).

22. Haider Bux Jatoi was a revolutionary leader of peasants in Sindh who advocated for the rights of the poor throughout the region. He was also a well-known Sindhi poet.

23. HRCP (2009, 130).

24. See http://www.hrcp-web.org/default.asp for details.

3. BRICKS AND BIDIS

1. Bidis are thin South Asian cigarettes filled with tobacco and wrapped in a tendu leaf, with a string tying it shut at one end.

2. India, Nepal, and Pakistan each have stipulated state, district, or province minimum wages for various roles at brick kilns; Bangladesh is the only country of the four that does not have industry-specific government or district-mandated minimum wages for work at brick kilns.

3. See chapter 7 of Kara (2009).

4. HRCP (2009, 230).

5. The All India Brick and Tile Manufacturers Association states its membership includes 35,000 chimney brick kilns and 15,000 small-kilns spread across twenty states in India. See http://www.brick-India.com.

6. While most kilns are seasonal, there is the possibility of some off-season work at some of the kilns near riverbeds, where sand is used in brickmaking rather than clay. At these kilns, a small number of workers may spend the off-season arduously gathering tons of sand from the riverbanks or from sand islands in the middle of the river, then transporting them to the kiln area to be used for brick molding the following season. I saw this practice most prevalent on either side of the Ichhamati River in Bangladesh and West Bengal.

7. The roles of the laborers at brick kilns in Pakistan and Bangladesh are roughly the same as at kilns in India and Nepal, though some of the names differ—*kumhars* are called *ghumhars*, and *beldars* are called *dabais* or *safai walas*.

8. Many kilns are also operated on leases from landowners, in which the lessee may pay the government royalties as well, though in many cases bribes and corruption help the lessee avoid paying the full royalty or any royalty at all. In a few cases, the landowner pays the government royalty himself.

9. Brothels and sex venues in Sonagachi are categorized into three tiers. Tier A comprises the top-end venues, in which sex workers occupy their own flats inside a multidwelling brothel and largely transact on their own or through a pimp; tier B comprises the traditional multidwelling brothels that are managed by *gharwalis* who transact on behalf of the sex workers; tier C comprises street prostitutes who are

managed by pimps and typically transact in low-end buildings, alleys, or customers' vehicles.

10. *Darshan Mashih vs. State*, 1990 PLD 1990 SC 513, 554: Darshan Mashih Case, telegram 30 July 1988.

11. Speech given in April 1886 commemorating the twenty-fourth anniversary of the emancipation of the District of Columbia.

12. Data from the All India Bidi, Cigar, and Tobacco Worker's Federation and the Tobacco Institute of India.

13. This includes bidis produced in India and exported abroad.

4. SHRIMP AND TEA

1. For an interesting discussion on the forces in Bangladesh that promote child labor, see Hoque (2007).

2. There can also be an intermediary step in which shrimp fry are first taken to a hatchery, grown for a period of time, then taken to larger farms to be fully grown and harvested.

3. See chapter 6 of Kara (2009).

4. There are seven primary species of shrimp exported from Bangladesh: black tiger shrimp (saline), green tiger shrimp (freshwater), Kuruma shrimp, Indian white shrimp, yellow shrimp, rainbow shrimp, and speckled shrimp.

5. Data from Bangladesh Frozen Food Exporters Association (BFFEA), available at http://www.bffea.net.

6. Thirty-three decimals is 14,400 square feet.

7. The Bangladesh Rural Advancement Committee (BRAC) was founded by Sir Fazle Hasan Abed in 1972, shortly after Bangladesh's independence from Pakistan. Primarily focused on antipoverty and rural development initiatives, BRAC is now present in over fourteen countries and is the largest NGO in the world as measured by number of employees, currently around 120,000.

8. Data from BFFEA.

9. Before freezing, shrimp are also randomly given five microbial tests and nine chemical tests under the Hazard Analysis Critical Control Point (HACCP) protocol for food safety.

10. The statistics in this paragraph are from FAO (2010, 6, 18, 20).

11. Data from BFFEA.

12. Ibid.

13. Data from the Food and Agriculture Association of the United States, available at http://www.fao.org.

14. Adding India lowers the average for South Asia by about 10 percentage points. Other countries in South Asia do not have shrimp aquaculture industries.

15. Data from the Food and Agriculture Association of the United States.

16. For an interesting discussion of bonded labor in the tea plantations of Assam, see Lahiri (2000).

17. The process of transforming a tea leaf into ground or curled tea was explained to me by the director of the Bangladesh Tea Research Institute near Srimangal. The process for black tea is as follows: The harvested tea leaves are loaded into a long steel bed, where they are dried, or "withered," for sixteen to eighteen hours. The withered leaves are then crushed in a machine, and the crushed leaves are oxidized in a long metal pan for up to one hour (this is when the tea leaves turn brown). The oxidized tea is placed in small trays inside a drying machine for thirty minutes, then the tea is packed into fifty-kilogram sacks for shipment. For "orthodox" or higher-quality tea, the second step (crushing) is replaced with "curling," which involves a machine that dries and curls the tea leaves rather than crushing them, providing enhanced flavor. For green tea, the process is as follows: The green tea leaves are first steamed in a machine for three minutes. Next they are spun in a centrifuge to remove the water. A giant curling machine then curls the tea leaves, after which the leaves are laid out to dry. A machine then separates the stalk from the leaves. The leaves are "polished" by mixing them with a powder to keep them dry. Women then hand separate any remaining stalks from the leaves, which are then packed for shipping. All the tea is shipped to Chittagong, where it is priced at auction by the Central Tea Board of Bangladesh before being sold domestically or for export abroad.

18. Across South Asia, my best estimate is that approximately 28 to 38 percent of the region's $3.4+ billion wholesale tea industry is tainted by bonded, forced, or child labor.

19. At the time of independence from the British (August 15, 1947), India and Pakistan were partitioned primarily so that Muslims could have a separate state in South Asia. Pakistan was further divided into West Pakistan (present-day Pakistan) and East Pakistan (present-day Bangladesh). Northern India geographically separated the two Pakistans, with Karachi in West Pakistan serving as the capital for both. Numerous social and economic differences led to ongoing tensions, and in 1971 a nine-month Liberation War was waged by East Pakistan. West Pakistani military forces engaged in a bloody campaign of rape, genocide, and murder, targeting civilians, intellectuals, journalists, and military forces. Over ten million refugees fled into West Bengal and Assam. Estimates of the slaughter range from one to three million people killed before Bangladesh's independence was finally won on December 16, 1971.

5. CONSTRUCTION AND STONE BREAKING

1. New Delhi was also the host for the first Asian Games, shortly after independence in 1951.

2. Article 23 includes the prohibition of traffic in human beings and forced labor, Article 24 includes the prohibition of employment of children, and Article 43 includes a mandate for living wages for workers.

3. Eventually, the president of India initiated an investigation into the corruption relating to the Commonwealth Games, headed by former Auditor General V. K. Shungulu. Shungulu's committee released its findings in April 2011 and found extensive graft, inefficiency, overspending, misplaced funds, and other issues among the two main agencies responsible for the games (the Delhi Development Authority and the Union Urban

Development Ministry) as well as the organizing committee for the games. All parties cited in the report denied any wrongdoing. Investigations are ongoing.

4. The report is available at http://www.cag.gov.in.

5. In India, some of these bodies include the Builder's Association of India (BIA), the Construction Industry Development Council (CIDC), the Government of India Planning Commission, and the Government of India Committee on Infrastructure (COI).

6. Data from "Housing Skyline of India," available at http://www.indicus.net.

7. The same is true of construction sectors that I have documented in many other countries, especially across Asia and the Middle East, but also in developed nations. Worldwide, construction is one of the most pervasive sectors involved in the slavelike exploitation of trafficked, forced, and bonded laborers.

8. The Indira Gandhi National Widow Pension Scheme (IGNWPS) is given to widows aged 45 to 64. Applicants must belong to a household below the poverty line. The pension amount is Rs. 200 ($4.44) per month per beneficiary, with the individual's state urged to match this sum. The pension is discontinued if the widow remarries, moves above the poverty line, or lives past the age of 64.

6. CARPETS AND OTHER SECTORS

1. A small proportion of the carpets are also "hand tufted." This process involves the use of a screwdriver-shaped, hand-operated "gun" that punches yarn into a canvas stretched on a frame. Once completed, the carpet is removed from the frame and glued to its backcloth. Though similar in appearance to knotted carpets, hand-tufted carpets can be made much more quickly. They are also much less durable and less expensive than knotted carpets.

2. Kara (2009, 62–63).

3. Jalaluddin Muhammad Akbar was the third Mughal emperor, following Babur and Humayun. Akbar's reign spanned 1556 to 1605, commencing at the age of fourteen. He was greatly interested in the arts, literature, and religion, and he was also a successful military leader, expanding the Mughal Empire to much of northern and central India before his death.

4. In India, the primary laws are the Mines Act, 1952; and the Mines and Minerals (Development and Regulation) Act, 1957. In Nepal, the relevant laws are the Mines Act, 1956; and the Mines and Minerals Act, 1985. The mining sectors of Pakistan and Bangladesh are still governed by a colonial law, called the Mines Act, 1923, which was passed before independence and covered all of India at that time. Also, the Consolidated Mines Rules, 1952, passed after independence but when both countries were still Pakistan, remains in effect in both countries today. There are also several mining laws that focus on specific types of mines and geographic areas across South Asia.

5. See http://ibm.nic.in/mpms.htm for more information.

6. The name "Firozabad" originally comes from the general Firoz Shah, who was sent by Emperor Akbar to clear the region of robbers and bandits. When the city was founded, it was named after the general.

7. Diamond dust is used because it is the hardest naturally occurring substance, with a Mohs scale rating of 10 out of 10. The Mohs rating of hardness is a nonlinear scale of 1 to 10 grading the hardness of naturally occurring minerals. Talc is at the bottom of the scale, at 1.

7. BONDED LABOR AND THE LAW

1. Article 23 in the Constitution of India, Article 20 in the Constitution of the Kingdom of Nepal, Article 11 in the Constitution of the Islamic Republic of Pakistan, and Article 34 in the Constitution of the People's Republic of Bangladesh all prohibit forced labor.

2. From his public speech delivered in Central Park, New York City, on May 21, 1944.

3. Banaji (1933, 214–215).

4. Gharpure (1939, 1210).

5. Ibid., 1210–1220.

6. Macnaghten (1828, 270–272).

7. Banaji (1933, 226).

8. Bailie (1957, 372–373).

9. See Macnaghten (1881) for further details on the legal treatment of slaves in the Muslim tradition of ancient India.

10. Bailie (1957, 367).

11. Banaji (1933, 241–242, 280).

12. There had also been a Draft Act issued two years earlier, in 1839, that attempted to protect slaves by making it a punishable offense to physically harm them. The governments of Bombay and Madras lobbied feverishly against the act, under the logic that if the British government abolished the only means a master had of punishing a slave for bad behavior or otherwise coercing labor from him, they would have to compensate the master for the associated losses. Ultimately, the act was not passed, as it was deemed virtually impossible that any slave would ever make a complaint under the act for fear of retribution from the master, as well as from the desire to avoid debates on whether or not the British would then have to compensate slavemasters for losses associated with a master's inability to discipline or coerce his slaves.

13. The 1859 act was partially repealed in 1874 and fully repealed in 1925.

14. *Bandhua Mukti Morcha vs. Union of India and Others*, 1983 2 S.C.R. at 67, 126.

15. 2011 U.S. dollar valuation based on CPI adjustment.

16. 2011 U.S. dollar valuation based on CPI adjustment.

17. There has not been much jurisprudence on the scope of the term "partly forced," but the PUDR, 1982; and BMM, 1983, cases seem to suggest that bonded labor can exist where one may consider the conditions of the labor not to be severely coercive or restrictive, including the "voluntary" entry into an agreement ("voluntary" often being vitiated by a devil's bargain between destitution and servitude), some level of freedom of movement, and some ability to enter into and out of the bonded state across periods

of time. These and other qualities of the agreement may have been considered "partly" forced by the drafters of the act so as to give scope for a wider interpretation of the conditions that follow after the laborer has entered into a bonded labor agreement and to limit the ability of the exploiter to maneuver the conditions past a theoretical line where coerced labor becomes some sort of reasonable labor arrangement that is based on an advance of credit.

18. 2011 U.S. dollar valuation based on CPI adjustment.

19. *People's Union for Democratic Rights vs. Union of India and Others*, 1982 1 S.C.R. at 456, 458.

20. Ibid., at 459. Justice Bhagwati further explained that "having regard to the peculiar socio-economic conditions prevailing in the country where there is considerable poverty, illiteracy and ignorance obstructing and impeding accessibility to the judicial process, it would result in closing the doors of justice to the poor and deprived sections of the community if the traditional rule of standing evolved by Anglo-Saxon jurisprudence that only a person wronged can sue for judicial redress were to be blindly adhered to and followed, and it is therefore necessary to evolve a new strategy by relaxing this traditional rule of standing in order that justice may become easily available to the lowly and the lost. Where a person or class of persons to whom legal injury is caused or legal wrong is done is by reason of poverty, disability or socially or economically disadvantaged position not able to approach the Court for judicial redress, any member of the public acting *bona fide* and not out of any extraneous motivation may move the Court for judicial redress of the legal injury or wrong suffered by such person or class of persons and the judicial process may be set in motion by any public spirited individual or institution even by addressing a letter to the court." *People's Union for Democratic Rights vs. Union of India and Others*, 1982 1 S.C.R. at 460.

21. *Begar* is a traditional form of forced labor in India in which a person is compelled to work without receiving any monetary remuneration.

22. *People's Union for Democratic Rights vs. Union of India and Others*, 1982 1 S.C.R., at 462. This point attracted some of Justice Bhagwati's most incisive reasoning, as he went on to explain that "to interpret Article 23 as contended would be reducing Article 23 to a mere rope of sand, for it would then be the easiest thing in an exploitative society for a person . . . to exact labour or service . . . by paying a negligible amount of remuneration and thus escape the rigour of Article 23," and "it makes no difference whether the person who is forced to give his labour or service to another is remunerated or not. Even if remuneration is paid, labour supplied by a person would be hit by Article 23 if it is forced labour, that is, labour supplied not willingly but as a result of force or compulsion." *People's Union for Democratic Rights vs. Union of India and Others*, 1982 1 S.C.R. at 463.

Justice Bhagwati further explained that the writers of the Indian constitution intended Article 23 to be wider than Article 4's prohibition of forced labor in the Universal Declaration of Human Rights (written one year earlier) and that the suggested interpretation of the Constitution would violate the earlier Supreme Court judgment of *Maneka Gandhi vs. Union of India*, 1962, in which the court held that "when interpreting the provisions of the Constitution conferring fundamental rights, the attempt of the court should be to expand the reach and ambit of the fundamental rights rather than to attenuate their meaning and content." *Maneka Gandhi vs. Union of India*, 1962 2 S.C.R. at 621, 670.

Justice Bhagwati amplified his reasoning by reminding the court of an essential legal principle from contract law that establishes bonded labor as a form of forced labor. Citing the 1911 U.S. Supreme Court case *Bailey vs. Alabama*, Bhagwati noted that the state of Alabama had passed a law that provided a fine for a person who enters into a contract whereby he agrees to provide work in exchange for an advance and then fails to complete the agreed-upon work and does not refund the advance. The U.S. Supreme Court held this to be a violation of the Thirteenth Amendment of the U.S. Constitution, which provides, *inter alia*, that "neither slavery nor involuntary servitude shall exist within the United States." Justice Hughes noted that the natural effect of the Alabama law is to provide a means of compulsion of involuntary servitude through the use of advances to be repaid by contractual labor (similar to the Workman's Breach of Contract Act, 1859): "The fact that a debtor contracted to perform the labor which is sought to be compelled does not withdraw the attempted enforcement from the condemnation of the statute. The full intent of the constitutional provision could be defeated with obvious facility if through the guise of contracts under which advances had been made, debtors could be held to compulsory service," and that the intention of the Thirteenth Amendment is to "abolish slavery of whatever name and form . . . to render impossible any state of bondage." *Bailey vs. Alabama*, 1911 219 U.S. at 219, 220, 241.

23. *People's Union for Democratic Rights vs. Union of India and Others*, 1982 1 S.C.R. at 464.

24. Ibid., at 465. Justice Bhagwati expanded this crucial point: "Where a person is suffering from hunger or starvation, when he has no resources at all to fight disease or to feed his wife and children or even to hide their nakedness, where utter grinding poverty has broken his back and reduced him to a state of helplessness and despair and where no other employment is available to alleviate the rigour of his poverty, he would have no choice but to accept any work that comes his way, even if the remuneration offered to him is less than the minimum wage. He would be in no position to bargain with the employer; he would have to accept what is offered to him. And in doing so he would be acting not as a free agent with a choice between alternatives but under the compulsion of economic circumstances and the labour of service provided by him would be clearly 'forced labour.' The word 'forced' should not be read in a narrow and restricted manner so as to be confined only to physical or legal 'force.'" *People's Union for Democratic Rights vs. Union of India and Others*, 1982 1 S.C.R at 465.

25. *Bandhua Mukti Morcha vs. Union of India and Others*, 1983 2 S.C.R. at 91.

26. Some of the points raised in this case relate to activating the provisions of the Mines Act, 1952; the Inter-state Migrant Workmen Act, 1979; and the Minimum Wage Act, 1948. More interesting issues relate to the fact that the court held that a writ petition attracts Article 32 of the Constitution of India (*Bandhua Mukti Morcha vs. Union of India and Others*, 1983 2 S.C.R. at 68–70), that a letter written to the court can be treated as a writ petition (71), that the court is empowered to investigate breaches of fundamental rights based on such a writ petition (71), and that the statements in the

writ petition do not need to be subjected to cross-examination in order to have evidentiary value (72–74). The court also found it "reprehensible" that the state of Haryana would attempt to evade responsibility for the condition of the workers in Faridabad and that it "should be anxious to satisfy the court . . . that it is discharging its constitutional obligation fairly and adequately and the workmen are being ensured social and economic justice" (102).

On the issue of the scope of Article 32, the court stated: "Article 32 confers the right to move the Supreme Court for enforcement of any of the fundamental rights, but it does not say as to who shall have this right. . . . There is no limitation in the words of . . . Article 32. . . . Any one can move the Supreme Court for enforcement of such fundamental right" (106).

The court also reiterated that PIL is a vital tool for the enforcement of rights of the poor of India and that, pursuant to doing so, the Supreme Court has wide power to issue directions or order investigations in pursuit of enforcing fundamental rights. Finally, there is no need for cross-examination of evidence proffered in a writ petition under Article 32: "It is not at all obligatory that an adversarial procedure, where each party produces his own evidence tested by cross examination by the other side . . . must be followed in a proceeding under Article 32 for enforcement of a fundamental right. . . . The strict adherence to the adversarial procedure can some times lead to injustice, particularly when the parties are not evenly balanced in social or economic strength. . . . Therefore, when the poor come before the court, particularly for enforcement of their fundamental rights, it is necessary to depart from the adversarial procedure and to evolve a new procedure which will make it possible for the poor and the weak to bring the necessary material before the court for the purpose of securing enforcement of their fundamental rights" (109).

27. *Bandhua Mukti Morcha vs. Union of India and Others*, 1983 2 S.C.R. at 131.

28. Ibid., at 92–93.

29. Andra Pradesh, Arunchal Pradesh, Bihar, Haryana, Karnataka, Kerala, Madhya Pradesh, Maharashtra, Orissa, Punjab, Rajasthan, Tamil Nadu, and Uttar Pradesh.

30. Some of the recommendations include that the government should provide immediate physical protection to released bonded laborers from harassment with regards the repayment of outstanding debts, a more comprehensive and sustained rehabilitation program for freed bonded laborers (including medical and psychological care), establishing more rigorous enforcement of the duties of district magistrates and vigilance committees, the creation of a bonded labor help line to provide assistance to organizations who work for the release of bonded laborers, and prioritization of poverty eradication programs.

31. Sources: Ministry of Labour, Government of India, Annual Reports: 1999–2000, 2008–2009.

32. *Bandhua Mukti Morcha vs. Union of India and Others*, 1983 2 S.C.R. at 133.

33. Report available at http://nhrc.nic.in.

34. Data from questionnaire responses, July 2010.

35. Report available at: http://nhrc.nic.in.

36. High Court of Judicature of Allahabad, Public Interest Litigation (PIL) no. 1605 of 2010.

37. High Court of Judicature of Allahabad, Public Interest Litigation (PIL) no. 68095 of 2009.

8. TACKLING BONDED LABOR

1. The "primary goods" that Sen posits are essential to human freedom include the "rights, liberties and opportunities, income and wealth, and the social bases of self-respect" (Sen 1992, 81) required to achieve what a person values.

2. Taking India as an example, vicarious liability mirrors the tort principles established in the Unites States and the United Kingdom. Lord Denning summarized the principle in *Jones vs. Manchester Corporation*, 1952: "In all these cases it is of importance to remember that when a master employs a servant to do something for him, he is responsible for the servant's conduct as if it were his own. If the servant commits a tort in the course of his employment, then the master is a tortfeasor as well as the servant. The master is never treated as an innocent party." The special relationships and industries that qualify for vicarious liability are primarily established as a matter of case law. At present, it is established in India that an employer is not liable for the acts of an independent contractor, unless one of three conditions apply: (1) strict liability in the case of hazardous activity, (2) negligence in selecting the proper person for the task, or (3) employment for the purpose of causing harm (see *Suppliers vs. Regional Provident Fund*, 2006; and *Commissioner, Corporation of the City of Bangalore and Another vs. Dr. N. A. Narayanaswamy*, 2001). The traditional "control test" for determining vicarious liability has been replaced by the more effective "integrated test" (see *Ram Singh vs. Union Territory, Chandigarh and Others*, 2003). This test includes considerations for "who has the power to select and dismiss, pay remuneration, deduct insurance contributions, organize the work, [and] supply tools and materials," and "the mere fact of formal employment by an independent contractor will not relieve the master of liability where the servant is, in fact, in his employment." Since *jamadars* almost always have the powers described in the *Ram Singh* case, and since established exceptions to the independent contractor exclusion from vicarious liability include strict liability for hazardous activity (such as brickmaking or construction), there are several precedents that can be used to ensure that the employer-*jamadar* relationship is captured by the principle of vicarious liability. Further, accepting the propositions that (1) the *jamadar* is an indispensible servant of his employer in numerous sectors in South Asia and (2) as a policy matter, allowing impunity in the employer-*jamadar* system directly facilitates the gross violation of labor laws and basic human rights, then it should be reasonable to conclude that the employer-*jamadar* relationship should be captured in the strictest sense by the principle of vicarious liability.

3. Government of India, Planning Commission (2010), 293. The Planning Commission report goes on to state: "Land reforms seem to have been relegated to the

background since the 1990s. More recently, initiatives of state governments have related to liberalisation of land laws in order to promote large-scale corporate farming. This is in sharp contrast to the policy environment soon after Independence when land reforms were meant to provide ownership rights to small and marginal farmers on equity considerations" (293), and "Alienation of tribals from their land is a major issue in tribal areas. States have passed legislation to restore alienated land to the tribal landholders. The progress in this regard, however, has been limited. The restoration proceedings have been challenged in courts, thwarting the restoration of land to tribals" (294).

4. A few simplifying assumptions must be made. First, in the formula for the real economic penalty, I have treated the prosecution and conviction probabilities as independent, though there several real-world conditions that might render them dependent. Either way, the output of the calculations is not materially different. Second, calculating the probability of being prosecuted can be simplified such that each bonded laborer in a country represents one criminal act of bonded labor each year. This may understate the number of criminal acts, but it allows for a more meaningful analysis.

5. *People's Union for Democratic Rights vs. Union of India and Others*, 1982 1 S.C.R. at 459.

6. See Kara (2011) for a full discussion of the concept of the EV of a slave as relates to the more effective design of laws to combat human trafficking.

7. Carpet weaving can be seen as a hybrid category, as the carpet looms in India and Pakistan would be highly fragmented, but those in Nepal would be more concentrated in the Kathmandu Valley.

8. The Self-Employment Scheme commenced in the 1970s under the Integrated Rural Development Programme (IRDP), to increase income of small farmers and landless laborers with subsidized credit and economic training. In the 1980s, this scheme was extended to scheduled castes and tribes, women, and rural artisans. Numerous shortfalls resulted in the replacement of this program with the Swarnjayanti Gram Swarozgar Yojana (SGSY) program in 1999, which focuses on microcredit and training through self-help groups.

The Wage Employment Program focuses on rural employment and infrastructure development. These programs commenced during the sixth five-year plan, in the form of the National Rural Employment Programme (NREP) and Rural Landless Employment Guarantee Programmes (RLEGP), which then merged in 1989 into the Jawahar Rozgar Yojana (JRY). The JRY became increasingly ineffective and was relaunched in 1999 as the Jawahar Gram Samridhi Yojana (JGSY). The JGSY suffered from a lack of funding, corruption, and mismanagement, so it was relaunched as the Sampoorna Gramin Rozgar Yojana (SGRY) in 2001. Reductions in funding in successive five-year plans, corruption, and mismanagement continue to hamper the efforts of the SGRY.

The Food Security Program was originally called the Universal Public Food Distribution System (UPDS). The main objective was to create a price stabilization of food grains. States are also supposed to identify households below the poverty line and provide them with twenty kilograms of food grains at subsidized prices. The primary problems with these programs are the stipulation that twenty kilograms of food be purchased at one time, which the poorest of the poor cannot afford, along with wastage, corruption, and stealing and reselling of food at inflated prices by government officials.

The Social Security Programs were launched under the National Social Assistance Program (NSAP) in 1995. The scheme was to provide an old-age pension of Rs. 75 ($1.67) per month to impoverished people above the age of sixty-five. The program has suffered from an inability to deliver income to the identified pensioners. Another scheme that is meant to provide ten kilograms of food grains per month to the elderly has also floundered under inefficiency and mismanagement. A third scheme involves payment of a lump sum of Rs. 10,000 ($222) to a family in which the primary income earner has died of natural or accidental causes. These funds are ineffectively delivered and compromised by graft and corruption.

The Urban Poverty Alleviation program is similar to the self-employment and wage employment programs but is set in urban areas. The first component is the Scheme of Urban Micro Enterprises (SUME), which provides training for microenterprises to urban poor. Unfortunately, very little support is provided in actually launching and sustaining a microenterprise after training. The second component is the Scheme of Urban Wage Employment (SUWE), in which the labor of urban poor is utilized to create economically useful public assets. This scheme is only applicable to small towns with populations under 100,000. The third component is the Scheme of Housing and Shelter Upgradation (SHASU), in which loans up to Rs. 9,950 ($221) are provided for housing upgrades in urban areas. The largest urban poverty alleviation program is the Urban Basic Services for Poor (UBSP), in which urban poor contribute to community development efforts. The primary deficiency with all these programs is the inadequate allocation of funding compared to the level of need.

9. For more information on the Grameen Bank model, see http://www.grameen.org.

10. See Chavan (2002) for a discussion of the proportions of microcredit in South Asia that reach the poorest of the poor, ranging from approximately one-eighth in India to approximately half with Grameen Bank in Bangladesh.

11. See *Nilabati Behera vs. State of Orissa*, 1993.

APPENDIX A: GLOBAL SLAVERY METRICS

1. The 95% confidence interval (CI) was determined by the formula: $x +/- t^*(s / (\sqrt{n}))$, where x equals the sample mean; t^* equals the upper $(1-C)/2$ critical value for the t distribution with $n-1$ degrees of freedom; s equals the sample standard deviation; and n equals the sample size. The first step in calculating the CI is to calculate the sample mean and standard deviation of the range of values. The second step is to compute the estimate of the standard error of the mean. The third step is to locate the appropriate t

value based on n–1 degrees of freedom. The final step is to calculate the upper and lower limits of the confidence interval using the formula above.

2. Capture-recapture (CR) is a methodology that was originally used to count and track animal populations. The methodology was later utilized to estimate the size of hidden or difficult-to-reach human populations, such as homeless people. There are four assumptions that must be met in order to generate reliable CR estimates: (1) the population under observation is closed, (2) each of the two captures are independent, (3) all members of the population have the same probability of being captured, and (4) the capture date of each member is accurate.

The CR formula used is: $n = (m \times c) / r$, where n equals the total population, m equals first capture, c equals second capture + recapture, and r equals recapture (captured both times).

3. The formula is $((\text{ending value/beginning value})^{(1 / \# \text{ of years})}) - 1$.

4. The global weighted average revenues and profits for each type of slavery were calculated as follows: For bonded labor, roughly 84 to 88 percent of slaves are in South Asia; the remainder are spread across East Asia and the Pacific, the Middle East, Africa, and Latin America at varying rates. I created unit economic models for bonded laborers who toil in the following industries: South Asia: brickmaking, tea harvesting, agriculture (rice, wheat, maize, sugar, citrus, legumes, spices), carpet weaving, textiles, fireworks, shrimp and fish aquaculture, construction, gem cutting and polishing, stonebreaking, bidi rolling, domestic work, mining (dimensional stones and minerals), leather processing, glass work, commercial sex; East Asia and the Pacific: tea harvesting, construction, domestic work shrimp and fish aquaculture and processing; Middle East: construction, domestic work, commercial sex; Africa: construction, coffee harvesting, agriculture (potato, wheat, citrus, legumes, spices), conveyance, commercial sex; Latin America and the Caribbean: dairy farm, coffee, agriculture (sugar, wheat, citrus, legumes), coal, construction, commercial sex.

For trafficked sex slaves, the numbers are updated from the global allocations and unit economic models included in appendix B of *Sex Trafficking* (Kara 2009).

For trafficked slaves in all other industries, my model includes allocations of slaves in all major regions of the world at varying rates derived from my calculations. I created unit economic models in the following industries: South Asia: brickmaking, tea harvesting, agriculture (rice, wheat, maize, sugar, citrus, legumes, spices), carpet weaving, textiles, fireworks, shrimp and fish aquaculture, construction, stonebreaking, domestic work, mining (dimensional stones and minerals), leather processing, glass work, commercial sex, begging, forced military service, organ harvesting; East Asia and the Pacific: tea harvesting, agriculture (rice, sugar, citrus, legumes, spices), textiles, construction, domestic work, shrimp and fish aquaculture and processing, begging, forced military service, organ harvesting; Middle East: construction, manufacturing, domestic work, camel jockey; Africa: construction, coffee harvesting, agriculture (potato, wheat, citrus, spices), conveyance, begging, forced military service; Latin America and the Caribbean: dairy farm, coffee, agriculture (sugar, wheat, citrus, legumes), coal, construction, organ harvesting; West Europe: textiles, domestic work, manufacturing, begging, organ harvesting; Central and Eastern Europe: textiles, domestic work, manufacturing, begging, organ harvesting; North America: agriculture (potato, wheat, citrus), textiles, domestic work, organ harvesting.

For forced labor slaves, my model includes allocations of forced laborers in all major regions of the world at varying rates derived from my calculations. The industries of exploitation are the same as trafficked labor slaves, with the addition of allocations in each region for commercial sex, as well as bidi rolling, gem cutting and polishing, and additional categories of carpet weaving in South Asia.

Finally, for all regions listed above there are calculated allocations of the number of slaves in each industry in each type of slavery.

5. 2011 U.S. dollar valuation based on averages of CPI and GDP deflator adjustments. GDP deflator was also used because unlike the CPI, it extends beyond consumer goods and services and provides a broader basis of comparison for the sales of human beings.

6. One could allocate some portion of the costs of the upkeep of the female slave who gave birth to the new slave as the cost of acquisition, but this value would not be very significant.

7. Many currencies in 1860, especially the U.S. dollar, were much weaker relative to 2011 than they were in 1810, which is also responsible for the increase in relative value in 1860 versus 1810.

8. Two finance concepts must be considered when multiplying monthly recurring contribution by the average duration of enslavement: the time value of money and the risk of future cash flows. The time value of money considers the fact that a dollar today is worth more than a dollar a year from now, primarily because of inflation. The risk of future cash flows is the risk that the exploiter will not possess the bonded laborer for as long as expected. Theoretically, the churn rate captures these risks, but to be conservative, the slaveowner's likelihood of achieving the average duration of enslavement can still be discounted. This discount rate is applied when calculating the operating EV to depreciate the value of future cash flows in relation to the time value of money and the risk of future cash flows. Most models used to calculate discount rates include applying a country's inflation rate to capture the time value of money as well as a risk premium on future cash flows. I have applied hefty discount rates of 25 percent to all countries covered in this book.

APPENDIX E: BONDED LABOR LAW AND CASES: PAKISTAN, NEPAL, BANGLADESH, INDIA

1. 2011 U.S. dollar valuation based on CPI adjustment.

2. See *Darshan Mashih vs. State*, 1990 PLD 1990 SC 513.

3. The *Sunnah* ("habit" or "usual practice" in Arabic), refers to the words, habits, and practices of the prophet Muhammad, as recorded in the *Hadith*. The *Sunnah* is consulted by Muslims for guidance in relation to Islamic principles for dealing with

family, friends, and the government, as demonstrated by the actions and habits of Muhammad. The *Sunnah* is consulted second, if an issue is not adequately addressed first by the Koran.

4. See Khair (2008, chap. 5) for a discussion of the development of public interest litigation in Bangladesh.

Works Cited

BOOKS AND REPORTS

Acemgolu, Daron, and Alexander Wolitzky. 2011. "The Economics of Labor Coercion." *Econometrica* 79, no. 2 (March): 555–600.

Bailie, Neil. 1957. *A Digest of Mohammedan Law*. Lahore.

Banaji, Dady Rustomji. 1933. *A General Survey of Slavery in British India*. Bombay: D. B. Taraporevala Sons & Co.

Barzel, Yoram. 1977. "An Economic Analysis of Slavery." *Journal of Law and Economics* 20:87–110.

Bista, Dor Bahadur. 1991. *Fatalism and Development: Nepal's Struggle for Modernization*. Hyderabad: Sangam Books.

Center for Education and Communication. 2004. *Debt Bondage in India: An Indicative Report*. New Delhi: CEC.

Chanana, Dev Raj. 1960. *Slavery in Ancient India as Depicted in Pali and Sanskrit Texts*. New Delhi: People's Publishing House.

Chavan, P., and R. Ramakumar. 2002. "Microcredit and Rural Poverty: An Analysis of Empirical Evidence." *Economic and Political Weekly* 37, no. 10 (March 9).

Cherney, H., and T. N. Srinivasan. 1988. *Handbook of Development Economics*. Vol. 1. Amsterdam: North Holland.

Conning, Jonathan. 2005. *Freedom, Servitude, and Voluntary Contract*. Department of Economics, Hunter College and the Graduate Center, City University of New York.

DellaVigna, Stefano. 2009. "Psychology and Economics: Evidence from the Field." *Journal of Economic Literature* 47, no. 2:315–372.

Emmer, P. C. 1985. "The Great Escape: The Migration of Female Indentured Servants from British India to Surinam, 1873–1916," in *Abolition and Its Aftermath: The Historical Context, 1790–1916*, ed. D. Richardson. London: Frank Cass and Co.

Fogel, Robert W., and Stanley L. Engerman. 1974. *Time on the Cross: The Economics of American Negro Slavery*. New York: Little, Brown.

Food and Agriculture Association (FAO) of the United Nations. 2010. *State of the World Fisheries and Aquaculture*. Rome, 2010.

Genicot, Garance. 2002. "Bonded Labour and Serfdom: A Paradox of Voluntary Choice." *Journal of Development Economics* 67, no. 1: 101–127.

Gharpure, V. J., trans. 1939. *Yajnavalkhya Smriti*. Vol. 2, part 4. 2nd ed. Bombay.

Government of India, Planning Commission. 2008. *Eleventh Five Year Plan: 2007–2012*. New Delhi: Oxford University Press.

Government of India, Planning Commission. 2010. *Poverty Alleviation in Rural India—Strategies and Programs*. New Delhi: Oxford University Press.

Guha, Ranajit. 1981. *A Rule of Property for Bengal: An Essay on the Idea of Permanent Settlement*. Hyderabad: Orient Longman.

Gupta, B. L. 1992. *Value and Distribution System in Ancient India*. New Delhi: Gian Publishing House.

Habib, Irfan. 1963. *The Agrarian System of Mughal India, 1562–1707*. Bombay: Oxford University Press India.

——. 2001. *The Economic History of Medieval India: A Survey*. New Delhi: Manohar Publishers.

Hoque, Ridwanul. 2007. "Elimination of the Worst Forms of Child Labour Through Law in Bangladesh: A Critique." *Dhaka University Law Journal* 18, no. 2 (December).

Human Rights Commission of Pakistan. 2010. *The State of Human Rights in 2009*. Lahore: HRCP.

Kara, Siddharth. 2009. *Sex Trafficking: Inside the Business of Modern Slavery*. New York: Columbia University Press.

——. 2011. "Designing More Effective Laws Against Human Trafficking." *Northwestern Journal of International Human Rights* 9, no. 2.

——. 2011b. "Supply and Demand: Human Trafficking in the Global Economy." *Harvard International Review* 33, no. 2.

Kautilya. 2010. *The Arthashastra*. Trans. R. Shamasastry. Bottom of the Hill Publishing.

Khair, Sumaiya. 2008. *Legal Empowerment for the Poor and Disadvantaged: Strategies Achievements and Challenges*. Dhaka: Colorline.

Kosambi, D. D. 1975. *An Introduction to the Study of Ancient Indian History*. Bombay: Sangham Books.

Kumar, D. 1965. *Land and Caste in South India*. Cambridge: Cambridge University Press.

Lahiri, Souperna. 2000. "Bonded Labour and the Tea Plantation Economy." *Revolutionary Democracy* 6, no. 2 (September).

Levi-Strauss, Claude. 1955. *Tristes Tropiques*. New York: Penguin.

Mackay, Earnest. 1976. *Early Indus Civilizations*. New Delhi: Indological Book Corporation.

Macnaghten, W. H. 1828. *Principles and Precedents of Hindu Law*. Calcutta.

——. 1881. *Principles and Precedents of Muslim Law*. Calcutta.

Maddison, Angus. 2006. *The World Economy*. 2 vols. Paris: Development Center Studies, OECD Publishing.

National Human Rights Commission, India. 2004–2009. *Annual Reports*. New Delhi.

Northrup, D. 1995. *Indentured Labour in the Age of Imperialism, 1834–1922*. New York: Cambridge University Press.

Pakistan Institute of Labour Education and Research (PILER). 2000. *Bonded Labour in Pakistan: An Overview*. Karachi: PILER.

Pete, Daniel R. 1990. *The Shadow of Slavery, Peonage in the South, 1901–1969*. Champaign: University of Illinois Press.

Platteau, Jean-Philippe. 1994. "A Framework for the Analysis of Evolving Patron-Client Ties in the Agrarian Economies." Centre de Recherche en Économie du Développement. Faculte de Sciences Economiques et Sociales, Belgium.

Poole, Jill. 2006. *Casebook on Contract Law*. 8th ed. Oxford: Oxford University Press.

Rabin, Matthew. 1998. "Psychology and Economics." *Journal of Economic Literature* 36, no. 1: 11–46.

Schultz, Theodore W. 1964. *Transforming Traditional Agriculture*. New Haven, Conn.: Yale University Press.

Sen, Amartya. 1975. *Employment, Technology, and Development*. Oxford: Oxford University Press.

——. 1992. *Inequality Reexamined*. Cambridge, Mass.: Harvard University Press.

Sheth, Arpan. 2010. *An Overview of Philanthropy in India*. New Delhi: Bain & Company.

Smith, Thomas C. 1959. *The Agrarian Origins of Modern Japan*. Palo Alto, Calif.: Stanford University Press.

Special Reports of the Indian Law Commissioners. 1842. *Report on Slavery in India: 1841*. London: East India House.

Srivastava, Ravi S. 2000. "Changes in Contractual Relations in Land and Labour." *Indian Journal of Agricultural Economics*, Keynote Paper, Conference Issue (October–December).

——. 2003. "An Overview of Migration, Its Impacts, and Key Issues." Paper no. 2, Migration and Development and Pro-poor Policy Choices in Asia. London: DFID.

——. 2005. "Microfinance in India: Odysseus or Interloper," *Economic and Political Weekly* 40, no. 33 (August 13–19).

Stephenson, Carl. 1952. *Mediaeval Feudalism*. Ithaca, N.Y.: Cornell University Press.

Stiglitz, Joseph. 1989. "Rational Peasants, Efficient Institutions, and a Theory of Rural Organization: Methodological Remarks for Development Economics." In *The Economic Theory of Agrarian Institutions*, ed. P. Bardham. Oxford: Oxford University Press.

Tinker, Hugh. 1974. *A New System of Slavery*. Oxford: Oxford University Press.

UNHCR. 1999. "Report of the Working Group on Contemporary Forms of Slavery." Geneva: UNHCR.

LAWS AND CONVENTIONS

Bangladesh

Constitution of the People's Republic of Bangladesh, 1972. Art. 34: Prohibition against forced labour.
Bangladesh Labour Act, 2006.
Consolidated Mines Rules, 1952.
Mines Act, 1923.

India

Constitution of India, 1949. Art. 21: Protection of life and personal liberty.
——. Art. 23: Prohibition of traffic in human beings and forced labour.
——. Art. 24: Prohibition of employment of children in factories, etc.
——. Art. 32: Remedies for enforcement of rights.
——. Art. 43: Living wage, etc for workers.
Bonded Labour System (Abolition) Act, 1976.
Building and Other Construction Workers (Regulation of Employment and Condition of Service) Act, 1996.
Children (Pledging of Labour) Act, 1933.
Child Labour (Prohibition and Regulation) Act, 1986.
Contract Labour (Regulation and Abolition) Act, 1970.
Equal Remuneration Act, 1976.
Factories Act, 1948.
Inter-State Migrant Workmen (Regulation of Employment and Condition of Service) Act, 1979.
Mines Act, 1952.
Mines and Minerals (Development and Regulation) Act, 1957.
Minimum Wages Act, 1948.
Narcotic Drugs and Psychotropic Substances Act of 1985.
Plantation Labour Act, 1951.
Right to Education Bill, 2009.
Scheduled Castes/Scheduled Tribes Prevention of Atrocities Act, 1989.

Nepal

Constitution of Kingdom of Nepal, 1990. Art. 20: Prohibition against traffic in human beings and forced labour.
Child Labour (Prohibition and Regulation) Act, 2000.
Contract Act, 1964.
Kamaiya Labour (Prohibition) Act, 2002.

Labour Act, 1991.
Laws on Migrant Workers (Foreign Employment), Act 1985.
Mines Act, 1956.
Mines and Minerals Act, 1985.
Muluki Ain, 1854.
Muluki Ain, 1964.

Pakistan

Constitution of the Islamic Republic of Pakistan, 1956. Art. 9: Security of person.
——. Art. 11: Prohibition against traffic in human beings and forced labour.
——. Art. 14: Protecting the dignity of man.
——. Art. 15: Protecting freedom of movement.
——. Art. 25: Prohibition of discrimination on basis of sex.
Consolidated Mines Rules, 1952.
Bonded Labour System (Abolition) Act, 1992.
Bonded Labour System (Abolition) Rules, 1995.
Employment of Children Act, 1991.
Land Reform Regulations, 1972.
Mines Act, 1923.
Sindh Tenancy Act, 1950.

United Kingdom

Act V of 1843.
Anti-Slavery Act, 1843.
Slave Trade Abolition Act, 1807.
Slavery Abolition Act, 1833.
Workman's Breach of Contract Act, 1859.

United Nations

League of Nations Convention to Suppress the Slave Trade and Slavery, 1926.
United Nations Supplementary Convention on the Abolition of Slavery, 1956.

CASES

India

Maneka Gandhi vs. Union of India, 1962.
People's Union for Democratic Rights vs. Union of India and Others, 1982.

Bandhua Mukti Morcha vs. Union of India and Others, 1983.
Sanjit Roy vs. State of Rajasthan Supreme Court, 1983.
Neeraja Chaudhary vs. State of Madhya Pradesh Supreme Court, 1984.
Mukesh Advani vs. State of Madhya Pradesh Supreme Court, 1985.
Bandhua Mukti Morcha vs. State of Tamil Nadu, 1986.
Nilabati Behera vs. State of Orissa, 1993.
People's Union for Civil Liberties vs. Union of India and Others, 1994.
Public Union for Civil Liberties vs. State of Tamil Nadu and Others, 1985.
Public Union for Civil Liberties vs. the State of Tamil Nadu and Others, 1994.
Commissioner, Corporation of the City of Bangalore and Another vs. Dr. N. A. Narayanaswamy, 2001.
Ram Singh vs. Union Territory, Chandigarh & Others, 2003.
Public Union for Civil Liberties vs. the State of Tamil Nadu and Others, 2004.
Suppliers vs. Regional Provident Fund, 2006.

Pakistan

Darshan Mashih vs. State, 1990.
Judgment of the Federal Shariat Court in the Bonded Labour System Abolition Case, 2005.

United Kingdom

Jones vs. Manchester Corporation, 1952.

United States

Bailey vs. Alabama, 1911.

Index

Bangladesh (*continued*)
Munshiganj, 107, 109, 111–13;
Pakistan war with, 130; poverty in,
111–12; research in, 105–6; *sab-e-barat*
in, 106
Bangladesh bonded labor, xiii; in shrimp
industry, 114–16, 121–22; in tea
industry, 122, 130. *See also* South Asia
bonded labor
Bangladesh bonded labor law:
Bangladesh Labour Act (2006), 269
Bangladesh brick kilns, 80, 82, 87;
laborers, 88
Bangladesh child labor: research of, 105;
in shrimp fry collection, *108*, 109, *110*,
114; in shrimp industry, *108*, 109, *110*,
114, 118–22; in shrimp processing,
118–20; in tea industry, 130
Bangladesh fishing industry, 121;
forced labor in, 121; slavery in,
107–8. *See also* Bangladesh shrimp
industry
Bangladesh forced labor: in fishing
industry, 121; in shrimp distribution,
117–18; in shrimp industry, 117–22; in
shrimp processing, 118–20; in tea
industry, 122, 130
Bangladesh human trafficking: climate
change and, 104–5; in shrimp
industry, 112, 113
Bangladesh Labour Act (2006), 269
Bangladesh Rural Advancement
Committee (BRAC), 114, 280n7
Bangladesh shrimp: black tiger, 113;
harvesting, 104; types of exported,
113, 280n4
Bangladesh shrimp distribution, 106,
116–18; economics of, 117; forced labor
in, 117–18
Bangladesh shrimp farming, 106, 112–16;
economics of, 115, 116, *251*; saltwater
shrimp farm, *113*; security of, 115–16;
testimonials about, 114

Bangladesh shrimp fry collection,
107–12; child labor in, *108*, 109, *110*,
114; testimonials about, 109
Bangladesh shrimp industry, 120–22:
bonded labor in, 114–16, 121–22; child
labor in, *108*, 109, *110*, 114, 118–22;
climate change and, 104–5, 113–14;
exports, 280n4; forced labor in,
117–22; hatchery, 280n2; human
trafficking in, 112, 113; research of,
106–7, 112; secrecy in, 118, 123, 131;
slavery in, 121. *See also specific
Bangladesh shrimp topics*
Bangladesh shrimp laborers: abuse of,
118; bonded labor of, 114–16, 121–22;
children as, *108*, 109, *110*, 114, 118–22;
conditions of, 109–15, 117–20;
exploitation of, 119–21; families as,
109–12; forced labor of, 117–22; *hari*
bonded laborers and, 112, 114; loans
to, 114; testimonials of, 109, 114
Bangladesh shrimp processing, 106,
118–20; business, 118–19; child labor
in, 118–20; economics of, 119;
exploitation in, 119–20; forced labor
in, 118–20; freezing in, 119, 280n9
Bangladesh slavery: climate change and,
104–5; in fishing industry, 107–8; in
shrimp industry, 121
Bangladesh tea industry: annual
production of, 130; bonded labor in,
122, 130; child labor in, 130; forced
labor in, 122, 130; guards, 123–24;
harvesting, 127–28; managers, 125;
plant, *123*; plantations, 123, 130;
processing, 125–26, 281n17; secrecy
in, 123–25, 131; tea weighing in, 128,
129
Bangladesh tea laborers, *129*; bonded labor
of, 122, 130; children as, 130; conditions
of, 125, *126*, 127–28, 130; exploitation of,
126–28, 130; forced labor of, 122, 130;
India human trafficking and, 25, 26,

122–23, 130; loans to, 127; research of,
  122–23; testimonials of, 127; wages of,
  126, 128, 130
begar (traditional India forced labor),
  196, 284n21
Bhagwati, P. N., 1, 36, 192, 194, 195, 199,
  200, 203, 215, 284n20, 284n22, 285n24
Bibi, Amina (bidi roller), 99–100
Bibi, Khadija (bidi roller), 98, 100
bidis, *101*, 279n1; South Asia bonded
  labor supply chain for, *260. See also*
  India bidi bonded labor
bigha (twenty *kattha*), 277n2
BMM. *See* Bandhua Mukti Morcha
BMM case. *See Bandhua Mukti Morcha
  vs. Union of India and Others*
bonded debts, 32; Bonded Labour System
  (Abolition) Act on, 192, 262; South
  Asia illegality of, 9, 29
bonded labor, xvi, 1–48: child labor and,
  xvii; compensation in, 33; consumers
  of products produced by, 209; debt
  bondage and, 4; definitions of, 31,
  276n45; essential form of, 3–4;
  exploitation value summary (2011),
  243, *244*, 245, 291n8; forced labor and,
  xvii; generational, 4; global economy
  and, 3, 14, 210–11; history of, xvi, 3–5,
  14–15; human trafficking and, xvi;
  lack of reasonable alternatives in,
  33–34, 37; numbers of, 3; products
  produced by, 209; research on, xvi,
  273nn1–2; slavery compared to, xvi, 3,
  7–8, 25, 27–28, 30, 31, 33–37; vicious
  cycle of, 4, *5*; voluntary agreements in,
  34–37, 276nn47–48. *See also* debt
  bondage; *specific South Asia bonded
  labor topics*
bonded labor agreements: in
  construction, 10; exit costs of, 12;
  exploitation of, 12; key features of,
  10–12; labor in, 11–12; loans in, 10–12;
  movement restrictions in, 12

bonded labor business, 14–16: global
  economy and, 14
bonded labor economics, 12–14;
  Bangladesh shrimp farming, *251*;
  caste system in, 13; exploitation
  of, 12–13; fair labor agreements
  compared to, 13–14; free market
  compared to, 12–13, 274n14; *hari,
  248*; human debasement in, 14;
  India bidi rolling, *250*; India
  brickmaking, *249*; India carpet
  weaving, *254*; India construction, *252*;
  India glass bangle, *256*; India mining,
  255; India stonebreaking, *253*;
  insurance premium, 13; *kamaiya,
  247*; laborer lack of alternatives in,
  13; loans in, 13
bonded laborers: conditions of, 1–3;
  strength of spirit of, 47–48. *See also*
  South Asia bonded laborers
bonded labor law: contacting lawmakers
  about, 46; contract law, 7–8. *See also*
  South Asia bonded labor law
bonded labor loans, 10–11; economics of,
  13; reasons for taking, *11*
Bonded Labour Debt Relief and
  Upliftment Program (Nepal), 60
Bonded Labour Liberation Front. *See*
  Bandhua Mukti Morcha
Bonded Labour System (Abolition) Act
  (India, 1976), 132, 133, 191–94, 265,
  283n17
Bonded Labour System (Abolition) Act
  (Pakistan, 1992), 265–66, 267, 268
Bonded Labour System (Abolition) rules
  (1995), 265–66
BRAC. *See* Bangladesh Rural
  Advancement Committee
Brahma, 19
brickmaking. *See* South Asia
  brickmaking business
British colonialism: *hari* system and, 75;
  South Asia bonded labor and, 16

British colonialism in India: agriculture and textiles expansion in, 24–25; British slavery law and, 189–91, 283nn12–13; debt bondage expansion during, 22–23, 276n33; East India Company in, 22; human trafficking and, 23–27, 122–23, 130; in India slavery and bondage history, 22–27, 276n33; India slavery law and, 187; land-revenue policy, 24–25, 276n40; second slavery expansion of, 24–27, 276n40; urban slave market expansion of, 23–24; wealth extraction, 26–27; *zamindars* and, 25–26

British slavery law: British colonialism in India, and, 189–91, 283nn12–13; colonial (1770–1920), 189–91, 283nn12–13; India slavery and, 189–91, 283nn12–13

brothels: *kothas* as, 136–37; in Sonagachi, India, 92, 279n92

Buddha, 158

buzgar system, 278n14

capture-recapture (CR), 237, 290n2

carpets: girl pulling yarn down loom, *172*; hand tufted, 282n1; hand weaving process, *171*; knotted, 158, 171, 282n1. *See also specific carpet weaving topics*

caste system: in bonded labor economics, 13. *See also* South Asia caste system

chakravriddhi (compound interest), 21

child labor: bonded labor and, xvii. *See also* South Asia child labor

Child Labour (Prohibition and Regulation) Act (2000), 268–69

chingri (shrimp): harvesting, 104. *See also* shrimp

CI. *See* confidence intervals

climate change: Bangladesh and, 104; Bangladesh human trafficking, 104–5; Bangladesh shrimp industry and, 104–5, 113–14; Bangladesh slavery and, 104–5; human trafficking and, 105

colonialism. *See* British colonialism

colonialism in India: in India slavery and bondage history, 22–27; urban slave market expansion of, 23–24. *See also* British colonialism in India

Commonwealth Games (2010): construction and India labor law violations, 133, 136, 138, 281n2; India construction industry and, 132–36, 138–39; India construction laborers and, 133–36, 138–39; India government corruption and, 134, 138, 281n3; India sex trafficking and, 137–38

confidence intervals (CI), 235, 289n1

construction. *See* South Asia construction industry

contemporary slavery, xiii, xvi; definitions of, 30–32

corruption: Commonwealth Games and, 134, 138, 281n3; in India construction industry, 134, 138, 142, 281n3; as South Asia bonded labor promotion force, 40, 211; in South Asia construction industry, 144, 145

CR. *See* capture-recapture

dalal (trafficker), 80, 92, 174

dalits (untouchables), 20, 79, 163, 233–34

Darshan Mashih vs. State (1990), 14, 74–75, 94–95, 267

dasas (slaves), 16–17; categories of, 18

debt bondage, 4–5; bonded labor and, 4; definitions of, 29; expansion during British colonialism in India, 22–23, 276n33; informal systems of, 5; of migrant domestic servants, 5, 274n6; South Asia promotion of vulnerability to, 38, 40, 210, 211. *See also* bonded labor

domestic servitude: migrant workers and, 5, 274n6. *See also* South Asia domestic servitude

slavery (*continued*)
chattel, 22, 25, 28, 30; compensation in, 33; contemporary, xiii, xvi, 30–32; definitions of, 28–32, 276n43; environmental disaster or transformation influences on, 70; forced labor compared to, 28–30; human trafficking as, 30, 130–31; illegality of, 32; labor cost minimization and, 15; lack of alternatives in, 33, 37; terminology usage of, 30; UN definitions of, 28, 29; voluntary agreements and, 34–37. *See also* bonded labor; domestic servitude; forced labor; global slavery metrics; human trafficking; South Asia slavery
slavery economics (2011), 238, 240, 242; global slavery profits, 238, *239*, 240; global weighted average revenues and profits calculations, 290n4; summary, 240, *241*, 242, 291nn5–7
slavery estimates (2011), 235–38, 289n1; slavery breakdown, 235, *236*; slavery breakdown (restrictive), 236, *237*; sources for, 237, 290n2; South Asia bonded laborers, 235, *236*
slavery law. *See* bonded labor law; British slavery law; South Asia slavery law
slave trading: definition of, 30, 276n43. *See also* human trafficking
South Asia: bonded debts illegality in, 9, 29; income inequality in, 6; poverty in, 6, 162; security and brick kiln laborers, 93–97
South Asia agricultural bonded labor, 55–56; average annual cash profits per laborer, 15–16; labor force-to-arable land ratio in, 277n6. *See also* India agricultural bonded labor systems; Nepal agricultural bonded labor; Pakistan agricultural bonded labor
South Asia agricultural bonded laborers: in Pakistan, 76, 77; physical violence

against, 71–72; sexual exploitation of women and children, 72
South Asia agricultural systems. *See specific agricultural systems*
South Asia agricultural workers, 52
South Asia bonded labor, xiii–xiv, xvi, 3, 5–6;: British colonialism and, 16; in carpet weaving industry, 162–66, 171–73; in construction industry, 133, 139, 144–48; documented cases by industry, 9; documented cases summary statistics, 8–9, *10*, 274n12; domestic servitude, 173–75; environmental disaster and, 42–43, 70–71, 97–101, 103, 211; generational, 4; in glasswork industry, 178–80; in global economy, 3; illegality of, 29; in mining industry, 176–78; numbers of, 3; other sectors involving, 173, 183; research, xiv–xvii; supply chain for brickmaking, *257*; supply chain for shrimp industry, *258*; voluntary agreements in, 36–37. *See also specific bonded labor topics*
South Asia bonded labor criminal penalties: bonded labor promotion force of insufficient, 39, 211; economic increases in, *45*, 214–18; in India, 215
South Asia bonded labor economic penalties: current, 214–15, 288n4; current bonded labor economic profits and, 215–17; determination of, 214–18; exploitation value and, 216–17; increases needed to diminish profits, 217–18; legal reform of increases in, *45*, 214–18
South Asia bonded labor elimination, 208–9. *See also* South Asia bonded labor law; South Asia bonded labor promotion forces; South Asia bonded labor tackling
South Asia bonded labor elimination initiatives, 44, *45*, 212; demand-side, *45*, 212–24; effective government

antipoverty programs, *45*, 225–29; fast-track courts, *45*, 223; free expanded rural education program, *45*, 229; *jamadar* system redesign or abolition, *45*, 223–24; legal reform, *45*, 212–18; national awareness and educational campaigns, *45*, 231–32; rapid-response environmental teams, *45*, 231; rapid-response registration and rehabilitation teams, *45*, 229–30; rural integration and information dissemination, *45*, 230; supply-side, *45*, 212, 224–32; transnational slavery intervention force, *45*, 219–23

South Asia bonded laborers: abuse of, 208; in caste system, 6–7, 19, 43; combinations of, 278n7; conditions of, 208–9; credit accessibility of, 7, 274n8; ethnicities of, 6–7, 19, 43; exploitation of, 208, 209; human dignity and, 208–9; human rights of, 208–9; key features of, 6–10; lack of education and literacy of, 7; lack of reasonable alternatives for, 7, 274n9; landlessness of, 7; numbers of, 56, 278n7; planting rice, *53*; poverty of, 6; social isolation of, 7. *See also specific bonded laborer topics*

South Asia bonded labor industries: documented cases, *9*; exploitation value in key, *216*, *217*; transnational slavery intervention force and, 220–21. *See also specific industry topics*

South Asia bonded labor industry supply chain: bidi rolling, *260*; brickmaking, *257*; categories, 220–21, 288n7; data, 15–16; fixed point of production, 220–22; fragmented point of production/cottage industry, 220–22; frozen shrimp (tiger), *258*; India carpet weaving, *259*

South Asia bonded labor law, 183–87, 265–70; Bangladesh, 269; failure to implement, 201–7; history of, 185–91.

See also specific bonded labor law topics

South Asia bonded labor law reform, *45*, 212; economic penalty increases, *45*, 214–18; fast-track courts, 223; *jamadars* in, 213; land ownership opportunity for poor, *45*, 213–14, 287n3; minimum wage increase, *45*, 212–13; vicarious liability law expansion, *45*, 213, 287n2

South Asia bonded labor promotion forces, 37–38, 43, 209–10; elimination initiatives, 44, *45*, 212–32; no-risk profit generation in, 37–38; tackling, 210, 211–12

South Asia bonded labor promotion forces (demand-side), 38, 210, 211–12; corruption in government, law enforcement and judiciary, 40, 211; insufficient criminal penalties, 39, 211; insufficient minimum wages, 38, 210; insufficient vicarious liability law, 38–39, 210, 277n50; *jamadars* in, 38–39, 40, 211; *jamadar* system labor subcontracting, 40, 211; laborer identification and freeing difficulties, 40, 211; labor law lack of enforcement, 39, 211; land law promoting peasant landlessness, 39, 211; legal deficiencies, 38–39, 210–11; substantial profit at no real risk, 38, 210; systemic barriers, 39–40, 211; unsafe reporting mechanisms, 40, 211

South Asia bonded labor promotion forces (supply-side), 38, 210, 211–12, 232; biases against subordinated caste and ethnic groups, 43, 211; environmental disaster or transformation, 42–43, 211; insufficient laborer rehabilitation packages, 42, 211; lack of health care and medicine, 43, 211; lack of literacy and education for poor, 41–42, 211; lack of poor's credit resources, 41, 211;